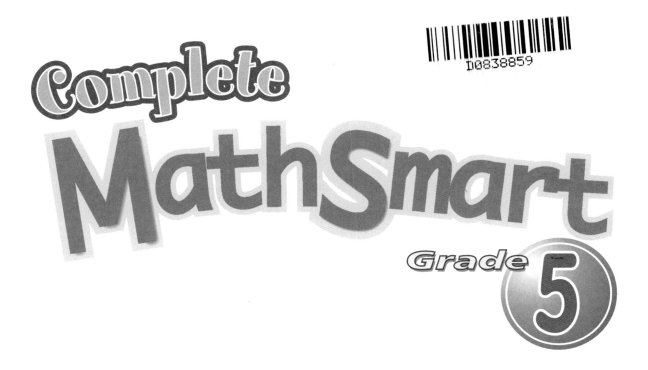

Consultant: Ann Bobker

Copyright © 2005 **Popular Book Company (Canada) Limited**

Printed in China

ontents

Section 1

Overview

In Grade 4, fraction skills were introduced. In this section, these skills are practised and expanded upon.

Concepts of equivalent fractions, improper fractions and mixed numbers are consolidated. Students learn how to add and subtract fractions with the same denominator. Ample practice in converting fractions to decimals and adding and subtracting decimals are provided.

Other skills include multiplying and dividing decimals by whole numbers.

Operations with Whole Numbers

EXAMPLES

1. Find the sum of 4297 and 970 and the difference between them.

$$
\begin{array}{r}
\overset{1\ \ \ 1}{4297} \\
+\ \ \ 970 \\
\hline
\end{array}
$$
sum ⟶ 5 2 6 7

$$
\begin{array}{r}
\overset{3\ 12}{4\!\!\!/297} \\
-\ \ \ 970 \\
\hline
\end{array}
$$
difference ⟶ 3 3 2 7

2. Find the product of 296 and 4.

$$
\begin{array}{r}
\overset{2}{296} \\
\times\ \ \ \ 4 \\
\hline
4
\end{array}
$$
↑
6 x 4 = 24

⟶

$$
\begin{array}{r}
\overset{3\ 2}{296} \\
\times\ \ \ \ 4 \\
\hline
84
\end{array}
$$
↑
9 x 4 + 2 = 36 + 2 = 38

⟶

$$
\begin{array}{r}
\overset{3}{296} \\
\times\ \ \ \ 4 \\
\hline
1184
\end{array}
$$
⟵ product
↑
2 x 4 + 3 = 8 + 3 = 11

3. Find the quotient when 511 is divided by 7.

$$
\begin{array}{r}
73 \\
7\,\overline{)511} \\
49 \\
\hline
21 \\
21 \\
\hline
\end{array}
$$

73 ⟵ quotient
49 ⟵ 7 x 7 = 49
51 − 49 = 2 ⟶ 21 ⟵ bring down 1
21 ⟵ 7 x 3 = 21

HINTS:

- Align all numbers on the right-hand side when doing vertical addition, subtraction and multiplication.

- In doing addition or multiplication, remember to carry groups of 10 to the column on the left if the sum or product of a column is greater than 10.

- In doing subtraction, borrow 10 from the column on the left if you can't take away.

- Continue to divide until the remainder is smaller than the divisor.

- Multiplication and division are done in order from left to right.

Find the answers mentally.

① 2 X 7 X 50 = _____

② 5700 ÷ 10 = _____

③ 5 X 8 X 20 = _____

④ 2000 X 35 = _____

⑤ 5 X 29 X 2 = _____

⑥ 27000 ÷ 300 = _____

⑦ 1000 X 20 ÷ 100 = _____

⑧ 2 X 62 X 5 = _____

⑨ 2000 ÷ 100 X 5 = _____

⑩ 30 X 100 ÷ 10 = _____

⑪ 500 ÷ 50 X 100 = _____

⑫ 400 ÷ 100 X 10 = _____

Do the calculation.

⑬ 2784 + 3796	⑭ 999 – 888

⑮ 2784 + 4370 – 401	⑯ 4983 + 3974 – 728

⑰ 595 ÷ 7	⑱ 314 x 8	⑲ 438 ÷ 6

⑳ 5 ⟌ 3 2 5	㉑ 3 ⟌ 8 7 3	㉒ 8 ⟌ 7 3 6

㉓ 5 3 7 X 9	㉔ 8 5 4 X 6	㉕ 2 1 3 X 5

Find the answers.

㉖ The sum of seven thousand two and four hundred ninety-nine.

_____

㉗ The difference between nine hundred eighty-four and five hundred seventy-eight.

_____

Write your answers in the puzzle below.

ACROSS

A	7 x 30
B	208 ÷ 4
C	270 ÷ 9
D	30 x 69
E	48 ÷ 12
F	5 x 150

DOWN

A	225 ÷ 9
C	5 x 75
E	322 ÷ 7
F	19 x 4
G	366 ÷ 3

㉘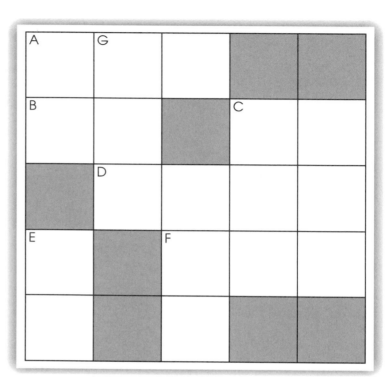

Do the division and write down the remainder in each case. The sum of the remainders is equal to the number of coconuts in the tree.

㉙ 218 ÷ 3   remainder = _____

㉚ 497 ÷ 7   remainder = _____

㉛ 100 ÷ 3   remainder = _____

㉜ 200 ÷ 5   remainder = _____

㉝ 124 ÷ 8   remainder = _____

㉞ 874 ÷ 4   remainder = _____

㉟ Sum of remainders   = _____

There are _____ coconuts in the tree.

Solve the problems. Show your work.

㊱ Jane is 7 years older than Jeff. Jane is 11 years old. How old is Jeff?

Jeff is _____ years old.

㊲ What is the perimeter of the rectangle?

12 m

2 m   2 m

12 m

㊳ Dan's heart beats 66 times a minute. How many times does it beat in an hour?

㊴ Farmer Fred's chickens lay 240 eggs per day. If he gets $2 for one dozen eggs, how much does he earn per day?

Solve the problems.

① Write the next 3 numbers in each of the following sequences.

    a.   77   88   99   _____   _____   _____

    b.   72   84   96   _____   _____   _____

② A number is divisible by 3 if the sum of its digits is divisible by 3. Circle the numbers which are divisible by 3. (Do not divide!)

    1234   5790   2927   9980   4563

Introducing Decimals

1. $0.94 = \dfrac{94}{100}$ or $\dfrac{9}{10} + \dfrac{4}{100}$ = 9 tenths and 4 hundredths

2. $0.4 = \dfrac{4}{10}$ or $\dfrac{40}{100}$ = 4 tenths or 40 hundredths

3. $0.02 = \dfrac{2}{100}$ = 2 hundredths

4. $1.43 = 1 + 0.43$

   $= 1 + \dfrac{43}{100}$

   $= 1$ and 43 hundredths

Complete the chart below.

	Decimal	Fraction
①	0.52	
②		$\dfrac{5}{100}$
③		$\dfrac{3}{10}$
④	0.09	
⑤		$7\dfrac{2}{10}$
⑥	4.1	

HINTS:

ones
↓   decimal point
↓ ↓
• **2.94** is a decimal number.
   ↑ ↑— hundredths
tenths

Read as two point nine four.

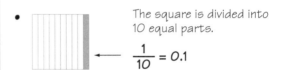

The square is divided into 10 equal parts.

$\dfrac{1}{10} = 0.1$

The square is divided into 100 equal parts.

$\dfrac{1}{100} = 0.01$

• 1 tenth is the same as 10 hundredths.

• Deleting the zeros at the end of a decimal number will not affect the numerical value of a decimal number.
   e.g. $2.30 = 2.3$

• When rounding decimal numbers, round up if the last digit is 5 or more; otherwise, round down.

Place the numbers on the number line below.

⑦

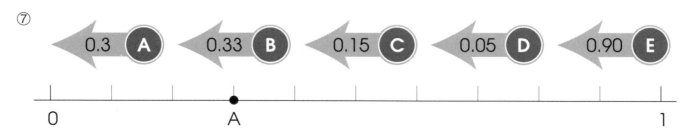

0.3 **A**   0.33 **B**   0.15 **C**   0.05 **D**   0.90 **E**

0   A   1

Write the numbers in order from least to greatest.

⑧   0.2, 0.15, 0.1, 0.02, 0.01

_____

⑨   1.45, 1.50, 1.4, 1.54, 1.05

_____

Write the numbers in order from greatest to least.

⑩   5.08, 5.80, 5.88, 0.58, 0.55, 0.50

_____

⑪   2.9, 2.09, 3.2, 2.39, 2.93, 2.3

_____

Write the quantities in decimal form.

⑫   5 cents = $ _____   ⑬   2 nickels = $ _____

⑭   3 quarters = $ _____   ⑮   4 dimes = $ _____

⑯   316 cm = _____ m   ⑰   37 mm = _____ cm

Write True (T) or False (F) in the ( ).

⑱   0.7 = 0.70   (   )   ⑲   1.02 = 1.2   (   )

⑳   3.0 = 3   (   )   ㉑   0.5 = .5   (   )

㉒ $9.1 = 9\frac{1}{100}$ (   )   ㉓ $2.3 = 2\frac{3}{100}$ (   )

Complete the expanded forms using decimals.

㉔ $7 + \frac{2}{100} =$ _____   ㉕ $3 + \frac{5}{10} + \frac{7}{100} =$ _____

㉖ $\frac{1}{10} + \frac{6}{100} =$ _____   ㉗ $2 + \frac{3}{10} + \frac{5}{100} =$ _____

Write an approximate decimal value for each of the numbers on the number line below.

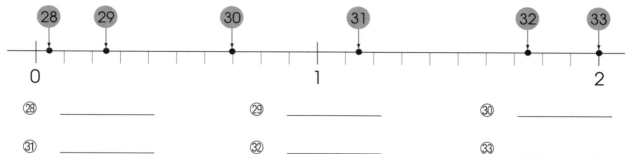

㉘ ________ ㉙ ________ ㉚ ________

㉛ ________ ㉜ ________ ㉝ ________

Write the place value and meaning of each underlined digit.

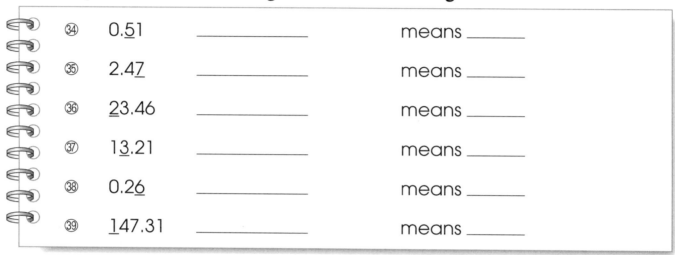

㉞ $0.\underline{5}1$ ____________ means ______

㉟ $2.4\underline{7}$ ____________ means ______

㊱ $\underline{2}3.46$ ____________ means ______

㊲ $1\underline{3}.21$ ____________ means ______

㊳ $0.2\underline{6}$ ____________ means ______

㊴ $\underline{1}47.31$ ____________ means ______

Round each of the following numbers to the nearest tenth.

㊵ 5.72 ________	㊶ 0.88 ________
㊷ 1.99 ________	㊸ 12.34 ________

Round each of the following numbers to the nearest hundredth.

㊹ 5.938 ________	㊺ 2.704 ________
㊻ 3.097 ________	㊼ 6.006 ________

Place < or > between each pair of decimal numbers.

㊽ 0.3 0.32	㊾ 0.09 0.9
㊿ 0.22 0.2	(51) 23.1 23.01

Answer the following questions.

(52) Ron finished a marathon race in 3 hours 57.8 minutes. John took 0.7 minutes longer.

a. How long did John take to finish the race? ____________

b. Did they both finish under 4 hours? ____________

(53) Ann spent $47.99 on a pair of jeans and $15.75 on a T-shirt. How much did she spend to the nearest dollar?

____

(54) Janice paid $0.80 for a chocolate bar. Write 2 different ways she could pay with 8 coins.

a. Use ____  ____  ____  ____ 

b. Use ____  ____  ____  ____ 

(55) Ming spent $195.55 at the mall. Write this amount in words.

____

Determine the value for each symbol. Each symbol has a different value. Write down all the possible solutions.

■ = ______ ♠ = ______

◆ = ______ ♥ = ______

	■	◆	.	9
+	♠	8	.	♥
	5	6	.	7

3 Adding Decimals

1.   57.23 + 85.9 + 0.78 + 30
     = 173.91

align the decimal points
↓
```
   57.23
   85.90 ←
    0.78      write "0"
              to fill the
 + 30.00 ←    empty
              places
 ───────
  173.91
```

2. Write 219.57 in expanded form.
   219.57 = 200 + 10 + 9 + 0.5 + 0.07

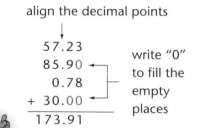

HINTS:

- Align the decimal points when doing vertical addition.

- Write zeros to fill the empty places.

- Add decimal numbers the same way we add whole numbers.

- Don't forget to add the decimal point in the answer.

Add these decimals in tenths.

①
```
   0.7
 + 0.8
 ─────
```

②
```
   1.9
 + 8.7
 ─────
```

③
```
   30.2
 + 16.6
 ──────
```

④
```
   23.4
 + 41.6
 ──────
```

⑤   10.2 + 12.7 = _____

⑥   0.9 + 12.8 = _____

Add these decimals in hundredths.

⑦
```
   50.93
 +  7.28
 ───────
```

⑧
```
    6.54
 + 27.69
 ───────
```

⑨
```
   27.84
 +  3.07
 ───────
```

⑩
```
   100.30
 +   6.84
 ────────
```

⑪   5.83 + 3.0   = _____

⑫   99.01 + 9.09   = _____

⑬   5.50 + 0.9   = _____

⑭   324.78 + 1.22 = _____

⑮   123.45 + 34.56 = _____

⑯   13.59 + 12.64 = _____

Add these decimals.

⑰ 5 + 7.8 = _____

⑱ 5.9 + 0.78 = _____

⑲ 2.73 + 4.9 = _____

⑳ 7 + 1.23 = _____

㉑ 5.9 + 8.73 = _____

㉒ 5.03 + 2.9 = _____

㉓ 11.67 + 40.9 = _____

㉔ 22.45 + 6.7 = _____

㉕ 52.93 + 109.2 = _____

㉖ 809 + 2.82 = _____

㉗ 141.05 + 26.4 = _____

㉘ 17.42 + 353 = _____

㉙ 0.98 + 3.2 + 12 = _____

㉚ 9 + 61.4 + 45.5 = _____

㉛ 14.07 + 6.67 + 9.91 = _____

㉜ 4.5 + 2.77 + 1.82 = _____

㉝ 5 + 4.23 + 12.6 = _____

㉞ 4.97 + 9.3 + 1.87 + 5 = _____

㉟ 902 + 77.13 + 0.87 = _____

Write these decimals in expanded form.

㊱ 25.87 = _____

㊲ 12.93 = _____

Write the decimals.

㊳ 500 + 70 + 0.8 = _____

㊴ 100 + 8 + 0.6 + 0.04 = _____

Add the money. If the sum is larger than the amount in the previous question, write it on the line in ㊼ and add the sums to find Sally's savings.

㊵ \$9.32 + \$0.95 = ____________

㊶ \$9.85 + \$1.32 = ____________

㊷ \$5.23 + \$6.09 = ____________

㊸ \$10.93 + \$0.21 = ____________

㊹ \$53.29 + \$6.78 = ____________

㊺ \$70.94 + \$0.50 = ____________

㊻ \$29.84 + \$39.99 = ____________

㊼ ____

㊽ sum = ______________________________

㊾ Sally saves ______________ .

Do the following addition. Write + or – in the ◯ to show the relation of P, Q, R and S.

(50) 5.9 + 12.8 = Ⓟ

(51) 15.2 + 9.4 = Ⓡ

(52) 19.4 + 3.9 = Ⓠ

(53) 7.8 + 9.6 = Ⓢ

(54) Ⓟ ◯ Ⓠ = Ⓡ ◯ Ⓢ

Solve the problems. Show your work.

(55) Casla and Sally go to a movie. The tickets cost \$5.50 each. Popcorn costs \$3.75 and drinks cost \$1.20 each. If they each have a drink and share the popcorn, how much do they pay altogether?

_______________________________ = __________

They pay __________ altogether.

(56) Ann's allowance in September is \$6.75 the first week, \$5.90 the second week, \$6.50 the third week and only \$5.00 the fourth week. How much does she get over the 4 week period?

(57) Ron is training for triathlon. He cycles 25.2 km on Monday, 22.1 km on Wednesday, 24.8 km on Friday and 28.2 km on Saturday. How far does he cycle during the week?

Bob has 17 coins. They are dimes, nickels and pennies. Their total value is \$0.90. How many of each coin does he have?

Bob has ________ dimes, ________ nickels and ________ pennies.

Subtracting Decimals

1. 29.43 − 17.86 = ?

$$
\begin{array}{r}
2\,9.\overset{3\ 13}{\cancel{4}\,\cancel{3}} \\
-\ 1\,7.8\,6 \\
\hline
7
\end{array}
$$
→
$$
\begin{array}{r}
2\,9.\overset{8\ 13}{\cancel{4}\,3} \\
-\ 1\,7.8\,6 \\
\hline
.5\,7
\end{array}
$$
→
$$
\begin{array}{r}
2\overset{8}{\cancel{9}}.4\,3 \\
-\ 1\,7.8\,6 \\
\hline
1.5\,7
\end{array}
$$
→
$$
\begin{array}{r}
2\,9.4\,3 \\
-\ 1\,7.8\,6 \\
\hline
1\,1.5\,7
\end{array}
$$

2. Jim ran 5.8 km and Andrea ran 7.25 km. How much farther did Andrea run?

7.25 − 5.8 = 1.45

$$
\begin{array}{r}
\overset{6\ \ 12}{\cancel{7}}.\cancel{2}\,5 \\
-\ \ 5.8\,0 \\
\hline
1.4\,5
\end{array}
$$

Andrea ran 1.45 km farther.

HINTS:

- Align the decimal points when doing vertical subtraction.
- Write zeros to fill the empty places.
- Subtract decimal numbers the same way we subtract whole numbers.
- Use addition to check your answer.
- Don't forget to add the decimal point in the answer.

Subtract these decimals in tenths.

①
$$
\begin{array}{r}
0.7 \\
-\ \ 0.2 \\
\hline
\end{array}
$$

②
$$
\begin{array}{r}
5\,8.3 \\
-\ \ \ 1.8 \\
\hline
\end{array}
$$

③
$$
\begin{array}{r}
9.2 \\
-\ \ 2.9 \\
\hline
\end{array}
$$

④
$$
\begin{array}{r}
5.0 \\
-\ \ 3.8 \\
\hline
\end{array}
$$

⑤ 45.3 − 16.9 = _____

⑥ 72.4 − 38.6 = _____

Subtract these decimals in hundredths.

⑦
$$
\begin{array}{r}
1\,7.0\,4 \\
-\ 1\,2.0\,0 \\
\hline
\end{array}
$$

⑧
$$
\begin{array}{r}
1.5\,7 \\
-\ \ 0.8\,8 \\
\hline
\end{array}
$$

⑨
$$
\begin{array}{r}
8.0\,4 \\
-\ \ 4.9\,8 \\
\hline
\end{array}
$$

⑩ 704.23 − 125.07 = _____

⑪ 32.16 − 8.45 = _____

Subtract these decimals.

⑫ 2.0 - 0.02 = _____

⑬ 9.03 - 4 = _____

⑭ 7.9 - 4.13 = _____

⑮ 10.4 - 2.13 = _____

⑯ 8.1 - 5.08 = _____

⑰ 15 - 3.62 = _____

⑱ 12.1 - 4.23 = _____

⑲ 9.5 - 7.68 = _____

⑳ 0.96 - 0.08 = _____

㉑ 0.72 - 0.5 = _____

㉒ 1.1 - 0.84 = _____

㉓ 2.3 - 1.49 = _____

㉔ 0.26 - 0.26 = _____

㉕ 0.36 - 0.3 = _____

㉖ 42.1 - 9.63 = _____

㉗ 98 - 71.6 = _____

㉘ 206.37 - 55.6 = _____

㉙ 58.9 - 8.9 = _____

㉚ 42.48 - 22.7 = _____

㉛ 1200 - 1000.6 = _____

Round each of the following differences to the nearest whole number.

㉜ 8.4 - 5.7 = _____

㉝ 3.1 - 1.7 = _____

㉞ 58.9 - 19.2 = _____

㉟ 14.2 - 5.4 = _____

㊱ 22.4 - 8.9 = _____

㊲ 36.4 - 22.8 = _____

Round each of the following differences to the nearest tenth.

㊳ 9.23 - 6.57 = _____

㊴ 7.63 - 5.87 = _____

㊵ 28.97 - 17.85 = _____

㊶ 32.04 - 13.68 = _____

㊷ 45 - 10.73 = _____

㊸ 19.4 - 6.83 = _____

Complete the number sentences and colour the boxes containing your answers in the number chart below.

(44) 9.2 − 7.8 = ____________

(45) 9.3 − ____________ = 1.3

(46) 9.23 − 5.87 = ____________

(47) 8.2 − ____________ = 5.8

(48) 5.2 + ____________ = 7.1

(49) 3 − 0.39 = ____________

(50) 2 + 3 − 0.8 = ____________

(51) 5.2 − 3.97 = ____________

(52) ____________ − 2.3 = 4.7

(53) 5 + ____________ + 2.3 = 7.9

(54) 15 − ____________ = 7.3

(55) 9.37 − 1.99 = ____________

(56) 27.62 − 13.49 = ____________

(57) 12.13 − ____________ = 2.67

(58)

11.4	7.7	7.38	7.0	6.94
17.0	5.8	1.4	10.6	9.17
7.5	0.2	14.13	5.2	3.61
15.1	9.3	4.2	14.0	15.2
14.8	3.63	9.46	41.11	12.3
12.3	22.3	2.61	2.60	11.36
2.63	0.6	8.0	1.23	3.27

(59) What is the letter formed by the coloured boxes?

The letter formed by the coloured boxes is ____________.

Solve the problems. Show your work.

60. Bill pays $35 for his groceries. How much change does he get if the total is $32.85?

_____ = _____

He gets _____ change.

61. Sue weighs 45.2 kg. Her sister weighs 41.5 kg. How much heavier is Sue than her sister?

62. The CN Tower in Toronto is 0.55 km high. The Calgary Tower is 0.19 km high. How much taller is the CN Tower?

63. At a high school track meet, Ben ran 100 m in 11.87 seconds and Carl ran the same distance in 12.13 seconds. How much longer did Carl take?

Just for Fun

Fill in the missing numbers in the magic square. All numbers from 1 to 9 must be used.

In a magic square, the sum of the numbers in a row, column or diagonal is the same.

	9	
3		7
8	1	

More Addition and Subtraction of Decimals

1. $5.93 + 17.29 - 3.74$ or $5.93 + 17.29 - 3.74$

    $= 23.22 - 3.74$ $= 5.93 - 3.74 + 17.29$ ◄── order of operations changed

    $= 19.48$ $= 2.19 + 17.29$

                           $= 19.48$ ◄── still the same answer

2. $2 - 3.1 + 1.93$

    $= 2 + 1.93 - 3.1$ ◄── Order of operations is changed because

    $= 3.93 - 3.1$ you can't take away 3.1 from 2.

    $= 0.83$

```
  2.00          3.93
+ 1.93        - 3.10
------        ------
  3.93          0.83
```

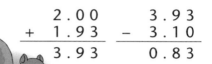

Find the answers mentally.

① $5.2 - 3.2 + 17.5$ = _____

② $3.75 - 1.25 - 0.5$ = _____

③ $5.99 - 3.99 + 4.99$ = _____

④ $12 - 0.5 + 2.5$ = _____

⑤ $7.55 + 3.45 - 0.50$ = _____

⑥ $3 - 0.75 - 0.75$ = _____

⑦ $1.9 - 0.5 - 1.4$ = _____

⑧ $9.99 + 10.01 - 5.00$ = _____

⑨ $13.25 - 5.5 + 2.25$ = _____

⑩ $26.5 - 2 + 3.5$ = _____

⑪ $45.85 - 70.5 + 25.15$ = _____

⑫ $175.5 - 155.5 - 2.5$ = _____

⑬ $115.50 - 100.00 - 5.50$ = _____

⑭ $125.75 + 25.25 - 51.0$ = _____

HINTS:

- To change the order of operations in multi-step operations, move the number together with the sign immediately in front of it.

  e.g. $5.1 + 3.2 - 4.9$

       $= 5.1 + 4.9 - 3.2$

       $= 10 - 3.2$

       $= 6.8$ ✗

       $5.1 + 3.2 - 4.9$

       $= 5.1 - 4.9 + 3.2$

       $= 0.2 + 3.2$

       $= 3.4$ ✓

- Remember to add zeros for missing decimal places in vertical addition or subtraction.

Find the answers. Show your work.

⑮ 19.2 − 3.75

= _____

⑯ 7 − 3.72

= _____

⑰ 22 − 3.5 − 9.7

= _____

⑱ 7.1 + 3 − 5.09

= _____

⑲ 1 − 0.09 + 3.78

= _____

⑳ 7.3 + 2.9 − 5.4

= _____

㉑ 123.55 − 17.55 + 3.25

= _____

㉒ 125 − 100.95 − 3.72

= _____

㉓ 197.8 + 188.7 − 142.9

= _____

㉔ 1000 − 1.2 + 5.00

= _____

㉕ 0.09 + 0.92 − 0.08

= _____

㉖ 77 + 29.2 − 5.93

= _____

㉗ 26.94 − 47.86 + 35.48

= _____

㉘ 6.73 − 28.45 + 32.38

= _____

Show your work for the following money problems.

29   $12.23 + $7.00 − $3.79

= _____

30   $100.00 − $7.55 − $19.35

= _____

31   $59.70 − $32.90 − $2.00

= _____

32   $100.00 − $3.50 + $1.50

= _____

33   $10.00 + 0.79 − $0.55

= _____

34   $15.25 − $6.75 + $3.02

= _____

Round each answer to the nearest cent.

35   59.7¢ − 3.9¢ + 2.8¢

= _____

36   39.8¢ − 5.2¢ − 1.3¢

= _____

37   120.1¢ + 9.8¢ − 108.2¢

= _____

38   0.9¢ + 0.7¢ + 5.3¢

= _____

Fill in the missing number in each of the following number sentences.

39   12.3 − [＿＿＿] + 1.7 = 5.9

40   0.23 + [＿＿＿] = 1.90

41   25.3 − 19.8 + [＿＿＿] = 7.0

42   [＿＿＿] − 7.8 = 12.2

43   [＿＿＿] + 15.77 − 8.69 = 7.73

44   12.51 − [＿＿＿] = 9.07

Solve the problems. Show your work.

㊺ Sam has saved $25.00 for a trip to town. He spends $4.55 on transportation and $6.99 on lunch. How much does he have left?

_____ = _____

He has _____ left.

㊻ Rebecca earns $35.00 from a baby-sitting job. She uses the money to buy gifts for Clara and Debbie. Clara's gift costs $5.95 and Debbie's gift costs $17.45. How much does Rebecca have left?

㊼ Adam, Bob & Colin went to the CNE together. The fare cost them $6.50 each and a 1-day pass cost $19.95 each. Lunch cost $7.50 each and they each had a discount coupon worth $2.00. How much did each of them spend?

㊽ Penny, Peter and Pam contribute $17.50 each to buy a birthday gift for Sue. They decide to buy 2 CDs which cost $20.95 each. The tax for 2 CDs is $6.30. Do they have enough money?

Answer Sally's question.

If you put 1¢ in your piggy bank on Monday, 2¢ on Tuesday, 4¢ on Wednesday, 8¢ on Thursday and so on, how much will you have saved at the end of 1 week?

I will have saved _____ at the end of 1 week.

6 Multiplying Decimals by Whole Numbers

1. $7.3 \times 9 = 65.7$

$$
\begin{array}{r}
\overset{2}{7}.3 \quad \leftarrow \text{1 decimal place} \\
\times \quad 9 \quad \leftarrow \text{align the numbers} \\
\hline
6\,5.7 \quad \leftarrow \text{1 decimal place in product}
\end{array}
$$

2. Danielle buys 5 books at $5.95 each. How much does she pay altogether?
   $5.95 \times 5 = \$29.75$

   She pays $29.75 altogether.

$$
\begin{array}{r}
\overset{4}{5}.\overset{2}{9}5 \quad \leftarrow \text{2 decimal places} \\
\times \quad 5 \quad \leftarrow \text{align the numbers} \\
\hline
2\,9.7\,5 \quad \leftarrow \text{2 decimal places in product}
\end{array}
$$

3. $0.75 \times 10 = 7.5 \leftarrow$ move the decimal point one place to the right

4. $0.75 \times 100 = 75. \leftarrow$ move the decimal point two places to the right

HINTS:

- Align all numbers on the right-hand side.

- Multiply the decimals as with whole numbers, from right to left.

- The number of decimal places in the product is the same as that in the question.

- Multiplying a decimal number
  by 10 → move the decimal point one place right
  by 100 → move the decimal point two places right
  and so on.

- Check if your answer is reasonable by rounding the decimal to the nearest whole number and estimate the answer.

Find the products mentally.

① 0.2×5 = _____

② 3.2×10 = _____

③ 0.1×7 = _____

④ 0.01×8 = _____

⑤ 3.0×4 = _____

⑥ 1.1×9 = _____

⑦ 4.01×6 = _____

⑧ 5.4×100 = _____

⑨ 9.15×10 = _____

⑩ 0.01×10 = _____

⑪ 0.1×100 = _____

⑫ 9.3×10 = _____

⑬ 100.4×2 = _____

⑭ 0.08×100 = _____

⑮ 0.62×10 = _____

⑯ 0.1×10 = _____

⑰ 24.8×10 = _____

⑱ 0.01×100 = _____

Write the decimal point in each product.

⑲
$$4.7 \times 3 = 141$$

⑳
$$2.69 \times 4 = 1076$$

㉑
$$10.9 \times 5 = 545$$

㉒ 6.47 × 7 = 4 5 2 9

㉓ 5.55 × 8 = 4 4 4 0

Find the products. Show your work.

㉔
$$7.3 \times 9$$

㉕
$$4.9 \times 7$$

㉖
$$12.2 \times 8$$

㉗
$$5.72 \times 5$$

㉘
$$9.89 \times 6$$

㉙
$$2.7 \times 4$$

㉚
$$0.98 \times 4$$

㉛
$$4.83 \times 7$$

㉜
$$0.18 \times 9$$

㉝
$$3.25 \times 9$$

㉞
$$1.38 \times 7$$

㉟
$$2.9 \times 8$$

㊱
$$72.3 \times 7$$

㊲
$$9.99 \times 3$$

㊳
$$0.76 \times 6$$

Estimate. Then find the exact products.

		Estimate	Exact Product
39	5.2 × 7		
40	3.7 × 2		
41	9.81 × 5		
42	8.23 × 6		
43	3.75 × 3		
44	0.36 × 8		
45	0.17 × 9		
46	8.44 × 4		

Check the answers of the following multiplication. Put a ✓ in the box if the answer is correct; otherwise, write the correct answer in the box.

47

$$\begin{array}{r} 2.31 \\ \times \quad 6 \\ \hline 1.386 \end{array}$$ ☐

48

$$\begin{array}{r} 0.02 \\ \times \quad 5 \\ \hline 0.10 \end{array}$$ ☐

49

$$\begin{array}{r} 1.03 \\ \times \quad 3 \\ \hline 3.9 \end{array}$$ ☐

Fill in the boxes.

50 $\quad 7.15 \times$ ☐ $= 715$

51 $\quad 5.1 \times$ ☐ $= 15.3$

52 ☐ $\times 3.2 = 32$

53 ☐ $\times 0.9 = 90$

54 $\dfrac{\boxed{}}{10} = 15.9$

55 $\dfrac{\boxed{}}{3} = 10.3$

Solve the problems. Show your work.

㊶ Sina buys 3 CDs at $23.99 each. How much does she pay altogether?

_____ = _____

She pays _____ altogether.

㊷ Ron buys 4 trees at $89.50 each. Calculate the total cost.

㊸ Adam walks 2.3 km each day to school. How far does he walk in a 5-day week?

㊹ How much space do 8 textbooks occupy on a book shelf if each is 3.2 cm thick?

㊺ Susanne buys 3 T-shirts at $12.95 each and 2 pairs of jeans at $39.99 each. How much does she pay altogether to the nearest dollar?

Help Bob solve the problem.

How can I add four + signs in the following number sentence to make it true?

4   4   4   4   4   4   4   4   =   500

Dividing Decimals by Whole Numbers

7

1. $5.7 \div 3 = 1.9$

$3\overline{)5.7} \longrightarrow$
$\begin{array}{r} 1 \\ 3\overline{)5.7} \\ \underline{3} \\ 2 \end{array}$
divisor — dividend

$\longrightarrow$
$\begin{array}{r} 1 \\ 3\overline{)5.7} \\ \underline{3}\downarrow \\ 2\,7 \end{array}$

$\longrightarrow$
$\begin{array}{r} 1.9 \nearrow \text{quotient} \\ 3\overline{)5.7} \\ \underline{3} \\ 2\,7 \\ \underline{2\,7} \end{array}$

2. $6.2 \div 4 = 1.55$

$\begin{array}{r} 1 \\ 4\overline{)6.2} \\ \underline{4} \end{array} \longrightarrow$
$\begin{array}{r} 1 \\ 4\overline{)6.2} \\ \underline{4}\downarrow \\ 2\,2 \end{array} \longrightarrow$
$\begin{array}{r} 1.5 \\ 4\overline{)6.2} \\ \underline{4} \\ 2\,2 \\ \underline{2\,0} \\ 2 \end{array} \longrightarrow$
$\begin{array}{r} 1.5 \\ 4\overline{)6.2\,0} \\ \underline{4} \\ 2\,2 \\ \underline{2\,0}\downarrow \\ 2\,0 \end{array} \longrightarrow$
$\begin{array}{r} 1.5\,5 \\ 4\overline{)6.2\,0} \\ \underline{4} \\ 2\,2 \\ \underline{2\,0} \\ 2\,0 \\ \underline{2\,0} \end{array}$

add extra zero

3. $7.5 \div 10 = 0.7\,5$ — move the decimal point one place to the left

4. $7.5 \div 100 = 0.0\,7\,5$ — move the decimal point two places to the left

Find the quotients mentally.

① $9.8 \div 10$ = _____

② $0.32 \div 10$ = _____

③ $75.0 \div 100$ = _____

④ $9.2 \div 1000$ = _____

⑤ $3.28 \div 10$ = _____

⑥ $0.05 \div 100$ = _____

⑦ $0.08 \div 10$ = _____

⑧ $154.93 \div 100$ = _____

⑨ $316.45 \div 100$ = _____

HINTS:

- Divide the decimals as with whole numbers, from left to right.

- If there is a remainder, add zeros to the right of the dividend after the decimal point. Continue to divide until the remainder is zero or you have enough decimal places.

- Don't forget to put a decimal point in the quotient above the one in the dividend.

- Always check if your answer makes sense.
  e.g. $6 \div 3 = 2$
  so $5.7 \div 3 = 1.9$ is reasonable.

- Dividing a decimal number
  by 10 → move the decimal point one place left.
  by 100 → move the decimal point two places left
  and so on.

Write the decimal point in each quotient. Add zeros where necessary.

⑩ $52.8 \div 3$ = 1 7 6

⑪ $0.84 \div 7$ = 1 2

⑫ $14.28 \div 7$ = 2 0 4

⑬ $2.08 \div 4$ = 5 2

Find the quotients. Show your work.

⑭ $7\,\overline{)\,8.05}$	⑮ $9\,\overline{)\,66.6}$	⑯ $7\,\overline{)\,73.5}$
⑰ $6\,\overline{)\,8.52}$	⑱ $4\,\overline{)\,0.24}$	⑲ $8\,\overline{)\,160.8}$
⑳ $3\,\overline{)\,12.09}$	㉑ $5\,\overline{)\,52.65}$	㉒ $8\,\overline{)\,36.4}$
㉓ $4\,\overline{)\,70.4}$	㉔ $5\,\overline{)\,10.4}$	㉕ $9\,\overline{)\,19.35}$

Divide. Show your work. Match the letters with the numbers in the boxes. What is the message?

㉖ (I)	㉗ (A)	㉘ (T)
4)9.2	3)0.57	2)5.1

㉙ (E)	㉚ (T)	㉛ (L)
7)35.84	5)760.5	5)35.05

㉜ (R)	㉝ (S)	㉞ (P)
8)10.4	7)380.1	4)503.4

㉟ (T)	㊱ (L)	㊲ (S)
5)0.45	9)58.77	6)502.38

㊳ What does Sally see in the night sky?

7.01	2.3	2.55	152.1	6.53	5.12

54.3	0.09	0.19	1.3	83.73

Solve the problems. Show your work.

㊴ John mails 10 equal packages. The total weight is 32.5 kg. How much does each package weigh ?

_____ = _____

Each package weighs _____ .

㊵ On his summer holidays Bob drove 7350 km in 100 hours. How far did he travel each hour?

㊶ Sam divides 36.4 metres of phone cable into 8 equal parts. How long is each part?

㊷ 8 students share the cost of a trip. If the total cost of the trip is $394.00, how much does each student pay?

㊸ An equilateral triangle has all sides equal. If the perimeter is 13.5 cm, what is the length of each side?

Look for the pattern. What are the next 3 numbers?

1 , 1 , 2 , 3 , 5 , 8 , 13 , , ,

More Multiplying and Dividing of Decimals

8

E X A M P L E S

1. 7.92 × 5 = 39.6

$$\begin{array}{r} \overset{4}{}\overset{1}{}\ \ \\ 7.9\,2 \\ \times \quad 5 \\ \hline 3\,9.6\,\cancel{0} \end{array}$$ ← delete the zero at the last decimal place

put a zero in the quotient

2. 10.25 ÷ 5 = 2.05

$$\begin{array}{r} 2.5 \\ 5\overline{)10.25} \\ 10 \\ \hline 25 \\ 25 \\ \hline \end{array}$$ ✗

$$\begin{array}{r} 2.05 \\ 5\overline{)10.25} \\ 10 \\ \hline 25 \\ 25 \\ \hline \end{array}$$ ✓

HINTS:

- The number of decimal places in the product is the same as that in the question, but a zero at the last decimal place can be deleted.

  e.g.   **7.92 × 5 = 39.6** ←

  only one decimal place in the product because the zero in the hundredths place is deleted

- Remember to put a zero in the quotient when the dividend is smaller than the divisor.

  e.g.   **10.25 ÷ 5 = 2.05**   but not 2.5

  a zero is put at the tenths place because 2 in the dividend is smaller than the divisor 5

Find the answers mentally.

①   7.34 × 10   = _____

②   9.23 ÷ 10   = _____

③   123.4 ÷ 100   = _____

④   2.42 ÷ 2   = _____

⑤   36.9 ÷ 3   = _____

⑥   1.2 × 100   = _____

⑦   0.15 ÷ 5   = _____

⑧   80.8 ÷ 8   = _____

⑨   342.9 ÷ 100   = _____

⑩   34.29 × 1000 = _____

⑪   1.25 × 100   = _____

⑫   0.02 ÷ 10   = _____

⑬   0.4 × 10   = _____

⑭   1.18 × 10   = _____

⑮   0.04 × 100   = _____

⑯   1.25 ÷ 100   = _____

⑰   0.02 × 10   = _____

⑱   63.5 × 10   = _____

Do the calculation. Show your work.

⑲ $4\overline{)94.4}$

⑳ $7\overline{)7.28}$

㉑ $3\overline{)45.09}$

㉒
$$\begin{array}{r} 3.92 \\ \times \quad 4 \\ \hline \end{array}$$

㉓
$$\begin{array}{r} 10.3 \\ \times \quad 7 \\ \hline \end{array}$$

㉔
$$\begin{array}{r} 5.91 \\ \times \quad 6 \\ \hline \end{array}$$

㉕ $6\overline{)7.92}$

㉖ $9\overline{)17.1}$

㉗ $5\overline{)6.2}$

㉘
$$\begin{array}{r} 0.47 \\ \times \quad 8 \\ \hline \end{array}$$

㉙
$$\begin{array}{r} 18.2 \\ \times \quad 9 \\ \hline \end{array}$$

㉚
$$\begin{array}{r} 36.7 \\ \times \quad 2 \\ \hline \end{array}$$

Find the answers.

㉛ 1.25 × 8   = _____

㉜ 1.75 × 4   = _____

㉝ 1.19 ÷ 7   = _____

㉞ 10.4 ÷ 4   = _____

㉟ 3.08 × 9   = _____

㊱ 76.8 ÷ 3   = _____

㊲ 89 × 10 ÷ 10 = _____

㊳ 1.9 × 10 × 10 = _____

Estimate. Then complete only those questions with a product greater than 15.

③⑨
$$\begin{array}{r} 7.2 \\ \times \quad 2 \\ \hline \end{array}$$

④⓪
$$\begin{array}{r} 7.9 \\ \times \quad 2 \\ \hline \end{array}$$

④①
$$\begin{array}{r} 3.8 \\ \times \quad 4 \\ \hline \end{array}$$

④②
$$\begin{array}{r} 1.9 \\ \times \quad 9 \\ \hline \end{array}$$

④③
$$\begin{array}{r} 3.1 \\ \times \quad 5 \\ \hline \end{array}$$

④④
$$\begin{array}{r} 0.25 \\ \times \quad 10 \\ \hline \end{array}$$

Estimate. Then complete only those questions with a quotient smaller than 2.

④⑤
$9\overline{)12.6}$

④⑥
$3\overline{)7.2}$

④⑦
$10\overline{)23.4}$

④⑧
$3\overline{)5.7}$

④⑨
$6\overline{)10.8}$

⑤⓪
$7\overline{)13.3}$

Fill in the blanks.

⑤① $12.7 \div \underline{\hspace{1.5cm}} = 0.127$

⑤② $3.92 \times \underline{\hspace{1.5cm}} = 39.2$

⑤③ $\underline{\hspace{1.5cm}} \div 3 = 1.14$

⑤④ $5.8 \times \underline{\hspace{1.5cm}} = 11.6$

⑤⑤ $2 \times \underline{\hspace{1.5cm}} = 12.4$

⑤⑥ $\underline{\hspace{1.5cm}} \div 7 = 1.3$

⑤⑦ $0.18 \times \underline{\hspace{1.5cm}} = 18$

⑤⑧ $54 \div \underline{\hspace{1.5cm}} = 5.4$

Answer the questions. Show your work.

(59) The Grade 5 class collects $58.20 to buy gifts for 3 children in a needy family. How much can they spend on each gift if the money is divided evenly?

______________________ = ______________

They can spend ______________ on each gift.

(60) Mrs Ling buys plants for her patio. She buys 3 plants at $19.95 each, 2 plants at $12.45 each and 10 plants at $1.25 each. How much does she pay altogether?

(61) 5 friends buy 2 pizzas at $12.99 each, 2 cans of juice at $1.29 each and 2 packets of chips at $1.49 each. They divide the total cost among them. How much must they each pay? Give the answer to the nearest cent.

(62) Carol is buying food for her dog. She can buy a 3-kg bag for $29.40 or a 5-kg bag for $39.50. Calculate the cost per kg for each bag. Which is the better buy?

What number am I?

I am a decimal number. Multiply me by 35. Divide the product by 7. The result is 2.5.

____

Calculate. Show your work.

①   3.75 + 4.2 + 11
 	
  = _____
	② 13.04 − 2.87 + 1.59
	
	  = _____

③   8.4 × 8
 	
  = _____
	④ 8.4 ÷ 8
	
	  = _____

⑤   3 × 5.42
 	
  = _____
	⑥ 5.58 ÷ 9
	
	  = _____

⑦   26.13 × 8
 	
  = _____
	⑧ 9.6 ÷ 3
	
	  = _____

Help Sally put the digits and decimal point in the right order to solve the problems.

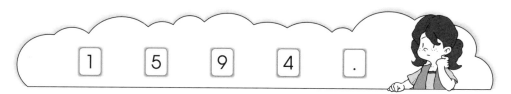

| 1 | 5 | 9 | 4 | . |

⑨   The largest decimal number with one decimal place   _____

⑩   The smallest decimal number with two decimal places   _____

⑪   The sum of the two decimals in ⑨ and ⑩   _____

⑫   The smallest decimal number with one decimal place and 9 at the ones place   _____

⑬   The largest decimal number with two decimal places and 9 at the hundredth place   _____

⑭   The difference of the two decimals in ⑫ and ⑬   _____

Complete the chart.

	Number	Number x 10	Number ÷ 10
⑮	52.0		
⑯	0.7		
⑰	0.12		
⑱		75.0	
⑲		3.0	
⑳			0.8
㉑			15.0

Circle the letter which represents the correct answer to each problem.

㉒   John earns $15.00 per hour. He works 9 hours a day, 5 days a week. How much does he earn per week?

    A. $135.00   B. $630.00   C. $450.00   D. $675.00

㉓   If $1.00 U.S. is worth $1.50 Canadian, how much is $7.00 U.S. worth in Canadian money?

    A. $8.50   B. $4.75   C. $10.50   D. $7.35

㉔   Mrs Wing earns 1.5 times her regular hourly wage on Sundays. She earns $8.00 per hour on weekdays. How much is her hourly wage on Sundays?

    A. $6.00   B. $10.00   C. $12.00   D. $16.00

㉕   John reads 10 pages per hour. How many pages does he read in 2.5 hours?

    A. 20   B. 22.5   C. 25   D. 27.5

㉖   If 1 cm = 0.39 inch, how many inches are there in 100 cm?

    A. 3.9   B. 39   C. 390   D. 3900

㉗ Mandy's mother buys her 2 new T-shirts at $9.50 each, 1 pair of jeans at $29.95 and 1 pair of sandals at $19.95. How much does Mandy's mother pay to the nearest dollar?

| A. $60 | B. $70 | C. $68 | D. $69 |

㉘ In August, Toronto's highest temperature is 35.5°C and the lowest temperature is 16.2°C. What is the difference between these temperatures?

| A. 51.7 °C | B. 19.3 °C | C. 26 °C | D. 29 °C |

㉙ The product of 1.6 and 2 is

| A. 3.6 | B. 0.8 | C. 3.2 | D. 1.4 |

㉚ When 1.2 is divided by 4, the quotient is

| A. 0.3 | B. 3.0 | C. 4.8 | D. 5.6 |

㉛ To calculate the average of 2 numbers is to add them up and then divide the sum by 2. The average of 13 and 10.2 is

| A. 23.2 | B. 11.6 | C. 1.6 | D. 3.2 |

㉜ When you divide a number by 10, the result is the same as multiplying the number by

| A. 10 | B. 0.1 | C. 0.01 | D. 100 |

㉝ When you multiply a number by 100, you move the decimal point

| A. 3 places to the right | B. 3 places to the left |
| C. 2 places to the right | D. 2 places to the left |

㉞ Which of the following statements is correct?

| A. $5 \div 2 = 0.5 \div 20$ | B. $5 \div 2 = 2 \div 5$ |
| C. $5 \div 2 = 50 \div 20$ | D. $5 \div 2 = 50 \div 0.2$ |

Ken's dog likes to run around in the backyard. Answer the questions using the measurements given in the diagram.

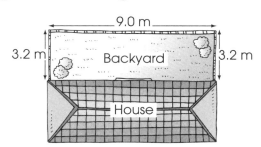

㉟	How much fencing is needed to enclose the backyard on 3 sides? _____ m fencing is needed.
㊱	The fencing costs $20 per m. What is the total cost of the fencing?
㊲	What is the perimeter of the backyard?
㊳	What is the area of the backyard?
㊴	If both the width and the length of the backyard are doubled, what effect would this have on the perimeter and the area of the backyard? a. perimeter b. area

Introducing Fractions

1. Write a fraction for the shaded area in each diagram.

    a. 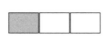 $\dfrac{1}{3}$

    b. $\dfrac{1}{4}$

    c. $\dfrac{3}{6} = \dfrac{1}{2}$

2. Write the fraction in its lowest terms.

    $$\dfrac{10}{15} = \dfrac{10 \div 5}{15 \div 5} = \dfrac{2}{3}$$

3. Label each of the divisions on the number line below. Write the fractions in lowest terms.

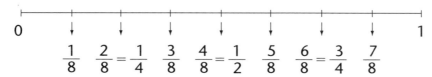

$\dfrac{1}{8}$ $\dfrac{2}{8} = \dfrac{1}{4}$ $\dfrac{3}{8}$ $\dfrac{4}{8} = \dfrac{1}{2}$ $\dfrac{5}{8}$ $\dfrac{6}{8} = \dfrac{3}{4}$ $\dfrac{7}{8}$

Write the fractions represented on the number line below.

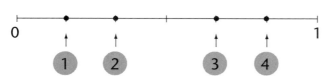

① _____   ② _____

③ _____   ④ _____

HINTS:

- A fraction represents a part of a whole or a part of a set.

  e.g.   3 slices of an 8-slice pizza
  $= \dfrac{3}{8}$ of the pizza

- To represent a fraction in lowest terms (or simplest form), divide both the numerator and denominator by the same number.

- A fraction in lowest terms means the only number that will divide into both the numerator and denominator is 1.

Write a fraction for each shaded part.

⑤  _____   ⑥ _____   ⑦ 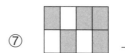 _____

⑧ _____   ⑨ _____   ⑩ _____

Colour the diagrams to show each fraction.

 ⑪ $\frac{5}{8}$

 ⑫ $\frac{7}{16}$

 ⑬ $\frac{4}{6}$

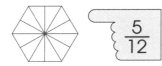 ⑭ $\frac{5}{12}$

⑮ $\frac{4}{10}$

⑯ $\frac{2}{5}$

Place the following fractions on the number line below.

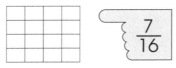

$\frac{1}{10}$ $\frac{2}{5}$ $\frac{1}{2}$ $\frac{9}{10}$ $\frac{1}{20}$ $\frac{4}{5}$

⑰ $\frac{1}{10}$

0   1

Write a fraction for the grey shapes of each set.

 ⑱

 ⑲

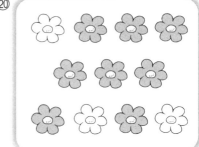 ⑳

_____   _____   _____

Colour the correct number of shapes grey to show each fraction.

 ㉑

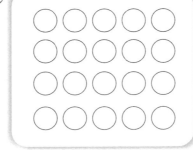 ㉒

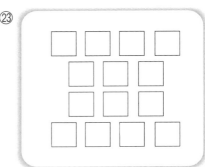 ㉓

$\frac{8}{12}$ $\frac{11}{20}$ $\frac{9}{14}$

Use the pictures to write the numbers.

㉔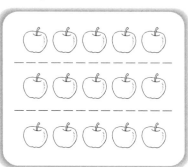

㉕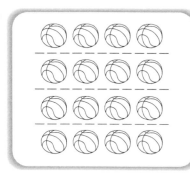

㉖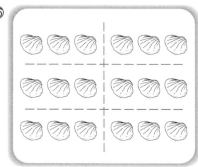

$\dfrac{1}{3}$ of 15 = _____

$\dfrac{3}{4}$ of 16 = _____

$\dfrac{2}{6}$ of 18 = _____

Fill in the boxes to express the following fractions in lowest terms.

㉗ $\dfrac{20}{30} = \dfrac{\square}{3}$

㉘ $\dfrac{5}{10} = \dfrac{1}{\square}$

㉙ $\dfrac{21}{28} = \dfrac{3}{\square}$

Write the following fractions in lowest terms.

㉚ $\dfrac{15}{20} =$ _____

㉛ $\dfrac{7}{21} =$ _____

㉜ $\dfrac{9}{18} =$ _____

㉝ $\dfrac{12}{18} =$ _____

㉞ $\dfrac{6}{16} =$ _____

㉟ $\dfrac{12}{15} =$ _____

Answer the following questions.

㊱ List any 3 fractions which lie between 0 and $\dfrac{1}{2}$. _____

㊲ What fraction of a dollar is represented by

    a. 7 nickels? _____

    b. 6 dimes? _____

㊳ Bill watches TV for 3 hours a day. What fraction of a day does he spend watching TV? _____

㊴ Margaret has 8 pairs of shoes. 6 pairs are black. What fraction of her shoes are not black? _____

㊵ Rick has finished reading 50 pages of a 250-page book. What fraction of the book has he read? _____

㊶ Pam is a rock climber. After she has climbed 30 m up a 45 m cliff, what fraction of the cliff must she climb to reach the top?

_____

㊷ 5 letters of the 26 letters in the alphabet are vowels. The others are consonants. What fraction of the alphabet do consonants make up?

_____

㊸ Tom worked 18 out of the 30 days in September. What fraction of the month did he work?

_____

㊹ Carol earns $7 per hour as a waitress. One weekend she worked for 10 hours and got $50 in tips. What fraction of her total earnings that day did her tips make up?

_____

㊺ Every day, Suzie sharpens her 16 cm long pencil and it loses 1 cm of its length. After 4 days, what fraction of its length remains?

_____

㊻ An ant crawls 50 cm along a 100-cm log the first day. The second day the ant crawls 25 cm and the third day it crawls 12 cm.

a. What fraction of the log has it covered in three days?

_____

b. What fraction of the log remains to be covered till it reaches the end?

_____

Look for the pattern.

① What are the next 3 fractions?

$\frac{1}{2}$ $\frac{1}{4}$ $\frac{1}{8}$ _____ _____ _____ .

② If you continue the pattern, will you get to zero?

_____

Equivalent Fractions and Ordering of Fractions

1. Fill in the boxes to find the equivalent fractions of $\frac{2}{3}$.

$$\frac{2}{3} = \frac{\boxed{4}}{6} = \frac{\boxed{20}}{30} = \frac{\boxed{10}}{15}$$

×2 ×5 ÷2

$\frac{2}{3} = \frac{4}{6}$

2. Order the following fractions from least to greatest.

$$\frac{2}{3} \, , \, \frac{5}{6} \, , \, \frac{7}{12} \, , \, \frac{1}{2}$$

$$\frac{2}{3} = \frac{8}{12} \qquad \frac{5}{6} = \frac{10}{12} \qquad \frac{1}{2} = \frac{6}{12}$$

×4   ×2   ×6

$$\therefore \quad \frac{1}{2} < \frac{7}{12} < \frac{2}{3} < \frac{5}{6}$$

HINTS:

- To find an equivalent fraction, multiply or divide the numerator and denominator by the same number.

- To compare the fractions, find their equivalent fractions with the same denominator first. Then compare their numerators.

- Equivalent fractions are fractions that are equal in value.

Fill in the boxes to find the equivalent fractions.

① $\frac{1}{2} = \frac{\boxed{}}{50}$

② $\frac{5}{6} = \frac{\boxed{}}{30}$

③ $\frac{5}{7} = \frac{\boxed{}}{21}$

④ $\frac{3}{4} = \frac{\boxed{}}{100}$

⑤ $\frac{\boxed{}}{8} = \frac{14}{56}$

⑥ $\frac{11}{12} = \frac{\boxed{}}{84}$

Write each fraction in lowest terms.

⑦ $\frac{25}{30} = \underline{\hspace{2cm}}$

⑧ $\frac{19}{38} = \underline{\hspace{2cm}}$

⑨ $\frac{22}{121} = \underline{\hspace{2cm}}$

⑩ $\frac{36}{84} = \underline{\hspace{2cm}}$

⑪ $\frac{250}{1000} = \underline{\hspace{2cm}}$

⑫ $\frac{32}{48} = \underline{\hspace{2cm}}$

Circle the smaller fraction in each pair of fractions.

⑬ $\dfrac{3}{4}$ $\dfrac{7}{8}$ ⑭ $\dfrac{1}{3}$ $\dfrac{1}{2}$ ⑮ $\dfrac{1}{5}$ $\dfrac{1}{6}$

⑯ $\dfrac{5}{6}$ $\dfrac{2}{3}$ ⑰ $\dfrac{3}{7}$ $\dfrac{8}{21}$ ⑱ $\dfrac{4}{5}$ $\dfrac{11}{15}$

Order the fractions from least to greatest using < .

⑲ $\dfrac{3}{5}$ $\dfrac{4}{5}$ $\dfrac{1}{2}$ $\dfrac{1}{5}$ $\dfrac{1}{10}$ $\dfrac{7}{10}$ _____

⑳ $\dfrac{1}{3}$ $\dfrac{1}{4}$ $\dfrac{3}{4}$ $\dfrac{2}{3}$ $\dfrac{2}{4}$ _____

Write True (T) or False (F) for each statement.

㉑ $\dfrac{2}{3} < \dfrac{4}{5}$ (   )   ㉒ $\dfrac{5}{9} < \dfrac{1}{2}$ (   )

㉓ $\dfrac{21}{28} < \dfrac{6}{7}$ (   )   ㉔ $\dfrac{24}{27} < \dfrac{7}{9}$ (   )

Fill in the boxes.

㉕ $\dfrac{9}{15} = \dfrac{\boxed{}}{5} = \dfrac{\boxed{}}{20}$ ㉖ $\dfrac{9}{45} = \dfrac{1}{\boxed{}} = \dfrac{\boxed{}}{10}$

㉗ $\dfrac{14}{35} = \dfrac{\boxed{}}{5} = \dfrac{\boxed{}}{10}$ ㉘ $\dfrac{11}{\boxed{}} = \dfrac{1}{5} = \dfrac{\boxed{}}{20}$

Write 3 equivalent fractions for each of the following fractions.

㉙ $\dfrac{1}{8}$ = ⬜ = ⬜ = ⬜   ㉚ $\dfrac{2}{3}$ = ⬜ = ⬜ = ⬜

㉛ $\dfrac{1}{4}$ = ⬜ = ⬜ = ⬜   ㉜ $\dfrac{5}{7}$ = ⬜ = ⬜ = ⬜

Order each group of fractions from greatest to least using >.

33 $\frac{3}{4}$ $\frac{7}{8}$ $\frac{1}{2}$ $\frac{5}{8}$ $\frac{3}{16}$ $\frac{1}{4}$ $\frac{3}{8}$

_____

34 $\frac{2}{3}$ $\frac{1}{6}$ $\frac{7}{18}$ $\frac{1}{2}$ $\frac{5}{6}$ $\frac{13}{18}$ $\frac{1}{3}$

_____

Compare each pair of fractions and write >, < or = between them.

35 $\frac{5}{6}$ $\frac{7}{8}$ 　　　　36 $\frac{14}{18}$ $\frac{7}{9}$ 　　　　37 $\frac{11}{12}$ $\frac{9}{10}$

38 $\frac{2}{3}$ $\frac{11}{15}$ 　　　　39 $\frac{5}{16}$ $\frac{3}{8}$ 　　　　40 $\frac{15}{30}$ $\frac{7}{16}$

Write each fraction in lowest terms and order the fractions from least to greatest.

41 $\frac{15}{20}$ = _____ 　　42 $\frac{75}{125}$ = _____ 　　43 $\frac{45}{54}$ = _____

44 $\frac{200}{450}$ = _____ 　　45 $\frac{14}{18}$ = _____ 　　46 $\frac{150}{175}$ = _____

47 _____ < _____ < _____ < _____ < _____ < _____

Find the missing numbers.

48
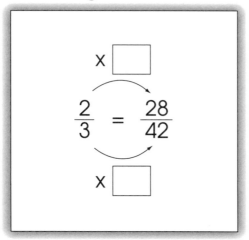

49
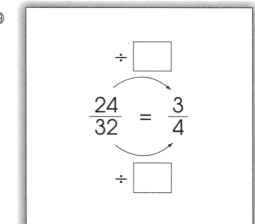

Answer the questions.

(50) John gets 22 out of 25 on a test. What is his mark out of 100?

$\frac{22}{25} = \frac{\quad}{100}$ His mark is ________.

(51) Nadine gets 9 out of 12 in a quiz. Danielle gets 14 out of 18 in another quiz. Who has the better score?

________ has the better score.

(52) The table below shows the world population in 1994 and the projected value in 2025. (Use your calculator to calculate, if necessary.)

World Population (in millions)		
	1994	2025
Africa	682	1583
North Africa	373	498
Europe	512	542
World Total	5421	8474

a. What is the fraction of the world's population living in Africa in 1994? And in 2025?

In 1994 ________ In 2025 ________

b. Is this fraction increasing or decreasing from 1994 to 2025? ________

c. What is the fraction of the world's population living in Europe in 1994? And in 2025?

In 1994 ________ In 2025 ________

d. Is this fraction increasing or decreasing from 1994 to 2025? ________

Look for the pattern. Write the next 3 terms.

1 $\frac{1}{4}$ $\frac{1}{9}$ ________ ________ ________

Adding Fractions with the Same Denominator

1. $\dfrac{1}{4} + \dfrac{3}{4} = \dfrac{1+3}{4} = \dfrac{4}{4} = \dfrac{4 \div 4}{4 \div 4} = 1$

add the numerators;
keep the denominator

reduce to lowest terms

HINTS:

- To add fractions with the same denominator, add the numerators and leave the denominator the same.

- Remember to reduce the sums to lowest terms.

- Reduce the fraction to 1 if its numerator and denominator are equal.

2. $\dfrac{1}{8} + \dfrac{5}{8} = \dfrac{1+5}{8} = \dfrac{6}{8} = \dfrac{3}{4}$

Find the sums mentally.

① $\dfrac{2}{3} + \dfrac{1}{3}$ = _____

② $\dfrac{1}{14} + \dfrac{13}{14}$ = _____

③ $\dfrac{1}{3} + \dfrac{1}{3}$ = _____

④ $\dfrac{1}{5} + \dfrac{1}{5}$ = _____

⑤ $\dfrac{1}{9} + \dfrac{4}{9}$ = _____

⑥ $\dfrac{1}{7} + \dfrac{3}{7}$ = _____

⑦ $\dfrac{3}{5} + \dfrac{1}{5}$ = _____

⑧ $\dfrac{1}{10} + \dfrac{9}{10}$ = _____

⑨ $\dfrac{5}{7} + \dfrac{2}{7}$ = _____

⑩ $\dfrac{1}{9} + \dfrac{7}{9}$ = _____

⑪ $\dfrac{1}{13} + \dfrac{10}{13}$ = _____

⑫ $\dfrac{5}{11} + \dfrac{3}{11}$ = _____

⑬ $\dfrac{2}{8} + \dfrac{5}{8}$ = _____

⑭ $\dfrac{6}{20} + \dfrac{7}{20}$ = _____

⑮ $\dfrac{5}{17} + \dfrac{4}{17}$ = _____

⑯ $\dfrac{6}{19} + \dfrac{3}{19}$ = _____

⑰ $\dfrac{4}{25} + \dfrac{17}{25}$ = _____

⑱ $\dfrac{5}{12} + \dfrac{5}{12}$ = _____

⑲ $\dfrac{4}{21} + \dfrac{13}{21}$ = _____

⑳ $\dfrac{7}{15} + \dfrac{1}{15}$ = _____

㉑ $\dfrac{1}{16} + \dfrac{5}{16}$ = _____

㉒ $\dfrac{1}{4} + \dfrac{1}{4}$ = _____

㉓ $\dfrac{5}{18} + \dfrac{7}{18}$ = _____

㉔ $\dfrac{11}{23} + \dfrac{11}{23}$ = _____

㉕ $\dfrac{1}{6} + \dfrac{3}{6}$ = _____

㉖ $\dfrac{14}{27} + \dfrac{11}{27}$ = _____

Add and reduce the answers to lowest terms. Show your work.

㉗ $\dfrac{6}{20} + \dfrac{7}{20}$ = _____

㉘ $\dfrac{4}{15} + \dfrac{8}{15}$ = _____

㉙ $\dfrac{2}{9} + \dfrac{1}{9}$ = _____

㉚ $\dfrac{11}{14} + \dfrac{1}{14}$ = _____

㉛ $\dfrac{5}{8} + \dfrac{1}{8}$ = _____

㉜ $\dfrac{3}{10} + \dfrac{3}{10}$ = _____

㉝ $\dfrac{3}{16} + \dfrac{5}{16}$ = _____

㉞ $\dfrac{1}{12} + \dfrac{5}{12}$ = _____

㉟ $\dfrac{1}{20} + \dfrac{3}{20}$ = _____

㊱ $\dfrac{1}{6} + \dfrac{1}{6}$ = _____

㊲ $\dfrac{3}{7} + \dfrac{1}{7}$ = _____

㊳ $\dfrac{1}{18} + \dfrac{2}{18}$ = _____

㊴ $\dfrac{1}{24} + \dfrac{5}{24}$ = _____

㊵ $\dfrac{5}{32} + \dfrac{3}{32}$ = _____

㊶ $\dfrac{2}{7} + \dfrac{3}{7} + \dfrac{2}{7}$ = _____

㊷ $\dfrac{2}{11} + \dfrac{2}{11} + \dfrac{3}{11} + \dfrac{4}{11}$ = _____

Complete each equation with a diagram. Then write each addition sentence using fractions. Give the sums in lowest terms.

43. + = $\dfrac{3}{8} + \dfrac{1}{8} =$ _____

44. + = _____

45. + = _____

46. + = _____

47. + = _____

48. + = _____

Fill in the boxes.

49. $\dfrac{3}{7} + \boxed{} = \dfrac{5}{7}$

50. $\dfrac{4}{11} + \boxed{} = \dfrac{5}{11}$

51. $\dfrac{1}{6} + \boxed{} = 1$

52. $\dfrac{1}{8} + \boxed{} = 1$

53. $\dfrac{1}{4} + \boxed{} = \dfrac{1}{2}$

54. $\dfrac{3}{8} + \boxed{} = \dfrac{1}{2}$

55. $\dfrac{8}{15} + \boxed{} = \dfrac{3}{5}$

56. $\dfrac{1}{10} + \boxed{} = \dfrac{1}{5}$

57. $\boxed{} + \dfrac{7}{20} = \dfrac{9}{10}$

58. $\boxed{} + \dfrac{7}{12} = 1$

59. $\boxed{} + \dfrac{9}{25} = \dfrac{4}{5}$

60. $\boxed{} + \dfrac{4}{9} = \dfrac{2}{3}$

Answer the questions. Show your work.

⑥₁ Suzie has 3 dogs. They each eat $\frac{1}{4}$ of a tin of dog food each day.
How much food do they eat among them each day?

They eat _____ tin of dog food.

⑥₂ Bob, Carrie and Dan go out for pizza. They order 1 pizza. Bob and
Carrie each eat $\frac{2}{6}$ of a pizza and Dan eats $\frac{1}{6}$ of a pizza.

a.   How many pizzas do they eat among them?

b.   Is there any pizza left?

⑥₃ Janet needs 2 pieces of ribbon, one of $\frac{5}{8}$ m and the other of $\frac{1}{8}$ m.

a.   How much ribbon does she need altogether?

b.   If she buys 1 m of ribbon, will she have enough?

⑥₄ Brenda spends $\frac{3}{10}$ of her weekly allowance on Monday and $\frac{1}{10}$ of
her allowance on Tuesday.

a.   What fraction of her allowance has she spent?

b.   What fraction of her allowance does she have left?

Find the missing fractions in the given magic square. The sum of each row, column and diagonal is the same.

$\frac{8}{15}$	$\frac{1}{15}$	$\frac{6}{15}$
	$\frac{5}{15}$	

 **Improper Fractions and Mixed Numbers**

1. Change $\frac{13}{6}$ to a mixed number.

$$\begin{array}{r} 2 \text{ R } 1 \\ 6\overline{)13} \\ 12 \\ \hline 1 \end{array}$$

$\frac{13}{6} = 2\frac{1}{6}$ ←— quotient
←— remainder
←— original denominator

2. Change $5\frac{3}{4}$ to an improper fraction.

$5 \times 4 = 20$

$5\frac{3}{4} = \frac{20}{4} + \frac{3}{4} = \frac{23}{4}$

3. Use a diagram to show that $3\frac{1}{4} = \frac{13}{4}$.

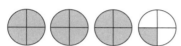

←— Divide each circle into 4 equal parts. Shade 13 quarters.

4. Put $\frac{9}{2}$, $\frac{15}{4}$, $\frac{17}{5}$ in order from least to greatest.

$\frac{9}{2} = 4\frac{1}{2}$ $\frac{15}{4} = 3\frac{3}{4}$ $\frac{17}{5} = 3\frac{2}{5}$

$= 4\frac{10}{20}$ $= 3\frac{15}{20}$ $= 3\frac{8}{20}$

$\therefore \frac{17}{5} < \frac{15}{4} < \frac{9}{2}$

HINTS:

- Proper fraction: the numerator is smaller than the denominator
  e.g. $\frac{3}{7}$

- Improper fraction: the numerator is greater than or equal to the denominator
  e.g. $\frac{10}{7}$, $\frac{7}{7}$

- Mixed number: formed by a whole number and a proper fraction
  e.g. $1\frac{3}{7}$

- To convert an improper fraction to a mixed number, divide the numerator by the denominator. The quotient is the whole number part of the mixed number. The remainder is the new numerator. The denominator is unchanged.

- To convert a mixed number to an improper fraction, the denominator is unchanged. The new numerator is the sum of the old numerator and the product of the whole number and the denominator.

Complete the table.

	Improper Fraction	Mixed Number
①	$\frac{15}{7}$	
②		$3\frac{3}{8}$
③	$\frac{11}{3}$	
④		$11\frac{1}{4}$
⑤	$\frac{7}{5}$	

Write the fractions or mixed numbers on the right screens.

$$3\frac{3}{10} \quad \frac{9}{9} \quad \frac{4}{7} \quad \frac{5}{20} \quad \frac{25}{20} \quad \frac{7}{9} \quad 3\frac{1}{2} \quad 1\frac{5}{20} \quad \frac{15}{8} \quad \frac{11}{12} \quad \frac{16}{7} \quad 1\frac{2}{5}$$

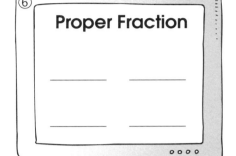

⑥ Proper Fraction

_____ _____

_____ _____

⑦ Improper Fraction

_____ _____

_____ _____

⑧ Mixed Number

_____ _____

_____ _____

Write the mixed numbers represented by each group of the following diagrams. Then convert each to an improper fraction.

⑨

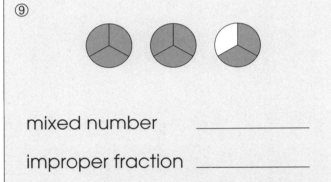

mixed number _____

improper fraction _____

⑩

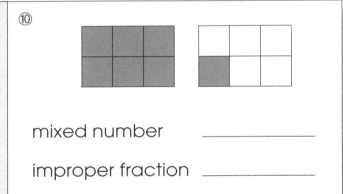

mixed number _____

improper fraction _____

Place the improper fractions on the number line below.

$$\frac{3}{2} \quad \frac{15}{4} \quad \frac{17}{5} \quad \frac{5}{2} \quad \frac{7}{3} \quad \frac{6}{5} \quad \frac{23}{5}$$

⑪

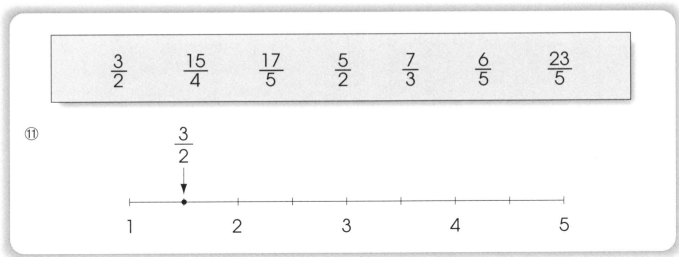

Write an improper fraction to represent each number on the number line below.

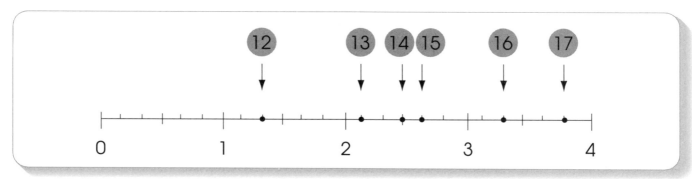

⑫ _____   ⑬ _____   ⑭ _____

⑮ _____   ⑯ _____   ⑰ _____

Order the fractions from greatest to least using > .

⑱ $\dfrac{5}{3}$ $\dfrac{7}{2}$ $\dfrac{9}{4}$ $\dfrac{7}{3}$ $\dfrac{15}{4}$ _____

⑲ $\dfrac{17}{2}$ $\dfrac{17}{5}$ $\dfrac{17}{6}$ $\dfrac{17}{3}$ $\dfrac{17}{4}$ _____

Circle the right numbers in each group.

⑳ The numbers between 3 and 4

$\dfrac{22}{3}$ $\dfrac{15}{7}$ $\dfrac{23}{6}$ $\dfrac{19}{6}$ $\dfrac{17}{4}$ $\dfrac{7}{2}$

㉑ The numbers between 8 and 9

$\dfrac{27}{4}$ $\dfrac{60}{7}$ $\dfrac{49}{6}$ $\dfrac{15}{2}$ $\dfrac{37}{5}$ $\dfrac{25}{3}$

Match the fractions and the mixed numbers.

㉒ $1\dfrac{1}{2}$ $4\dfrac{1}{2}$ $\dfrac{2}{3}$ $\dfrac{12}{9}$ $1\dfrac{3}{8}$ $1\dfrac{2}{5}$ $\dfrac{36}{5}$

$\dfrac{9}{2}$ $\dfrac{12}{18}$ $\dfrac{36}{24}$ $\dfrac{7}{5}$ $7\dfrac{1}{5}$ $1\dfrac{1}{3}$ $\dfrac{11}{8}$

Answer the questions. Show your work. Drawing diagrams may be helpful.

㉓ 5 friends each drink $\frac{1}{2}$ L of juice. How much juice do they drink? Write your answer

    a.   as a mixed number.   _____ L

    b.   as an improper fraction.   _____ L

㉔ Joanne has $2\frac{1}{4}$ dollars in her pocket. The coins are all quarters. How many quarters does she have?

                                               _____ quarters

㉕ Each worker paves $\frac{1}{5}$ of a driveway per day. How many driveways do 8 workers pave per day?

                                          _____ driveways

㉖ A group of students eat $4\frac{1}{2}$ pizzas among them. If they eat $\frac{1}{2}$ pizza each, how many students are there?

                                          _____ students

㉗ Candy says that $\frac{15}{4}$ is greater than $\frac{13}{3}$ since $15 > 13$ and $4 > 3$. Is this statement true or false? Explain.

How many sixteenths are there in three and a half?

There are _____ sixteenths.

Adding Improper Fractions and Mixed Numbers

EXAMPLES

1. $\dfrac{13}{7} + \dfrac{1}{7} = \dfrac{13 + 1}{7}$ ← add the numerators; keep the denominator

$= \dfrac{14}{7}$

$= 2$ ← reduce to lowest terms

2. $1\dfrac{1}{4} + 2\dfrac{1}{4} = \dfrac{5}{4} + \dfrac{9}{4}$ ← change mixed number to improper fraction

$= \dfrac{14}{4}$

$= 3\dfrac{1}{2}$ ← change back to mixed number

3. $1\dfrac{1}{4} + 2\dfrac{1}{4} = 1 + \dfrac{1}{4} + 2 + \dfrac{1}{4}$ ← split the mixed numbers into whole numbers and fractions

$= 3 + \dfrac{1 + 1}{4}$ ← add the whole numbers and fractions separately

$= 3\dfrac{2}{4}$

$= 3\dfrac{1}{2}$ ← reduce to lowest terms

HINTS:

- Adding mixed numbers:

  change the mixed numbers to improper fractions and add the fractions;

  or

  add the whole numbers and fractions separately.

- Remember to reduce the sums to lowest terms.

- If the sum is an improper fraction, change back to a mixed number.

Find the sums mentally. All the answers are whole numbers.

① $1\dfrac{1}{2} + \dfrac{1}{2} =$ _____

② $2\dfrac{1}{3} + \dfrac{2}{3} =$ _____

③ $4\dfrac{1}{4} + \dfrac{3}{4} =$ _____

④ $\dfrac{8}{3} + \dfrac{1}{3} =$ _____

⑤ $\dfrac{11}{2} + \dfrac{3}{2} =$ _____

⑥ $\dfrac{11}{5} + \dfrac{4}{5} =$ _____

⑦ $5\dfrac{3}{5} + \dfrac{2}{5} =$ _____

⑧ $\dfrac{17}{3} + \dfrac{4}{3} =$ _____

⑨ $\dfrac{2}{9} + 2\dfrac{7}{9} =$ _____

⑩ $\dfrac{11}{6} + \dfrac{1}{6} =$ _____

⑪ $1\dfrac{2}{7} + \dfrac{5}{7} =$ _____

⑫ $\dfrac{5}{8} + 2\dfrac{3}{8} =$ _____

⑬ $\dfrac{3}{10} + 3\dfrac{7}{10} =$ _____

⑭ $\dfrac{13}{11} + \dfrac{9}{11} =$ _____

Find the sums. Show your work. Write the answers in lowest terms as mixed numbers.

⑮ $2\frac{1}{8} + \frac{1}{8}$ = _____

⑯ $4\frac{2}{5} + 2\frac{1}{5}$ = _____

⑰ $3\frac{1}{5} + \frac{1}{5}$ = _____

⑱ $5\frac{1}{4} + \frac{1}{4}$ = _____

⑲ $\frac{11}{5} + \frac{6}{5}$ = _____

⑳ $1\frac{3}{4} + 1\frac{3}{4}$ = _____

㉑ $\frac{3}{8} + \frac{9}{8}$ = _____

㉒ $2\frac{2}{3} + 1\frac{2}{3}$ = _____

㉓ $\frac{3}{10} + \frac{13}{10}$ = _____

㉔ $2\frac{7}{16} + \frac{7}{16}$ = _____

㉕ $2\frac{7}{8} + \frac{3}{8}$ = _____

㉖ $\frac{3}{10} + \frac{17}{10}$ = _____

㉗ $1\frac{3}{8} + 3\frac{3}{8}$ = _____

㉘ $\frac{13}{6} + \frac{1}{6}$ = _____

㉙ $4\frac{1}{5} + 3\frac{2}{5} + 1\frac{4}{5}$ = _____

㉚ $\frac{5}{6} + 1\frac{1}{6} + 4$ = _____

Fill in the boxes.

31. $1\frac{1}{4} + \boxed{} = 2$

32. $3\frac{3}{8} + \boxed{} = 4$

33. $\boxed{} + 1\frac{1}{5} = 3$

34. $\boxed{} + 3\frac{1}{2} = 5$

35. $\frac{3}{2} + \boxed{} = 2$

36. $\frac{7}{5} + \boxed{} = 2$

37. $5\frac{1}{3} + \boxed{} = 6$

38. $\frac{11}{6} + \boxed{} = 3$

39. $\boxed{} + \frac{4}{5} = 4$

40. $\boxed{} + 4\frac{1}{4} = 5$

Write True (T) or False (F) for each of the following statements.

41. $\frac{2}{3} + \frac{2}{3} > 1$ ( )

42. $1\frac{3}{4} + \frac{1}{2} > 2$ ( )

43. $\frac{1}{3} + \frac{1}{3} > \frac{5}{6}$ ( )

44. $2\frac{1}{2} < 2\frac{4}{7}$ ( )

45. $1\frac{3}{8} + \frac{3}{4} > 2$ ( )

46. $1\frac{1}{3} > 1\frac{4}{11}$ ( )

47. $1\frac{2}{5} = \frac{7}{5}$ ( )

48. $3\frac{1}{3} > 3\frac{1}{2}$ ( )

Answer only the questions that have a sum greater than 3.

49. $2\frac{2}{3} + \frac{2}{3} = \underline{}$

50. $2\frac{1}{3} + \frac{1}{3} = \underline{}$

51. $\frac{15}{7} + \frac{5}{7} = \underline{}$

52. $1\frac{5}{8} + 1\frac{7}{8} = \underline{}$

53. $\frac{9}{4} + \frac{5}{4} = \underline{}$

54. $\frac{4}{5} + \frac{12}{5} = \underline{}$

55. $\frac{5}{6} + 1\frac{5}{6} = \underline{}$

56. $1\frac{7}{9} + 1\frac{7}{9} = \underline{}$

Answer the questions. Show your work.

㊼ Ann has 3 cats. Shadow eats $1\frac{1}{4}$ cans of food per week. Rocky eats $2\frac{1}{4}$ cans and Peppy eats $1\frac{3}{4}$ cans. How many cans of food do they eat among them per week?

㊽ Shares in Riverview International were sold for $45\frac{3}{8}$ ¢ per share. They increase in value by $2\frac{1}{8}$ ¢. What is the new selling price?

㊾ Janet is sewing 2 dresses. One needs $3\frac{1}{8}$ m of fabric and the other needs $4\frac{3}{4}$ m.

   a.   How much fabric must she buy?

   b.   Would 8 m be enough?

㉖⓪ Peggy keeps a record of her weekly TV watching in the chart below.

Day	Sun.	Mon.	Tue.	Wed.	Thu.	Fri.	Sat.
Time (hours)	$1\frac{1}{4}$	$1\frac{1}{4}$	$\frac{3}{4}$	$1\frac{1}{4}$	2	$1\frac{3}{4}$	$2\frac{3}{4}$

How much TV did she watch during the week?

Just f⓪r Fun

Look for the pattern. Fill in the missing number.

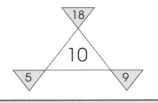
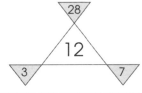
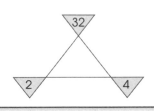

Subtracting Fractions with the Same Denominator

1. $\dfrac{3}{8} - \dfrac{1}{8} = \dfrac{3-1}{8}$ ← subtract the numerators; keep the denominator

$\quad = \dfrac{2}{8}$

$\quad = \dfrac{1}{4}$ ← reduce to lowest terms

2. $\dfrac{6}{10} - \dfrac{1}{10} = \dfrac{6-1}{10} = \dfrac{5}{10} = \dfrac{1}{2}$

HINTS:

- To subtract fractions with the same denominator, subtract the numerators and leave the denominator the same.

- Remember to reduce the difference to lowest terms.

- If the difference is an improper fraction, change back to a mixed number.

Find the differences mentally.

① $\dfrac{3}{7} - \dfrac{1}{7} = $ _____

② $\dfrac{11}{12} - \dfrac{10}{12} = $ _____

③ $\dfrac{8}{9} - \dfrac{1}{9} = $ _____

④ $\dfrac{9}{11} - \dfrac{7}{11} = $ _____

⑤ $\dfrac{3}{7} - \dfrac{1}{7} = $ _____

⑥ $\dfrac{5}{10} - \dfrac{4}{10} = $ _____

⑦ $\dfrac{16}{17} - \dfrac{13}{17} = $ _____

⑧ $\dfrac{5}{12} - \dfrac{5}{12} = $ _____

⑨ $\dfrac{8}{15} - \dfrac{7}{15} = $ _____

⑩ $\dfrac{5}{8} - \dfrac{3}{8} = $ _____

⑪ $\dfrac{11}{13} - \dfrac{9}{13} = $ _____

⑫ $\dfrac{13}{14} - \dfrac{9}{14} = $ _____

Complete each equation with a diagram.

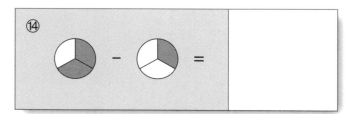

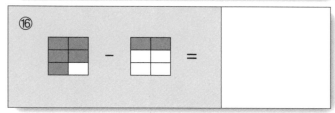

Subtract and reduce the answers to lowest terms. Show your work.

⑰ $\dfrac{9}{10} - \dfrac{4}{10} =$ _____

⑱ $\dfrac{5}{8} - \dfrac{1}{8} =$ _____

⑲ $\dfrac{4}{9} - \dfrac{1}{9} =$ _____

⑳ $\dfrac{7}{12} - \dfrac{4}{12} =$ _____

㉑ $\dfrac{5}{6} - \dfrac{1}{6} =$ _____

㉒ $\dfrac{13}{16} - \dfrac{1}{16} =$ _____

㉓ $\dfrac{3}{4} - \dfrac{1}{4} =$ _____

㉔ $\dfrac{10}{14} - \dfrac{2}{14} =$ _____

㉕ $\dfrac{7}{9} - \dfrac{1}{9} =$ _____

㉖ $\dfrac{3}{8} - \dfrac{1}{8} =$ _____

㉗ $\dfrac{17}{20} - \dfrac{2}{20} =$ _____

㉘ $\dfrac{42}{50} - \dfrac{12}{50} =$ _____

㉙ $\dfrac{16}{24} - \dfrac{8}{24} =$ _____

㉚ $\dfrac{13}{25} - \dfrac{3}{25} =$ _____

㉛ $\dfrac{19}{26} - \dfrac{6}{26} =$ _____

㉜ $\dfrac{6}{12} - \dfrac{1}{12} - \dfrac{2}{12} =$ _____

Fill in the missing number in each box.

㉝ $\frac{1}{4} + \square = 1$

㉞ $\square + \frac{4}{7} = \frac{5}{7}$

㉟ $\frac{5}{7} - \square = \frac{1}{7}$

㊱ $\frac{3}{4} - \square = \frac{1}{4}$

㊲ $\square + \frac{1}{2} = \frac{3}{4}$

㊳ $\square - \frac{1}{9} = \frac{7}{9}$

㊴ $\square + \frac{4}{5} = 1$

㊵ $\frac{5}{9} + \square = 1$

㊶ $\frac{5}{6} - \square = \frac{2}{3}$

㊷ $\square - \frac{1}{4} = \frac{1}{2}$

㊸ $\frac{1}{9} + \square = \frac{7}{9}$

㊹ $\frac{3}{9} + \square = \frac{5}{9}$

㊺ $\square - \frac{1}{3} = \frac{1}{3}$

㊻ $\frac{1}{5} + \square = \frac{3}{5}$

㊼ $\square - \frac{1}{10} = \frac{1}{5}$

㊽ $\frac{3}{11} + \square = \frac{8}{11}$

㊾ $\frac{3}{10} + \frac{1}{10} = \square$

㊿ $\frac{5}{8} - \square = \frac{1}{2}$

Find the answers.

(51) $\frac{1}{7} + \frac{5}{7} - \frac{4}{7} = \frac{1+5-4}{7} =$ ________

(52) $\frac{4}{12} + \frac{7}{12} - \frac{5}{12} =$ ________ $=$ ________

(53) $\frac{11}{18} - \frac{7}{18} + \frac{1}{18} =$ ________ $=$ ________

Answer the questions. Show your work.

54. Ron read $\frac{5}{8}$ of his book on Monday and $\frac{3}{8}$ on Tuesday. How much more did he read on Monday than on Tuesday?

He read _____ more of his book on Monday.

55. Ben takes $\frac{3}{4}$ hour to do his Math homework but Carla only takes $\frac{1}{4}$ hour. How much longer does Ben take?

56. Carol takes $\frac{5}{6}$ hour to walk to school. Dave takes $\frac{1}{6}$ hour for the same walk. How much less time does Dave take?

57. Paula takes 40 minutes to wash her car.

   a. What fraction of the job will she have done after 10 minutes?

   b. What fraction of the job still remains?

58. Bob buys 10 plants for his garden. 2 are violet and 4 are red.

   a. What fraction of the plants are violet? What fraction are red?

   b. What fraction of the plants are neither red nor violet?

Just for Fun

Fill in the missing numbers.

$$\begin{array}{r} \square\,7\;4\;5\;6\;1 \\ -\quad\; 8\;\square\,1\;\square\,3 \\ \hline 7\;\square\,7\;\square\,7\;\square \end{array}$$

Subtracting Improper Fractions and Mixed Numbers

1. $1 - \frac{3}{5} = \frac{5}{5} - \frac{3}{5}$ ← $\frac{5}{5} = 1$

   $= \frac{2}{5}$

2. $2\frac{4}{5} - 1\frac{3}{5} = \frac{14}{5} - \frac{8}{5}$ ← change mixed numbers to improper fractions

   $= \frac{14 - 8}{5}$ ← subtract the numerators; keep the denominator

   $= \frac{6}{5}$

   $= 1\frac{1}{5}$ ← change back to mixed number

   or

3. $2\frac{4}{5} - 1\frac{3}{5} = 2 + \frac{4}{5} - 1 - \frac{3}{5}$ ← split the mixed numbers

   $= 2 - 1 + \frac{4 - 3}{5}$ ← subtract the whole numbers and fractions separately

   $= 1\frac{1}{5}$

HINTS:

- Subtracting mixed numbers:

  Change mixed numbers to improper fractions and subtract the fractions; or

  subtract the whole numbers and fractions separately.

- Remember to reduce the difference to lowest terms.

- If the difference is an improper fraction, change back to a mixed number.

Find the differences mentally.

① $2\frac{4}{7} - \frac{3}{7}$ = _____

② $2\frac{3}{5} - \frac{1}{5}$ = _____

③ $\frac{11}{9} - \frac{4}{9}$ = _____

④ $1\frac{7}{8} - 1\frac{6}{8}$ = _____

⑤ $\frac{21}{4} - \frac{18}{4}$ = _____

⑥ $5\frac{3}{4} - 5$ = _____

⑦ $\frac{3}{2} - \frac{3}{2}$ = _____

⑧ $12\frac{3}{9} - 12\frac{1}{9}$ = _____

⑨ $5\frac{1}{3} - 2\frac{1}{3}$ = _____

⑩ $1\frac{4}{9} - 1\frac{3}{9}$ = _____

⑪ $8\frac{7}{13} - 8\frac{4}{13}$ = _____

⑫ $\frac{13}{10} - \frac{3}{10}$ = _____

⑬ $10\frac{7}{8} - 10$ = _____

⑭ $\frac{10}{3} - \frac{8}{3}$ = _____

⑮ $3\frac{5}{6} - 3\frac{1}{6}$ = _____

⑯ $9\frac{7}{8} - 4\frac{7}{8}$ = _____

Find the differences. Show your work. Write the answers in lowest terms.

⑰ $1\frac{1}{2} - \frac{3}{2} = $ _____

⑱ $2\frac{3}{4} - \frac{1}{4} = $ _____

⑲ $\frac{6}{5} - \frac{1}{5} = $ _____

⑳ $\frac{9}{4} - \frac{3}{4} = $ _____

㉑ $5\frac{1}{4} - 4\frac{3}{4} = $ _____

㉒ $3\frac{1}{8} - 2\frac{7}{8} = $ _____

㉓ $\frac{11}{4} - \frac{3}{4} = $ _____

㉔ $\frac{12}{10} - \frac{8}{10} = $ _____

㉕ $2\frac{1}{6} - 1\frac{5}{6} = $ _____

㉖ $\frac{20}{9} - \frac{11}{9} = $ _____

㉗ $2\frac{3}{8} - \frac{9}{8} = $ _____

㉘ $1\frac{1}{11} - \frac{12}{11} = $ _____

㉙ $\frac{21}{10} - 1\frac{1}{10} = $ _____

㉚ $\frac{21}{3} - 5\frac{1}{3} = $ _____

㉛ $5\frac{3}{4} - 2\frac{1}{4} - \frac{2}{4} = $ _____

㉜ $9 - 6\frac{1}{5} - 1\frac{3}{5} = $ _____

Fill in the missing number in each box.

㉝ $1\dfrac{1}{4} - \dfrac{3}{4} = \boxed{}$

㉞ $\dfrac{13}{5} - \boxed{} = \dfrac{9}{5}$

㉟ $\dfrac{5}{3} + \boxed{} = 2$

㊱ $\boxed{} - 1\dfrac{3}{4} = 3\dfrac{1}{4}$

㊲ $\boxed{} - \dfrac{1}{4} = 1\dfrac{1}{4}$

㊳ $\boxed{} + 2\dfrac{1}{4} = 3$

㊴ $\boxed{} - 3\dfrac{3}{8} = \dfrac{5}{8}$

㊵ $\dfrac{5}{3} - \boxed{} = 0$

㊶ $\dfrac{5}{4} + \boxed{} = 2$

㊷ $\boxed{} + \dfrac{4}{7} = 3$

㊸ $\dfrac{7}{5} - \boxed{} = 1$

㊹ $\dfrac{1}{2} + \boxed{} = 4$

㊺ $2 - \boxed{} = 1\dfrac{1}{3}$

㊻ $\boxed{} - \dfrac{1}{9} = \dfrac{8}{9}$

㊼ $\boxed{} + \dfrac{3}{4} = 1\dfrac{1}{4}$

㊽ $\boxed{} + \dfrac{6}{5} = 2$

Find the answers.

㊾ $3\dfrac{4}{6} + 4\dfrac{1}{6} - 2\dfrac{2}{6}$ = _____ = _____

㊿ $9 - 3\dfrac{1}{8} + 1\dfrac{2}{8}$ = _____ = _____

51 $4\dfrac{1}{6} - 3\dfrac{3}{6} + 1\dfrac{4}{6}$ = _____ = _____

52 $3\dfrac{2}{7} + 2\dfrac{4}{7} - 1\dfrac{5}{7}$ = _____ = _____

Answer the questions. Show your work. Write the fractions in lowest terms.

㊳ On Monday, Jonathan watched TV for $2\frac{3}{4}$ hours and Pat watched TV for $3\frac{1}{4}$ hours. How much longer did Pat spend watching TV?

㊴ On Monday, Ron ran $8\frac{3}{8}$ km and on Wednesday he ran $6\frac{5}{8}$ km. How much farther did he run on Monday?

㊵ ABC shares sell for $3\frac{1}{5}$ dollars each and BFI share sell for $2\frac{4}{5}$ dollars each. What is the difference between the share prices?

㊶ The perimeter of the triangle is 1 m. What is the length of the third side?

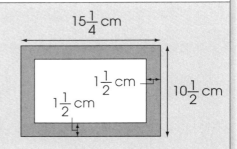

$\frac{1}{8}$ m $\frac{3}{8}$ m

㊷ The dimensions of a framed picture are $15\frac{1}{4}$ cm by $10\frac{1}{2}$ cm. The frame is $1\frac{1}{2}$ cm wide. What are the dimensions of the unframed part of the picture?

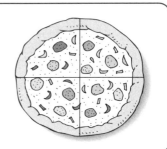

$15\frac{1}{4}$ cm

$1\frac{1}{2}$ cm $10\frac{1}{2}$ cm

$1\frac{1}{2}$ cm

7 people eat $\frac{1}{4}$ of a pizza each. If they buy 2 pizzas, how much pizza is left?

_____ pizza is left.

16 Relating Decimals and Fractions

1. Convert 0.7 and 0.55 to fractions.

   $0.7 = \dfrac{7}{10}$ ← put 1 zero in the denominator since 0.7 has 1 decimal place

   $0.55 = \dfrac{55}{100} = \dfrac{11}{20}$ ← reduce the fraction to lowest terms

   put 2 zeros in the denominator since 0.55 has 2 decimal places

2. Convert $\dfrac{1}{4}$ and $2\dfrac{1}{5}$ to decimals.

   $\dfrac{1}{4} = 0.25$

   $\begin{array}{r} 0.25 \\ 4\overline{)1.0} \\ 8 \\ \hline 20 \\ 20 \end{array}$ ← divide numerator by denominator and continue dividing until the remainder is zero

   $2\dfrac{1}{5} = 2 + \dfrac{1}{5} = 2 + 0.2 = 2.2$

   $\begin{array}{r} 0.2 \\ 5\overline{)1\ 0} \\ 1\ 0 \end{array}$

   change the fraction part to decimal

HINTS:

- Change decimals to fractions:

  Write the decimal part as numerator with a denominator of 10, 100, 1000 etc.

  e.g. $0.07 = \dfrac{7}{100}$ ← number of zeros in the denominator equals the number of decimal places

  Remember to reduce the fractions to lowest terms.

- Change fractions to decimals:

  Find the equivalent fraction with a denominator of 10, 100, 1000 etc, and then write the fraction as a decimal number.

  e.g. $\dfrac{1}{4} = \dfrac{1 \times 25}{4 \times 25} = \dfrac{25}{100} = 0.25$ or

  Divide the numerator by the denominator; continue dividing until the remainder is zero or there are enough decimal places.

  e.g. $\dfrac{2}{3} = 0.67$ ← round to the nearest hundredth

Change the following fractions to decimals.

Fraction	Decimal
① $\dfrac{1}{10}$	_____
② $\dfrac{7}{10}$	_____
③ $\dfrac{3}{100}$	_____
④ $\dfrac{49}{100}$	_____
⑤ $\dfrac{9}{100}$	_____
⑥ $\dfrac{73}{100}$	_____

Change the following decimals to fractions.

Decimal	Fraction	Decimal	Fraction
⑦ 0.3	_____	⑧ 0.7	_____
⑨ 0.9	_____	⑩ 0.01	_____
⑪ 0.09	_____	⑫ 0.07	_____
⑬ 0.31	_____	⑭ 0.19	_____
⑮ 0.47	_____	⑯ 0.03	_____

Use division to convert each of the following fractions to decimals.

Fraction	Decimal	Fraction	Decimal
⑰ $\frac{1}{2}$	_____	⑱ $\frac{1}{5}$	_____
⑲ $\frac{3}{4}$	_____	⑳ $\frac{3}{5}$	_____
㉑ $\frac{1}{8}$	_____	㉒ $\frac{5}{8}$	_____
㉓ $\frac{3}{8}$	_____	㉔ $\frac{4}{5}$	_____

Convert the following fractions to decimals. Round the answers to the nearest hundredth if necessary.

㉕ $1\frac{5}{8}$ = _____   ㉖ $3\frac{4}{7}$ = _____   ㉗ $12\frac{4}{5}$ = _____

㉘ $2\frac{3}{8}$ = _____   ㉙ $3\frac{5}{6}$ = _____   ㉚ $5\frac{4}{9}$ = _____

㉛ $1\frac{2}{3}$ = _____   ㉜ $2\frac{3}{5}$ = _____   ㉝ $4\frac{1}{4}$ = _____

㉞ $10\frac{2}{5}$ = _____   ㉟ $8\frac{6}{7}$ = _____   ㊱ $6\frac{7}{10}$ = _____

Change the decimals to fractions. Give your answers in lowest terms.

③⑦ $0.65 = \dfrac{65}{100} =$ _____

③⑧ $0.75 =$ _____ $=$ _____

③⑨ $0.05 =$ _____ $=$ _____

④⓪ $0.12 =$ _____ $=$ _____

④① $0.45 =$ _____ $=$ _____

④② $0.36 =$ _____ $=$ _____

④③ $1.45 =$ _____ $=$ _____

④④ $6.55 =$ _____ $=$ _____

④⑤ $2.8 =$ _____ $=$ _____

④⑥ $2.25 =$ _____ $=$ _____

How many cents are there in each of the following fractions of a dollar?

④⑦ $\$\dfrac{1}{4} =$ _____ ¢

④⑧ $\$\dfrac{3}{4} =$ _____ ¢

④⑨ $\$\dfrac{2}{5} =$ _____ ¢

⑤⓪ $\$\dfrac{3}{5} =$ _____ ¢

⑤① $\$\dfrac{7}{10} =$ _____ ¢

⑤② $\$\dfrac{9}{10} =$ _____ ¢

Circle the larger number in each pair.

⑤③ $0.65 \quad \dfrac{1}{2}$

⑤④ $\dfrac{4}{5} \quad 0.9$

⑤⑤ $1.3 \quad 1\dfrac{2}{5}$

⑤⑥ $\dfrac{2}{3} \quad 0.62$

⑤⑦ $4.26 \quad 4\dfrac{1}{4}$

⑤⑧ $0.57 \quad \dfrac{8}{15}$

⑤⑨ $3.69 \quad 3\dfrac{3}{5}$

⑥⓪ $8.38 \quad 8\dfrac{1}{3}$

⑥① $6\dfrac{3}{8} \quad 6.37$

Arrange the following numbers in order from least to greatest.

⑥② $1\dfrac{7}{8} \quad 1.54 \quad 1\dfrac{8}{9}$ _____ $<$ _____ $<$ _____

⑥③ $2.68 \quad 2\dfrac{3}{5} \quad 2\dfrac{4}{7}$ _____ $<$ _____ $<$ _____

⑥④ $5\dfrac{9}{10} \quad 5\dfrac{4}{5} \quad 5.83$ _____ $<$ _____ $<$ _____

Complete the table. Then list the fractions in order from least to greatest.

Fraction	$\frac{1}{8}$	$\frac{1}{4}$	$\frac{3}{4}$	$\frac{3}{8}$	$\frac{7}{8}$	$\frac{1}{5}$	$\frac{7}{10}$
㉒ Decimal							

㉖ _____ < _____ < _____ < _____ < _____ < _____ < _____

Answer the questions.

㉗ Canada produces about 0.24 of the world's supply of
nickel ore. Express this as a fraction in lowest terms. _____

㉘ Paul climbs 100 steps up a 160-step tower.

    a.   What fraction of the tower has he climbed? _____

    b.   Express your answer as a decimal. _____

㉙ $\frac{2}{5}$ of the cost of a litre of gas is tax.

    a.   Express this fraction as a decimal. _____

    b.   If gas costs 75¢ a litre, how much is the tax? _____

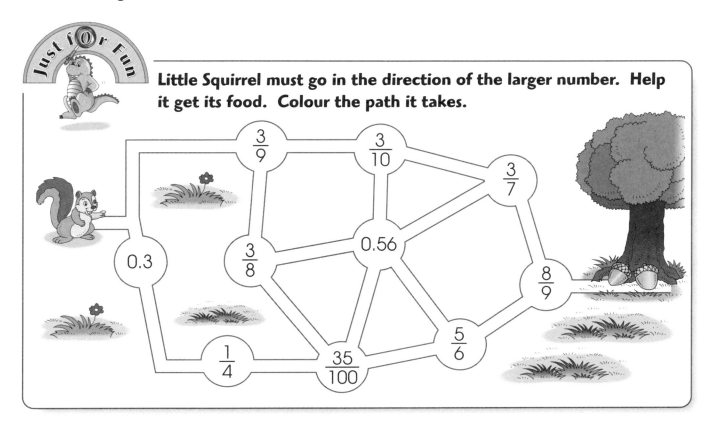

Just for Fun

Little Squirrel must go in the direction of the larger number. Help it get its food. Colour the path it takes.

Final Review

Circle the letter which represents the correct answer in each problem.

① A fraction equivalent to $\frac{3}{4}$ is

   A. $\frac{5}{6}$ B. $\frac{6}{8}$ C. $\frac{35}{45}$ D. $\frac{9}{16}$

② The fraction $\frac{36}{92}$ expressed in lowest terms is

   A. $\frac{1}{2}$ B. $\frac{18}{46}$ C. $\frac{9}{23}$ D. $\frac{2}{5}$

③ The fraction $\frac{1}{8}$ expressed as a decimal is

   A. 0.12   B. 0.2   C. 0.1   D. 0.125

④ The decimal 0.95 expressed as a fraction in lowest terms is

   A. $\frac{19}{20}$ B. $\frac{9}{10}$ C. $\frac{9.5}{10}$ D. $\frac{9}{100}$

⑤ The mixed number $3\frac{1}{3}$ expressed as an improper fraction is

   A. $\frac{1}{2}$ B. $\frac{10}{3}$ C. $\frac{31}{3}$ D. $\frac{10}{9}$

⑥ The improper fraction $\frac{27}{7}$ expressed as a mixed number is

   A. $3\frac{1}{7}$ B. $27\frac{1}{7}$ C. $4\frac{6}{7}$ D. $3\frac{6}{7}$

⑦ The sum of $\frac{3}{11}$ and $\frac{7}{11}$ is

   A. $\frac{10}{11}$ B. $\frac{10}{22}$ C. $\frac{21}{121}$ D. $\frac{21}{11}$

⑧ The difference between $\frac{7}{9}$ and $\frac{2}{9}$ is

   A. $\frac{1}{7}$ B. 5   C. $\frac{5}{9}$ D. $\frac{14}{81}$

⑨ The improper fraction $\frac{24}{5}$ expressed as a decimal is

   A. 2.8   B. 4.8   C. 24.2   D. 5.2

Represent each diagram as a fraction in lowest terms and also as a decimal.

⑩

Fraction _____

Decimal _____

⑪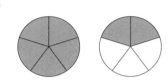

Fraction _____

Decimal _____

⑫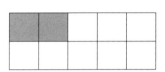

Fraction _____

Decimal _____

Write the numbers labelled A - E on the number line below as fractions and decimals.

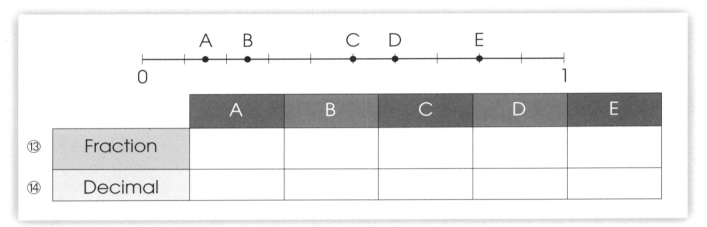

	A	B	C	D	E
⑬ Fraction					
⑭ Decimal					

Change the fractions to mixed numbers. Place the fractions on the number line below.

⑮ $\dfrac{15}{4}$ = _____

⑯ $\dfrac{3}{2}$ = _____

⑰ $\dfrac{17}{5}$ = _____

⑱ $\dfrac{19}{9}$ = _____

⑲ $\dfrac{4}{3}$ = _____

⑳ $\dfrac{7}{2}$ = _____

㉑ $\dfrac{14}{3}$ = _____

㉒ $\dfrac{25}{6}$ = _____

㉓ $\dfrac{35}{8}$ = _____

㉔ $\dfrac{7}{4}$ = _____

㉕ $\dfrac{13}{5}$ = _____

㉖ $\dfrac{24}{5}$ = _____

㉗

Add or subtract. Write your answers in lowest terms.

㉘ $\dfrac{10}{3} - \dfrac{10}{3} =$ _____

㉙ $\dfrac{9}{2} - \dfrac{5}{2} =$ _____

㉚ $7\dfrac{1}{4} - 3\dfrac{1}{4} =$ _____

㉛ $6\dfrac{3}{8} - 5\dfrac{1}{8} =$ _____

㉜ $\dfrac{16}{5} + \dfrac{6}{5} =$ _____

㉝ $5\dfrac{1}{4} + 3\dfrac{3}{4} =$ _____

㉞ $5\dfrac{1}{4} - 4\dfrac{3}{4} =$ _____

㉟ $3\dfrac{1}{5} - 2\dfrac{3}{5} =$ _____

The chart below shows the minimum hourly wage in a number of Canadian provinces. Read the chart and answer the questions. Write the number sentences where necessary.

Province	B.C.	Alberta	Manitoba	Ontario	Quebec	PEI	Nova Scotia
Wage ($)	7.60	5.90	6.00	6.85	6.90	5.40	5.60

㊱ What is the difference between the highest and lowest wages?

_____ = _____

㊲ How much would a student working for 5 hours at minimum wage earn in

  a. Ontario? _____ = _____

  b. B.C.? _____ = _____

㊳ What is the difference between the two amounts in ㊲ ?

_____ = _____

㊴ Write the minimum wage in Quebec as

  a. a mixed number.　　　　　　　 _____

  b. an improper fraction.　　　　　 _____

㊵ Brenda lives in Alberta and earns $ $\dfrac{3}{4}$ per hour more than the minimum wage. How much does she earn per hour?

_____ = _____

Solve the problems. Show your work.

㊶ In 1969, Canada's population was 21.3 million and in 1994, it was 29.2 million.

    a. Express each of these numbers as a mixed number in lowest terms.

    b. What was the increase in Canada's population between 1969 and 1994? Express your answer as a decimal and also as a mixed number.

    c. If this trend continues, what will the population of Canada be in 2019?

㊷ Dan is training for a Marathon race. His monthly goal is 100 km. He ran 35 km during the first week of the month.

    a. What fraction of his monthly goal has he run? Express your answer as a proper fraction in lowest terms and as a decimal.

    b. What distance does he still have to run during the month to achieve his goal?

    c. What fraction of the total distance does he still have to run? Express your answer as a fraction and as a decimal.

    d. What is the difference between the fraction of the total distance run in the first week and the fraction run during the rest of the month?

㊸ Mr King drinks an average of $2\frac{1}{4}$ cups of tea each day. Mrs King drinks an average of $3\frac{3}{4}$ cups per day.

   a. How many cups of tea do they drink between them each day?

   b. What is the difference between the amounts they drink per day?

   c. Change the amount Mr King drinks to a decimal. How much tea will Mr King drink per week?

   d. Change the amount Mrs King drinks to a decimal. How much tea will Mrs King drink per week?

㊹ Peter watches TV for $8\frac{1}{5}$ hours per week. David watches $9\frac{3}{5}$ hours and Ruth watches $7\frac{1}{5}$ hours.

   a. How much TV do they watch among them in a week?

   b. How much longer does David watch TV than Peter?

   c. How much longer does David watch TV than Ruth?

   d. Ruth's mother says that Ruth must cut down watching TV by $1\frac{3}{5}$ hours. How much TV can she watch now?

Overview

In Section I, fraction and decimal skills were practised. In this section, these skills are expanded to include percent, reducing fractions to simplest form, and multiplying decimals by decimals.

Students also practise solving simple equations, analysing line graphs and dealing with inverse proportion. New arithmetic skills include rounding large numbers, identifying prime and composite numbers, and finding G.C.F. (greatest common factor) and L.C.M. (least common multiple).

In the Measurement units, students learn how to find the area of triangles and parallelograms. They also practise the calculation of volume of rectangular prisms and capacity of containers.

In the Geometry units, students carry out transformations of points as well as shapes. Time applications include the calculation of the duration of an event. Money applications involve finding change and calculating sale prices.

1 Large Numbers

Rounding - expressing a number to the nearest ten, hundred, thousand or other value

Help Dave write the price of each house in standard form.

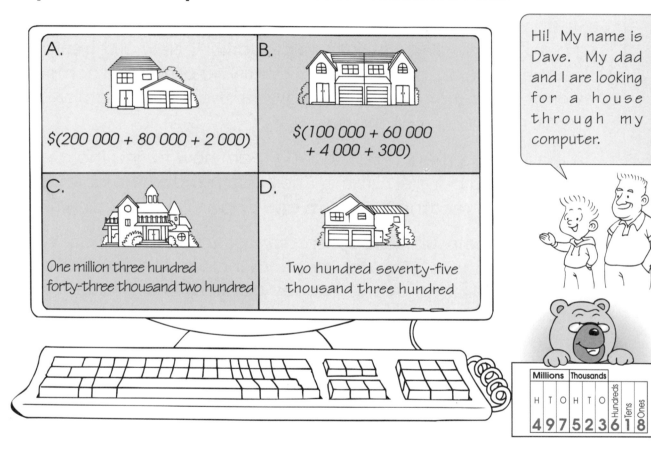

A. $(200 000 + 80 000 + 2 000)

B. $(100 000 + 60 000 + 4 000 + 300)

C. One million three hundred forty-three thousand two hundred

D. Two hundred seventy-five thousand three hundred

Hi! My name is Dave. My dad and I are looking for a house through my computer.

Millions			Thousands			Hundreds	Tens	Ones
H	T	O	H	T	O			
4	9	7	5	2	3	6	1	8

① House A : $_____

② House B : $_____

③ House C : $_____

④ House D : $_____

Write the place value of each underlined digit.

⑤ 46<u>5</u> 200 623 _____

⑥ 1 <u>6</u>20 973 _____

⑦ 1<u>2</u>6 305 704 _____

⑧ 248 2<u>7</u>3 046 _____

Read what Dave says. Then help him round the price of the houses.

Round 123 205 to the nearest ten thousand.

1st	Mark in multiples of 10 000 on a number line; look at the thousands digit.

123 205

110 000   120 000   130 000

2nd	123 205 is between 120 000 and 130 000 but closer to 120 000.

123 205 rounds to 120 000.

Price of the houses	Rounded to the nearest		
	hundred	thousand	ten thousand
⑨ 123 205			120 000
⑩ 174 158		174 000	
⑪ 246 523	246 500		
⑫ 477 099		477 000	
⑬ 1 205 103			1 210 000
⑭ 985 804		986 000	

Round up if a number is halfway between 2 multiples.

  **A C T I V I T Y**

Which of these numbers have been rounded? Tick ✔ the right boxes.

A	**CITY NEWS** 
	About 2 500 000 people living in Toronto

B	**GAZETTE** 
	42 436 cases of flu reported

C	**SUN WEEKLY** 
	Exactly $140 000 stolen in bank robbery

D	**THE SYSTEM** 
	Over 20 000 people go south for vacation

Prime and Composite Numbers

WORDS TO LEARN

Composite number — any number greater than 1 that has more than 2 factors

Prime number — any number with only 1 and itself as factors

Find the number of stickers in each group and write composite or prime.

 $6 = 2 \times 3$; 6 can form a rectangle.

6 is a _composite_ number.

① _____ = 2 × 4 ;

8 is a _____ number.

> If the number can form a rectangle, it is a composite number.

②

_____ = 1 × 7 ;   7 is a _____ number.

③

_____ = 1 × 5 ;   5 is a _____ number.

④ _____ = 2 × 2 ;

4 is a _____ number.

Write prime or composite for the following numbers.

⑤ 12 _____   ⑥ 11 _____   ⑦ 18 _____

⑧ 36 _____   ⑨ 41 _____   ⑩ 47 _____

Follow the directions to find all the prime numbers within 100. Colour the board and fill in the blanks.

⑪ Colour 1 orange.

⑫ Colour all the multiples of 2 (except 2) red.

⑬ Colour all the uncoloured multiples of 3, 5 and 7 (except 3, 5 and 7) yellow.

⑭ There are _____ uncoloured numbers. All of them are _____ numbers.

1	2	3	4	5	6	7	8	9	10
11	12	13	14	15	16	17	18	19	20
21	22	23	24	25	26	27	28	29	30
31	32	33	34	35	36	37	38	39	40
41	42	43	44	45	46	47	48	49	50
51	52	53	54	55	56	57	58	59	60
61	62	63	64	65	66	67	68	69	70
71	72	73	74	75	76	77	78	79	80
81	82	83	84	85	86	87	88	89	90
91	92	93	94	95	96	97	98	99	100

⑮ All the coloured numbers (except 1) are _____ numbers.

Write True or False.

⑯ All prime numbers except 2 are odd numbers. _____

⑰ 5 is the only prime number ending in 5. _____

⑱ From 1 to 100, there are 24 prime numbers. _____

ACTIVITY

Read what Dave says. Then try out Goldbach's theory on the following numbers.

1. 20 = _____ + _____

2. 24 = _____ + _____

3. 32 = _____ + _____

4. 98 = _____ + _____

A mathematician called Goldbach believes <u>all</u> even numbers can be made by adding 2 prime numbers together.

e.g.

$$10 = 7 + 3, \quad 8 = 5 + 3$$

3 Fractions

Fraction	- a number showing a part of a whole	e.g. $\dfrac{3}{8}$ are shaded. ← numerator ← denominator
Proper fraction	- a fraction with the numerator smaller than the denominator	e.g. $\dfrac{2}{5}$
Improper fraction	- a fraction with the numerator greater than or equal to the denominator	e.g. $\dfrac{11}{7}$
Mixed number	- a number formed by a whole number and a proper fraction	e.g. $2\dfrac{3}{5}$
Simplest form	- a fraction in which the numerator and denominator have only 1 as their common factor	

See how much food the children ate. Write the answers in simplest form.

① Dave and 3 friends each ate $\dfrac{2}{3}$ of a pizza. How many pizzas did they eat in all?

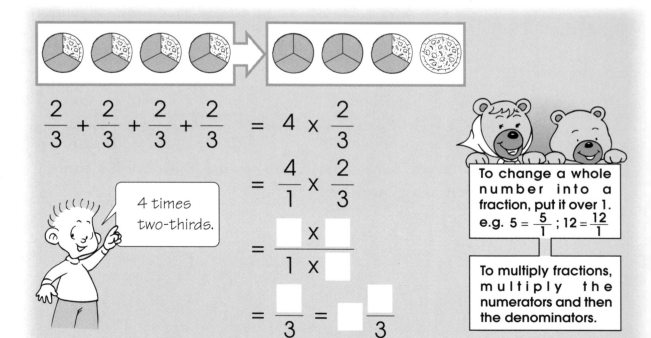

$$\frac{2}{3} + \frac{2}{3} + \frac{2}{3} + \frac{2}{3} = 4 \times \frac{2}{3}$$

$$= \frac{4}{1} \times \frac{2}{3}$$

$$= \frac{\boxed{} \times \boxed{}}{1 \times \boxed{}}$$

$$= \frac{\boxed{}}{3} = \boxed{}\frac{\boxed{}}{3}$$

4 times two-thirds.

To change a whole number into a fraction, put it over 1.
e.g. $5 = \dfrac{5}{1}$; $12 = \dfrac{12}{1}$

To multiply fractions, multiply the numerators and then the denominators.

They ate _____ pizzas in all.

② Dave ate $\frac{1}{2}$ of $1\frac{1}{2}$ cakes. What fraction of a cake did he eat?

$$\frac{1}{2} \text{ of } 1\frac{1}{2} = \frac{1}{2} \times 1\frac{1}{2} = \frac{1}{2} \times \frac{\square}{2}$$

$$= \frac{1 \times \square}{\square \times \square}$$

$$= \frac{\square}{\square} $$

To multiply a mixed number, change it to an improper fraction first.

Dave ate _____ of a cake.

Try these. Write the answers in simplest form.

③ $2 \times \dfrac{3}{5}$ = _____

④ $3 \times \dfrac{3}{7}$ = _____

⑤ $\dfrac{1}{4} \times \dfrac{2}{3}$ = _____

⑥ $\dfrac{2}{9} \times \dfrac{2}{3}$ = _____

⑦ $3 \times 2\dfrac{5}{6}$ = _____

⑧ $1\dfrac{1}{3} \times \dfrac{3}{8}$ = _____

⑨ $\dfrac{5}{9} \times \dfrac{3}{10}$ = _____

⑩ $\dfrac{6}{7} \times 1\dfrac{2}{3}$ = _____

⑪ There are 28 students in a class. $\dfrac{4}{7}$ of them are boys. How many boys are there? _____ boys

⑫ There were $\dfrac{5}{6}$ of a cake. Steve ate $\dfrac{3}{5}$ of it. What fraction of the cake did he eat? _____ cake

See how Steve divided his pizza. Follow his method to solve the problems and write the answers in simplest form.

 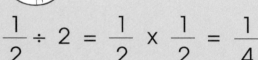 

I shared $\frac{1}{2}$ of a pizza with Dave.

$$\frac{1}{2} \div 2 = \frac{1}{2} \times \frac{1}{2} = \frac{1}{4}$$

Dave and Steve each got $\frac{1}{4}$ of a pizza.

To divide fractions, invert the divisor and then multiply.
e.g. $5 \div n = 5 \times \frac{1}{n}$

⑬ $\dfrac{1}{3} \div 5 =$ _____

⑭ $\dfrac{4}{7} \div 2 =$ _____

⑮ $\dfrac{5}{9} \div 10 =$ _____

⑯ $\dfrac{3}{4} \div 9 =$ _____

⑰ $\dfrac{4}{3} \div 2 =$ _____

⑱ $\dfrac{8}{5} \div 4 =$ _____

See how Dave cut the cakes. Follow his method to solve the problems and write the answers in simplest form.

Each piece is $\frac{1}{4}$ of a cake.
How many pieces are there in 2 cakes?

$$2 \div \frac{1}{4} = 2 \times \frac{4}{1}$$

Invert the fractions first. Then multiply.

$$= 8$$

There are 8 pieces in 2 cakes.

Dividing by $\frac{1}{n}$ is the same as multiplying by n.

⑲ $3 \div \dfrac{3}{4} =$ _____

⑳ $5 \div \dfrac{5}{6} =$ _____

㉑ $9 \div \dfrac{3}{4}$ = _____

㉒ $6 \div \dfrac{3}{10}$ = _____

㉓ $3 \div \dfrac{2}{5}$ = _____

㉔ $4 \div \dfrac{8}{9}$ = _____

㉕ Dave eats $\dfrac{2}{5}$ of a box of cereal every day. In how many days will he finish 4 boxes of cereal? _____ days

Follow Dave's method to solve the problems and write the answers in simplest form.

I had $\dfrac{2}{3}$ of a pizza. Each person ate $\dfrac{1}{9}$ of the pizza. How many people were there?

$\dfrac{2}{3} \div \dfrac{1}{9} = \dfrac{2}{3} \times \dfrac{9}{1} = 6$

Invert the divisor first. Then multiply.

There were 6 people.

㉖ $\dfrac{3}{7} \div \dfrac{1}{2}$ = _____

㉗ $\dfrac{3}{4} \div \dfrac{1}{8}$ = _____

㉘ $\dfrac{7}{8} \div \dfrac{1}{4}$ = _____

㉙ $\dfrac{5}{9} \div \dfrac{2}{3}$ = _____

ACTIVITY

Put +, −, X or ÷ in the ☐.

1. $\dfrac{1}{2} \ \boxed{} \ \dfrac{1}{3} = \dfrac{5}{6}$

2. $4 \ \boxed{} \ \dfrac{1}{12} = \dfrac{1}{3}$

3. $\dfrac{2}{3} \ \boxed{} \ \dfrac{1}{6} = 4$

4. $\dfrac{5}{7} \ \boxed{} \ \dfrac{1}{14} = \dfrac{9}{14}$

Distributive Property of Multiplication

**Distributive property
of multiplication**   -   for any three numbers a, b and c, it is true that:

a x (b + c) = a x b + a x c

Find the perimeter of the picture for Dave and Steve. Circle Yes or No.

5 cm

3 cm

① Perimeter = 2 x 5 + 2 x 3

= _____ + _____

= _____ cm

② Perimeter = 2 x (5 + 3)

= _____ X _____

= _____ cm

③ Is 2 x (5 + 3) the same as 2 x 5 + 2 x 3?   Yes   No

Try these.

④ 7 x (3 + 5)

= 7 x _____ + 7 x _____

= _____ + _____

= _____

Distributive property
of multiplication
$a \times (b + c) = a \times b + a \times c$

⑤ 4 x (18 – 7)

= 4 x _____ – 4 x _____

= _____ – _____

= _____

⑥ 5 x 12 – 5 x 7

= 5 x (_____ – _____)

= 5 x _____

= _____

Follow Dave and Steve's method to solve the problems.

$$4 \times 82 = 4 \times (80 + 2)$$
$$= 4 \times 80 + 4 \times 2$$
$$= 320 + 8$$
$$= 328$$

82 = 80 + 2

$$5 \times 99 = 5 \times (100 - 1)$$
$$= 5 \times 100 - 5 \times 1$$
$$= 500 - 5$$
$$= 495$$

99 = 100 - 1

⑦ 5×73

$= 5 \times ($ _____ $+$ _____ $)$

$= 5 \times$ _____ $+ 5 \times$ _____

$=$ _____ $+$ _____

$=$ _____

⑧ 6×98

$= 6 \times ($ _____ $-$ _____ $)$

$= 6 \times$ _____ $- 6 \times$ _____

$=$ _____ $-$ _____

$=$ _____

⑨ $7 \times 102 =$ _____

⑩ $9 \times 49 =$ _____

⑪ $6 \times 93 =$ _____

⑫ $4 \times 83 =$ _____

⑬ $9 \times 62 =$ _____

⑭ $5 \times 79 =$ _____

ACTIVITY

Use the distributive property of multiplication to find the answers.

1. $10 \times 5\frac{1}{5}$

$= 10 \times (5 + \boxed{})$

$= 10 \times \boxed{} + 10 \times \boxed{}$

$= \boxed{} + \boxed{}$

$= \boxed{}$

2. $6 \times 54\frac{1}{5}$

$= 6 \times (50 + 4 + \boxed{})$

$= 6 \times \boxed{} + 6 \times \boxed{} + 6 \times \boxed{}$

$= \boxed{} + \boxed{} + \boxed{}$

$= \boxed{}$

5 Simple Equations

Equation - a number sentence with an equal sign

     e.g. $2 \times 5 = 10$, $y - 5 = 12$

Read what Uncle Ray says and help Dave tick ✔ the right equations.

① 5 more than a number y is 12.

☐ $5 - y = 12$ ☐ $5 + y = 12$

② 6 less than a number n is 8.

☐ $n \div 6 = 8$ ☐ $6 - n = 8$ ☐ $n - 6 = 8$

③ 3 times a number m is 12.

☐ $3 \times m = 12$ ☐ $m = 12 \times 3$ ☐ $m \div 3 = 12$

④ A number k divided by 5 is 2.

☐ $5 \div k = 2$ ☐ $k = 5 \div 2$ ☐ $k \div 5 = 2$

Use the balance below to find the weight of Dave's toy cars and check the answers.

⑤

To solve an addition equation, subtract the same amount from both sides.

$$\text{🚗} + 20 = 50 + \underline{\hspace{1.5cm}}$$

$$\text{🚗} + 20 - 20 = \underline{\hspace{1.5cm}} - \underline{\hspace{1.5cm}}$$

$$\text{🚗} = \underline{\hspace{1.5cm}}$$ **Check:** $\underline{\hspace{1.5cm}} + 20 = 60$

The weight of is $\underline{\hspace{1.5cm}}$ g.

⑥

 x 2 = _____ + _____

 x 2 ÷ 2 = _____ ÷ 2

 = _____

Check: _____ x 2 = 70

The weight of is _____ g.

Solve these equations and check the answers.

⑦ $x + 3 = 12$

$x + 3 -$ ____ $= 12 -$ ____

$x =$ ____

Check : ____ $+ 3 = 12$

Substitute the answer for the letter. If two sides of the equation are equal, the answer is correct.

⑧ $7 \times n = 28$

$7 \times n \div$ ____ $= 28 \div$ ____

$n =$ ____

Check : $7 \times$ ____ $=$ ____

⑨ $m \div 2 = 9$

$m \div 2 \times$ ____ $= 9 \times$ ____

$m =$ ____

Check : ____ $\div 2 =$ ____

⑩ $p - 9 = 26$

$p - 9 +$ ____ $= 26 +$ ____

$p =$ ____

Check : ____ $- 9 =$ ____

⑪ $q \times 5 = 35$

$q \times 5 \div$ ____ $= 35 \div$ ____

$q =$ ____

Check : ____ $\times 5 =$ ____

See how Dave set up the equations. Then use his equations to complete the tables.

In my birthday party, I have 2 sandwiches for each guest.

Number of guests

Equation : n × 2 = Total number of sandwiches

Number of sandwiches	Equation	Number of guests (n)
6	n × 2 = 6	3
⑫ 10		
⑬ 14		
⑭ 18		
⑮ 36		

You can use this equation to find the number of guests in my party.

n × 2 = 6
n × 2 ÷ 2 = 6 ÷ 2
n = 3

Each box holds 6 cupcakes.

Total number of cupcakes

Equation : m ÷ 6 = Number of boxes

Number of boxes	Equation	Number of cupcakes (m)
3	m ÷ 6 = 3	18
⑯ 4		
⑰ 6		
⑱ 8		
⑲ 9		

You can use this equation to find the number of cupcakes I have.

m ÷ 6 = 3
m ÷ 6 × 6 = 3 × 6
m = 18

Complete the equation for each problem. Then solve and check the answers.

⑳ For a game, Dave divided his guests into 3 groups. There were 5 people in each group. How many guests were there?

$$m \div \underline{\hspace{1cm}} = \underline{\hspace{1cm}}$$

$$m \div \underline{\hspace{1cm}} \times \underline{\hspace{1cm}} = \underline{\hspace{1cm}} \times \underline{\hspace{1cm}}$$

$$m = \underline{\hspace{1cm}}$$

There were ___ guests.

Check : ___ ÷ ___ = ___

㉑ There was p L of juice in the bottle. Dave drank 0.5L leaving 0.125L behind. How much juice was in the bottle at the beginning?

$$p - \underline{\hspace{1cm}} = \underline{\hspace{1cm}}$$

$$p - \underline{\hspace{1cm}} + \underline{\hspace{1cm}} = \underline{\hspace{1cm}} + \underline{\hspace{1cm}}$$

$$p = \underline{\hspace{1cm}}$$

There was ___ L of juice.

Check : ___ − ___ = ___

ACTIVITY

Tick ✔ the child who wrote the equivalent equations.

A
| $x + 5 = 14$ |
| $5 + x = 14$ |

B
| $p \div 6 = 4$ |
| $6 \div p = 4$ |

C
| $y - 10 = 5$ |
| $10 - y = 5$ |

D
| $q \times 2 = 8$ |
| $2 \times q = 8$ |

6 Time

WORDS TO LEARN

Duration - how long an event lasts

e.g. $\frac{1}{2}$ hour or 30 minutes

Complete Dave's schedule.

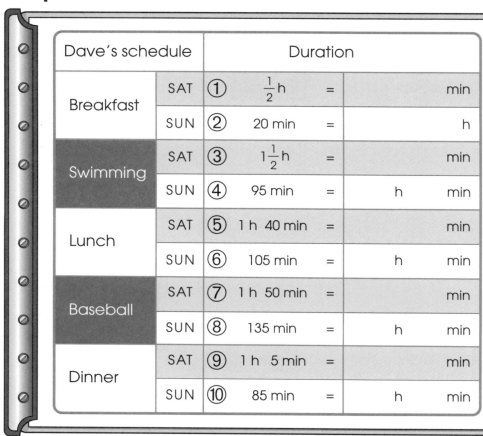

Dave's schedule			Duration			
Breakfast	SAT	①	$\frac{1}{2}$ h	=		min
	SUN	②	20 min	=		h
Swimming	SAT	③	$1\frac{1}{2}$ h	=		min
	SUN	④	95 min	=	h	min
Lunch	SAT	⑤	1 h 40 min	=		min
	SUN	⑥	105 min	=	h	min
Baseball	SAT	⑦	1 h 50 min	=		min
	SUN	⑧	135 min	=	h	min
Dinner	SAT	⑨	1 h 5 min	=		min
	SUN	⑩	85 min	=	h	min

$\frac{1}{4}$ h = $\frac{1}{4}$ × 60 min

= 15 min

65 min = 60 min + 5 min

= 1 h 5 min

Convert hours to minutes
Multiply each hour by 60.

Convert minutes to hours
Divide the minutes by 60; leave the remainder as minutes.

Follow Dave's method to solve the problems.

Addition

1st Add the minutes.

2nd Trade every 60 minutes (1 hour) to the hours.

3rd Add the hours.

$$\begin{array}{r} \overset{1}{4} \text{ h } 25 \text{ min} \\ + \quad 2 \text{ h } 55 \text{ min} \\ \hline 7 \text{ h } 20 \text{ min} \end{array}$$

Subtraction

1st Subtract the minutes.

2nd If the minutes can't take away, trade 1 hour (60 minutes) to the minutes.

3rd Subtract the hour.

$$\begin{array}{r} \overset{3}{4} \text{ h } \overset{8\,5}{25} \text{ min} \\ - \quad 2 \text{ h } 55 \text{ min} \\ \hline 1 \text{ h } 30 \text{ min} \end{array}$$

⑪ 3 h 40 min
  +   30 min
   _____
     h   min

⑫ 8 h 12 min
  − 5 h 49 min
   _____
     h   min

⑬ 4 h 30 min
  − 3 h 50 min
   _____
     h   min

⑭   06 : 17
  + 02 : 53
   _____
        :

⑮   12 : 00
  − 09 : 13
   _____
        :

⑯   02 : 16
  + 04 : 44
   _____
        :

Read what Uncle Ray says and answer the questions.

⑰

The ball game lasted 1 h 5 min. It ended at 5:00 p.m.
What time did it start?

_____ = _____

It started at _____ p.m.

⑱

My favourite TV programme starts at 7:30 p.m. and
ends at 9:15 p.m. How long does it last?

_____ = _____

Uncle Ray's favourite programme lasts

_____h_____min .

A C T I V I T Y

Help Dave write the times.

		Start	End	Duration
1.	Swimming Class	9:35 a.m.	10:10 a.m.	
2.	Hockey Class	12:05 p.m.		45 min
3.	Baseball Class		4:55 p.m.	1 h 10 min

7 Area

WORDS TO LEARN

Area - the number of square units of a surface

e.g.

1cm
1cm ☐ ← Area = 1 cm²

1m
1m ☐ ← Area = 1 m²

Height - the distance straight down from top to bottom of an object or a shape

Base - the length of the bottom edge

Count the squares for each shape to complete the table.

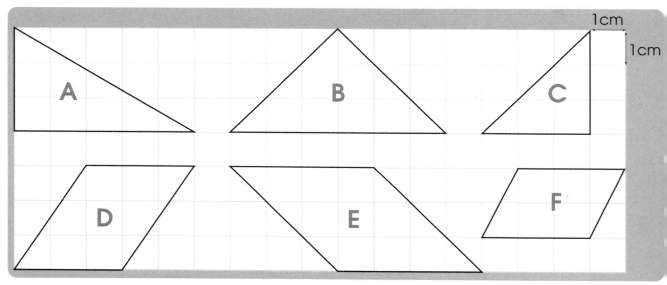

	Height (cm)	Base (cm)	Area (cm²)
① Triangle A	3		
② Triangle B		6	
③ Triangle C			
④ Parallelogram D	3		
⑤ Parallelogram E		4	
⑥ Parallelogram F			

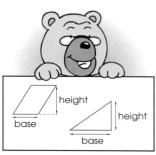

Count the fully covered squares first. Then combine the partly covered squares to make whole squares.

Read what Dave says. Then help him find the base, height and area of each parallelogram.

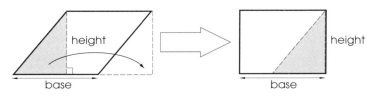

I can make a rectangle from a parallelogram by cutting out a triangle and put it on the other side.

Area of a parallelogram = Area of a rectangle
= base X height

⑦

7 cm   8 cm

9 cm

Base   = _____ cm

Height = _____ cm

Area   = _____ cm²

⑧

14 cm   12 cm

10 cm

Base   = _____ cm

Height = _____ cm

Area   = _____ cm²

b = base, h = height

⑨

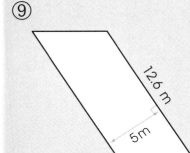

12.6 m

5 m

6 m

Base   = _____ m

Height = _____ m

Area   = _____ m²

⑩

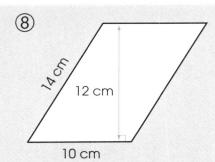

13 m

11.2 m

8 m

Base   = _____ m

Height = _____ m

Area   = _____ m²

⑪

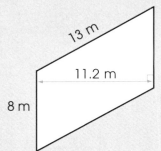

17 m

5m

6 m

Base   = _____ m

Height = _____ m

Area   = _____ m²

Follow Steve's method to find the base, height and area of each triangle.

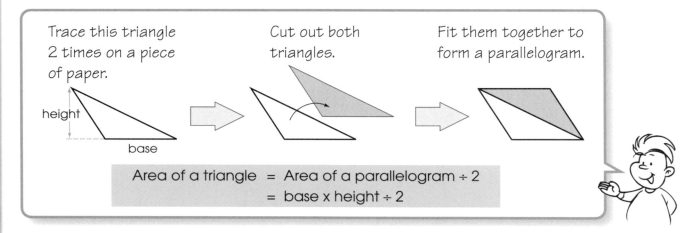

Trace this triangle 2 times on a piece of paper.

height
base

Cut out both triangles.

Fit them together to form a parallelogram.

Area of a triangle = Area of a parallelogram ÷ 2
= base × height ÷ 2

⑫

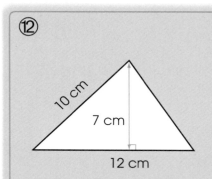

10 cm
7 cm
12 cm

Base = _____ cm

Height = _____ cm

Area = _____ cm²

⑬

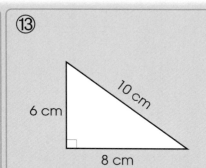

6 cm
10 cm
8 cm

Base = _____ cm

Height = _____ cm

Area = _____ cm²

b = base, h = height

⑭

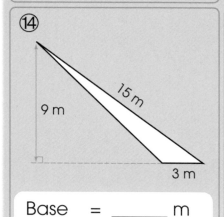

9 m
15 m
3 m

Base = _____ m

Height = _____ m

Area = _____ m²

⑮

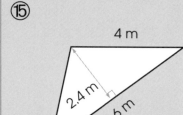

4 m
2.4 m
6 m

Base = _____ m

Height = _____ m

Area = _____ m²

⑯

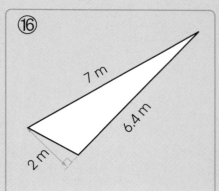

7 m
6.4 m
2 m

Base = _____ m

Height = _____ m

Area = _____ m²

Find the area of the shapes.

⑰
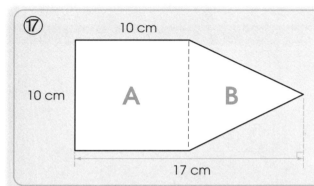

Area of A = _____ cm²

Area of B = _____ cm²

Area of (A + B) = _____ cm²

⑱
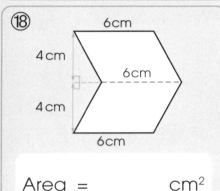

Area = _____ cm²

⑲
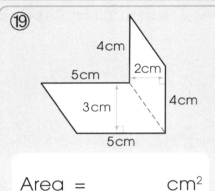

Area = _____ cm²

Cut the shapes into squares, triangles, parallelograms etc. Then add up the areas.

⑳
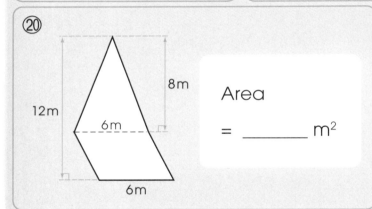

Area = _____ m²

㉑
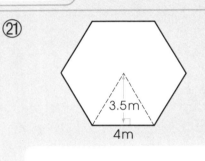

Area = _____ m²

ACTIVITY

Find the area of the shaded parts. Each ☐ = 1 cm².

1.
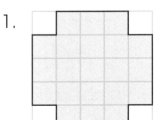

Area = _____ cm²

2.
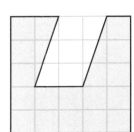

Area = _____ cm²

Directions

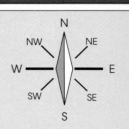

WORDS TO LEARN

Direction - a point toward which a person or thing looks or faces

Look at the map and write North, East, South or West.

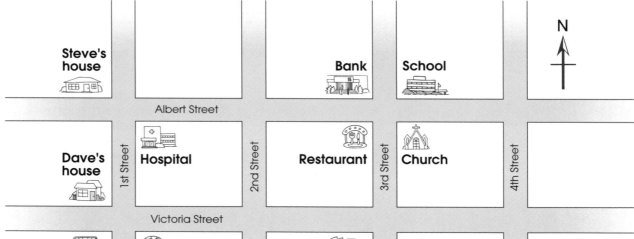

My house is to the north of the playground.

① Dave's house is to the _____ of Steve's house.

② The hospital is to the _____ of the restaurant.

③ The bank is to the _____ of the shopping mall.

④ The cinema is to the _____ of the playground.

⑤ If Dave wants to go to school from his house, he needs to go 1 block north and 2 blocks _____ .

⑥ If Dave wants to go to the cinema from the bank, he needs to go 2 blocks _____ and 1 block _____ .

Look at the map on P.22 again and use Uncle Ray's direction board to answer the questions.

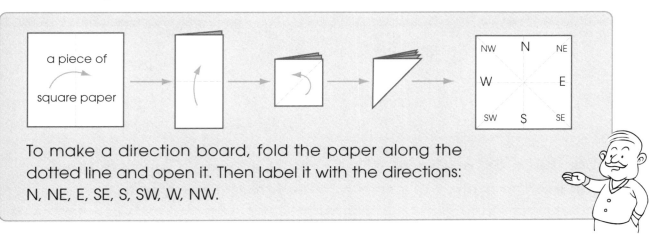

To make a direction board, fold the paper along the dotted line and open it. Then label it with the directions: N, NE, E, SE, S, SW, W, NW.

⑦ The church is to the _____ of the shopping mall.

⑧ The cinema is to the _____ of Dave's house.

⑨ The restaurant is to the _____ of the school.

⑩ Steve's house is to the _____ of the hospital.

⑪ The playground is to the _____ of the bank.

⑫ The hospital is to the _____ of the shopping mall.

NE	:	North-east
NW	:	North-west
SE	:	South-east
SW	:	South-west

ACTIVITY

Follow Dave's instruction to draw this shape ▢ without taking your pencil off the paper.

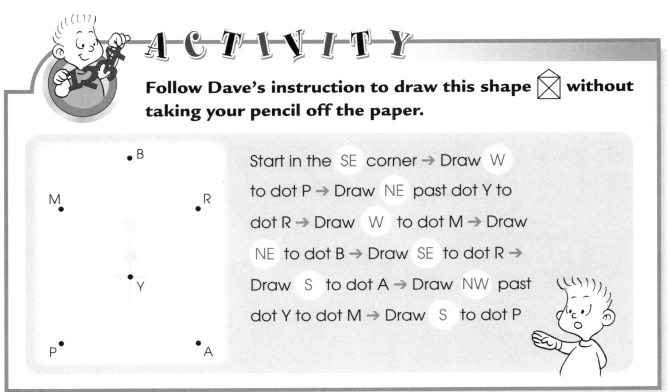

Start in the SE corner → Draw W to dot P → Draw NE past dot Y to dot R → Draw W to dot M → Draw NE to dot B → Draw SE to dot R → Draw S to dot A → Draw NW past dot Y to dot M → Draw S to dot P

Graphs

WORDS TO LEARN

Bar graph - a graph using bars to show information
Line graph - a graph using points and lines to show information

The table shows the profits of ABC Centre last week. Complete the table and use the rounded figures to complete the bar graph.

①	SUN	MON	TUE	WED	THU	FRI	SAT
Profit ($)	4 372	2 139	1 426	2 547	2 982	3 759	5 236
Round to the nearest thousand	4 000						

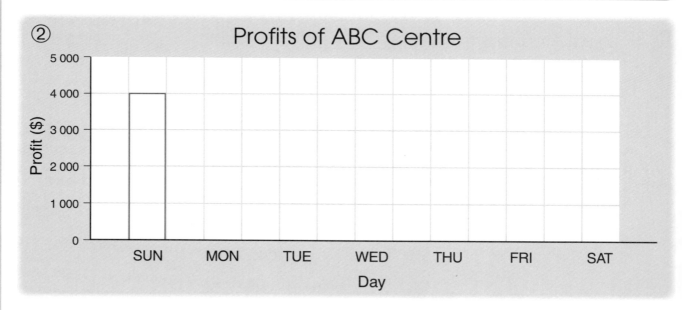

Read the bar graph and answer the questions.

③ On which day did ABC Centre have the highest profit? _____

④ On which day did ABC Centre have the lowest profit? _____

⑤ About how many times more profit was there on

Sunday than on Monday? _____ times

Study the line graph and answer the questions.

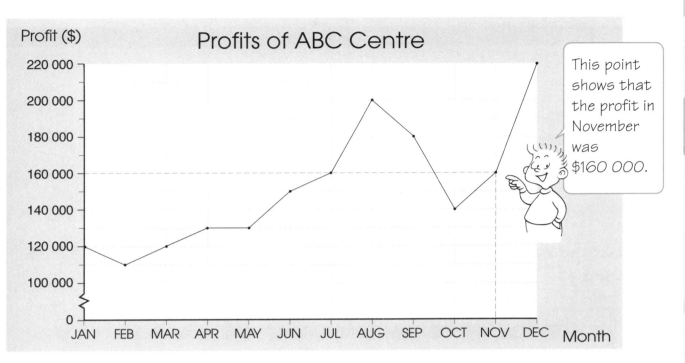

⑥ In which month did the profit reach $200 000? _____

⑦ In how many months was the profit over $170 000? _____

⑧ What was the difference in profits between July

and March? $ _____

⑨ About how many times more profit was there in

December than in February? _____ times

ACTIVITY

Read the table and help Dave complete the vertical and horizontal scales.

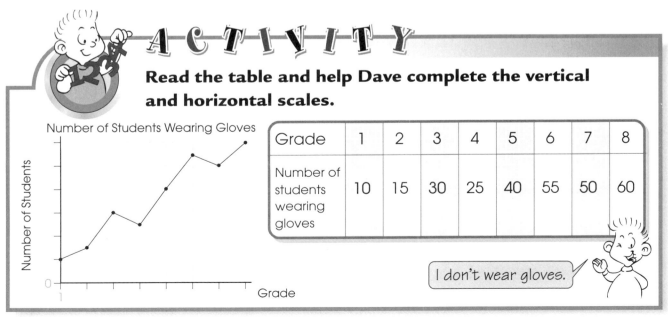

Grade	1	2	3	4	5	6	7	8
Number of students wearing gloves	10	15	30	25	40	55	50	60

I don't wear gloves.

10 Factorization

Factor	-	a number that can divide a larger number exactly
Composite number	-	any number greater than 1 that has more than 2 factors
Prime number	-	any number with only 1 and itself as factors
Prime factor	-	a factor that is a prime number

Look at the 10-column board. Put a cross (x) on every multiple of 2, 3, 5, 7, 11 and 13. Then answer the question.

①

101	1̶0̶2̶	103	1̶0̶4̶	1̶0̶5̶	1̶0̶6̶	107	1̶0̶8̶	109	1̶1̶0̶
1̶1̶1̶	1̶1̶2̶	113	114	115	116	117	118	119	120
121	122	123	124	125	126	127	128	129	130
131	132	133	134	135	136	137	138	139	140
141	142	143	144	145	146	147	148	149	150
151	152	153	154	155	156	157	158	159	160
161	162	163	164	165	166	167	168	169	170
171	172	173	174	175	176	177	178	179	180
181	182	183	184	185	186	187	188	189	190
191	192	193	194	195	196	197	198	199	200

All multiples of 2 end in 2, 4, 6, 8 or 0.
All multiples of 5 end in 5 or 0.

All multiples of 3 have digits that add to a multiple of 3.

② Which is the largest prime number under 200? _____

Write prime or composite for each number.

③ 67 _____ ④ 85 _____ ⑤ 71 _____

⑥ 326 _____ ⑦ 213 _____ ⑧ 367 _____

Follow Dave's method to write each number as a product of prime factors.

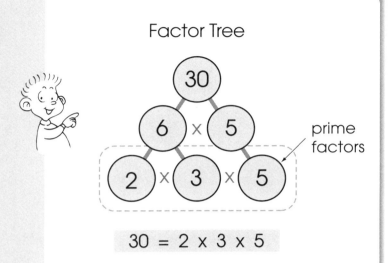

1st Write the number as the product of two factors.

2nd Continue to factorize each composite number until all factors are prime numbers.

3rd Write the number as a product of prime numbers.

Factor Tree

prime factors

30 = 2 x 3 x 5

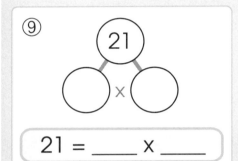

⑨

21 = _____ x _____

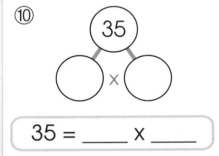

⑩

35 = _____ x _____

The number 1 is not used in factor trees.

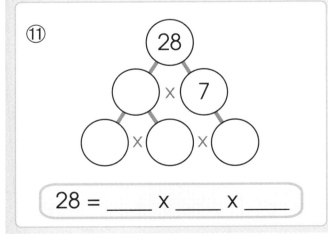

⑪

28 = _____ x _____ x _____

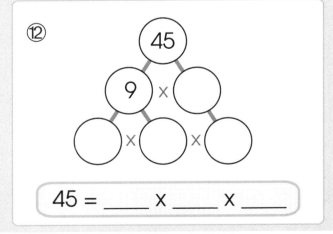

⑫

45 = _____ x _____ x _____

Write each number as a product of prime factors.

⑬ 36 = _____

⑭ 54 = _____

⑮ 64 = _____

⑯ 72 = _____

Follow Dave's method to find the GCF of the following numbers.

Find the GCF of 16 and 20.

16　　= 2 x 2 x 2 x 2
20　　= 2 x 2 x 5

Common prime factors : 2 , 2
GCF　= 2 x 2 = 4

Steps to find GCF:

1st　Write each number as a product of prime factors.

2nd　Multiply all prime factors common to both numbers.

⑰　26 = ＿＿ x ＿＿

39 = ＿＿ x ＿＿

Common
prime factor : ＿＿＿

GCF = ＿＿

⑱　30 = ＿＿ x ＿＿ x ＿＿

45 = ＿＿ x ＿＿ x ＿＿

Common
prime factors : ＿＿ , ＿＿

GCF = ＿＿ x ＿＿ = ＿＿

⑲　28 = ＿＿ x ＿＿ x ＿＿

42 = ＿＿ x ＿＿ x ＿＿

Common
prime factors : ＿＿ , ＿＿

GCF = ＿＿ x ＿＿ = ＿＿

⑳　50 = ＿＿ x ＿＿ x ＿＿

75 = ＿＿ x ＿＿ x ＿＿

Common
prime factors : ＿＿ , ＿＿

GCF = ＿＿ x ＿＿ = ＿＿

Find the GCF.

㉑　12 and 20 ＿＿＿＿＿＿

㉒　18 and 30 ＿＿＿＿＿＿

㉓　80 and 100 ＿＿＿＿＿＿

㉔　56 and 64 ＿＿＿＿＿＿

Follow Steve's method to find the LCM of the following numbers.

Find the LCM of 16 and 20.

$16 = 2 \times 2 \times 2 \times 2$
$20 = 2 \times 2 \qquad \times 5$

$LCM = 2 \times 2 \times 2 \times 2 \times 5$
$\qquad = 80$

Steps to find LCM:

1st Write each number as a product of prime factors.

2nd Sort out the prime factors common to both numbers and multiply them to all other factors on the list.

㉕ $12 = \underline{\quad} \times \underline{\quad} \times \underline{\quad}$
$18 = \underline{\quad} \times \underline{\quad} \times \underline{\quad}$

LCM
$= \underline{\quad} \times \underline{\quad} \times \underline{\quad} \times \underline{\quad}$
$= \underline{\quad}$

㉖ $15 = \underline{\quad} \times \underline{\quad}$
$21 = \underline{\quad} \times \underline{\quad}$

LCM
$= \underline{\quad} \times \underline{\quad} \times \underline{\quad}$
$= \underline{\quad}$

Find the LCM.

㉗ 10 and 15 _____

㉘ 9 and 24 _____

㉙ 16 and 24 _____

㉚ 8 and 20 _____

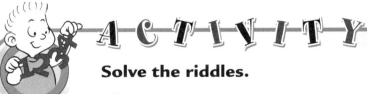

Solve the riddles.

1. It is a 3-digit prime number under 200. The 2nd and 3rd digits are the same and greater than 4. What number is it?

2. It is a 3-digit prime number under 200. The difference between the 2nd digit and the 3rd digit is 9. What number is it?

Midway Test

Write the numbers in words. (4 marks)

① 20 681 _____

② 433 000 _____

Write the numbers in order from the greatest to the least. (4 marks)

③ 387 425, 378 425, 387 245, 378 245

_____

④ 941 756, 914 576, 941 576, 914 756

_____

Write the place value of the underlined digits. (4 marks)

⑤ 4 5̲86 042 _____   ⑥ 1̲ 732 469 _____

Tick ✔ the right equations. (3 marks)

⑦ 6 more than a number *n* is 15.

☐ $6 \times n = 15$ ☐ $n - 6 = 15$ ☐ $n + 6 = 15$

⑧ 3 times a number *m* is 18.

☐ $m = 18 \times 3$ ☐ $3 \times m = 18$ ☐ $18 \times m = 3$

⑨ 5 less than a number *k* is 9.

☐ $5 - k = 9$ ☐ $k - 5 = 9$ ☐ $k = 9 - 5$

Solve the equations. (4 marks)

⑩
$$y + 2 = 21$$
$$y = \underline{\hspace{2em}}$$

⑪
$$m - 6 = 5$$
$$m = \underline{\hspace{2em}}$$

⑫
$$4 \times n = 24$$
$$n = \underline{\hspace{2em}}$$

⑬
$$p \div 9 = 3$$
$$p = \underline{\hspace{2em}}$$

Complete the table and use the rounded figures to complete the bar graph.

(8 marks)

⑭

City	Fairmount	Lakeview	Pinedale	Orchid
Population	680 462	886 217	275 176	239 421
Rounded to the nearest hundred thousand				

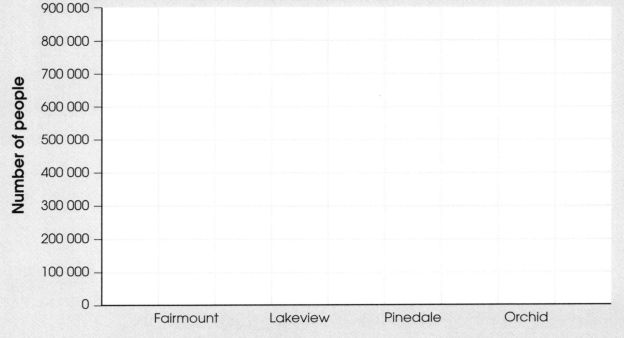

Population of Cities

⑮ Number of people — City

Read the graph and answer the questions. (10 marks)

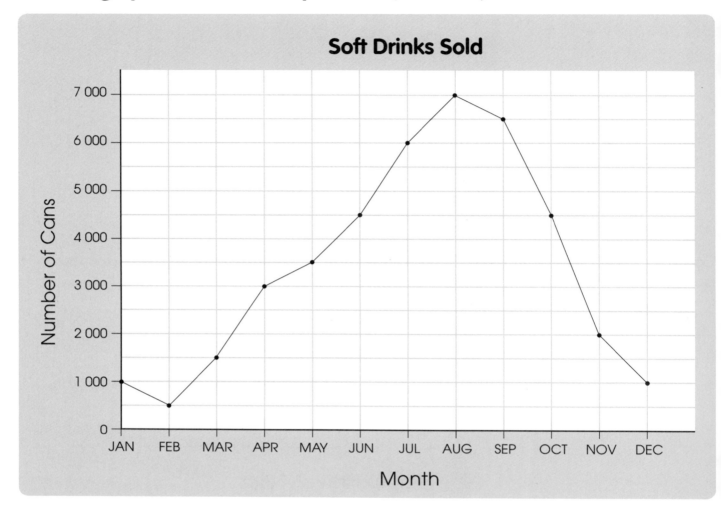

Soft Drinks Sold

⑯ How many cans of soft drink were sold in March? _____ cans

⑰ In which month were 7000 cans sold? _____

⑱ How many cans of soft drink were sold in February and September? _____ cans

⑲ How many cans of soft drink were sold in May and December? _____ cans

⑳ How many more cans of soft drink were sold in October than April? _____ cans

Find the area of each shape. (12 marks)

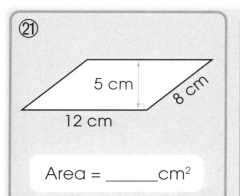

㉑ Area = _____ cm²

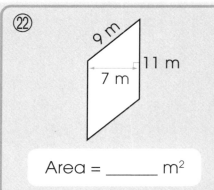

㉒ Area = _____ m²

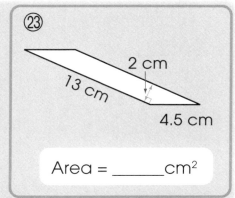

㉓ Area = _____ cm²

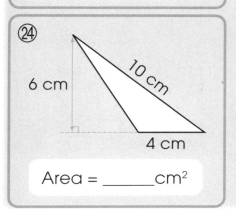

㉔ Area = _____ cm²

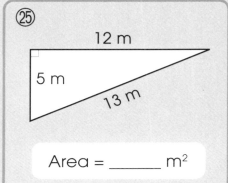

㉕ Area = _____ m²

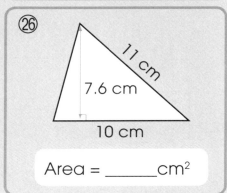

㉖ Area = _____ cm²

Write the answers in simplest form. (20 marks)

㉗ $8 \times \dfrac{2}{3} =$ _____

㉘ $\dfrac{1}{2} \times \dfrac{4}{7} =$ _____

㉙ $7 \div \dfrac{1}{2} =$ _____

㉚ $\dfrac{2}{3} \div \dfrac{1}{6} =$ _____

㉛ $6 \times \dfrac{1}{4} =$ _____

㉜ $\dfrac{3}{5} \times 1\dfrac{2}{3} =$ _____

㉝ $\dfrac{8}{9} \times \dfrac{3}{4} =$ _____

㉞ $\dfrac{5}{8} \div 10 =$ _____

㉟ $1\dfrac{1}{3} \times \dfrac{3}{8} =$ _____

㊱ $\dfrac{6}{7} \div 1\dfrac{5}{7} =$ _____

Write each number as a product of prime factors. Then find the GCF of each pair of numbers. (12 marks)

③⑦ 42 = _____

72 = _____

GCF = _____

③⑧ 16 = _____

24 = _____

GCF = _____

③⑨ 15 = _____

45 = _____

GCF = _____

④⓪ 20 = _____

32 = _____

GCF = _____

Write each number as a product of prime factors. Then find the LCM of each pair of numbers. (12 marks)

④① 28 = _____

35 = _____

LCM = _____

④② 18 = _____

20 = _____

LCM = _____

④③ 24 = _____

36 = _____

LCM = _____

④④ 30 = _____

40 = _____

LCM = _____

Read Dave's map. Then fill in the blanks and answer the questions. (7 marks)

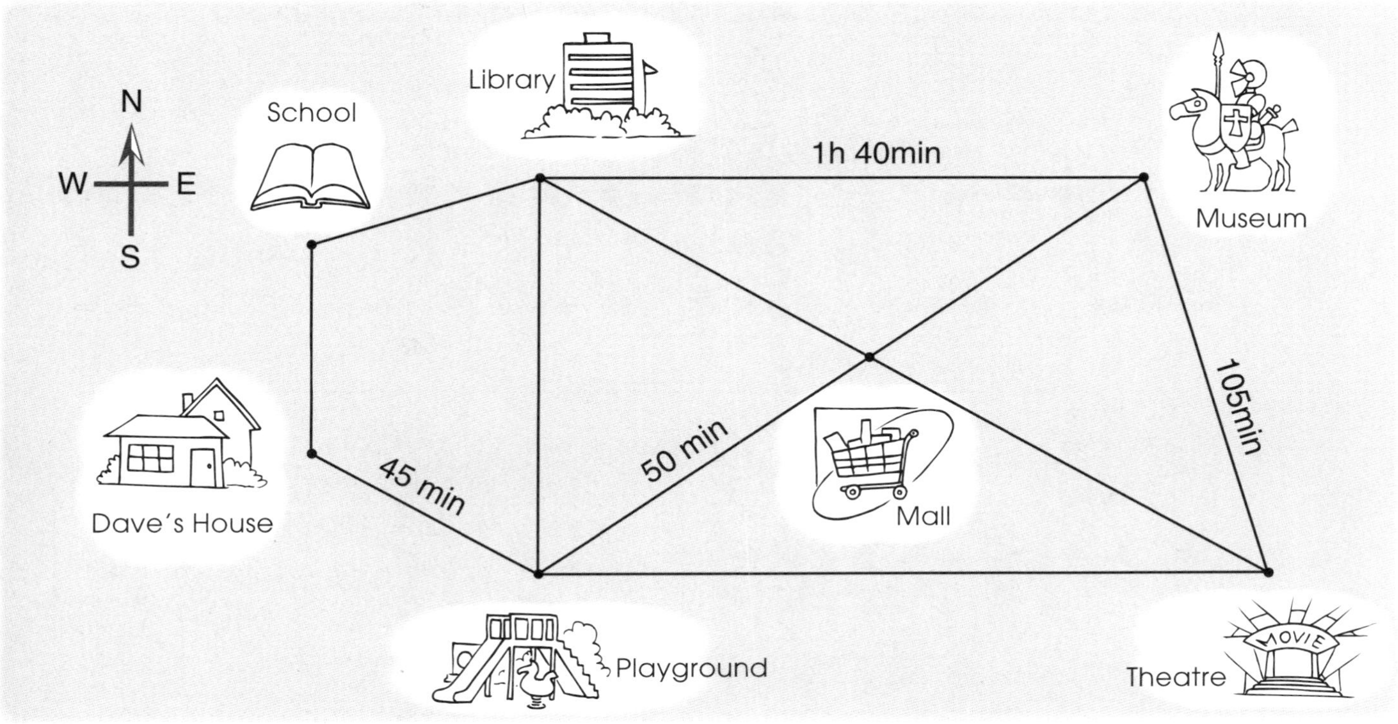

㊺ The museum is to the ____________ of the mall.

㊻ The playground is to the ____________ of the library.

㊼ The playground is to the ____________ of the mall.

㊽ Where would Dave be if he travelled NW from the mall? ____________

㊾ How many minutes did Dave take to travel from the library to the museum? ________ min

㊿ How long did Dave take to travel from home to the mall passing the playground? _____ h _____ min

(51) If Dave left the museum at 9:25 a.m., when did he reach the theatre? __________ a.m.

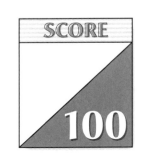

SCORE

100

Inverse Proportion

WORDS TO LEARN

Increase	-	becoming greater in size, number or degree
Decrease	-	becoming smaller in size, number or degree
Inverse proportion	-	the relation of two values with one increasing and the other decreasing

Today is my birthday. I've got some candies for my friends. If only 2 of my friends come, I can give each of them 12 candies. But if 4 of my friends come, how many candies can each one get?

1st Find the number of candies that Dave has.

$12 \times 2 = 24$

Dave has 24 candies.

2nd Divide the number of candies by the number of friends.

$24 \div 4 = 6$

Each friend gets 6 candies.

Help Dave solve the problems. Complete the table.

	No. of friends coming	Total no. of candies	No. of candies each friend can get
①	2		$24 \div 2 =$
②	3		$=$
③	4	$12 \times 2 = 24$	$=$
④	6		$=$
⑤	8		$=$
⑥	12		$=$

The more friends that come to my party, the fewer candies each one will get. This is inverse proportion.

My friends will come to help me make the sandwiches. 3 people will take 60 minutes to finish the work.

Help Dave find the answers.

⑦ How long will 6 people take to finish the work?

_____ X _____ ÷ _____ = _____

6 people will take _____ minutes.

⑧ How long will 9 people take to finish the work?

_____ X _____ ÷ _____ = _____

9 people will take _____ minutes.

First, find the time needed for 1 person to finish the work.

48 of my friends have come to my party. I want to group them with the same number of people in each group.

How does Dave group his friends? Fill in the table.

⑨

No. of groups	2	3	4			
No. of people in each group				8	6	4

ACTIVITY

Write the number of glasses or mugs needed.

I want to pour this jar of juice into different kinds of mugs or glasses.

	1. 300mL	2. 250mL	3. 200mL	4. 150mL	5. 100mL	6. 50mL
Number needed	10					

Decimals and Fractions

12

WORDS TO LEARN

Thousands Hundreds Tens Ones Tenths Hundredths Thousandths

$$1\ 2\ 3\ 4\ .\ 5\ 6\ 7$$

Decimal point

Equivalent Fractions - fractions that represent the same value

e.g. $\frac{1}{2}$ and $\frac{2}{4}$ are equivalent fractions.

Numerator - the top number in a fraction

Denominator - the bottom number in a fraction

e.g. $\frac{4}{5}$ — numerator — denominator

 My brother, Tony, is a marathon runner.

Read how far Tony runs. Write the answers as decimal numbers.

① 16 and 25 hundredths of a kilometre. ☐ km

② 14 and 62 thousandths of a kilometre. ☐ km

③ 15 and 2 tenths of a kilometre. ☐ km

④ 13 and 424 thousandths of a kilometre. ☐ km

⑤ 17 and 7 hundredths of a kilometre. ☐ km

Write the place value of each underlined digit.

⑥ 14.3<u>3</u>4 ☐

⑦ 1.37<u>5</u> ☐

⑧ 16.01<u>6</u> ☐

⑨ <u>1</u>1.52 ☐

There is another way to write my records.

$15.2 = 15\frac{2}{10}$	$16.25 = 16\frac{25}{100}$	$13.424 = 13\frac{424}{1000}$
$= 15\frac{2 \div 2}{10 \div 2}$	$= 16\frac{25 \div 25}{100 \div 25}$	$= 13\frac{424 \div 8}{1000 \div 8}$
$= 15\frac{1}{5}$	$= 16\frac{1}{4}$	$= 13\frac{53}{125}$
$15.2 \text{ km} = 15\frac{1}{5} \text{ km}$	$16.25 \text{ km} = 16\frac{1}{4} \text{ km}$	$13.424 \text{ km} = 13\frac{53}{125} \text{ km}$

Find the fractions and put them in simplest form.

⑩ 16.3 = ☐   ⑪ 18.2 = ☐   ⑫ 19.4 = ☐

⑬ 13.16 = ☐   ⑭ 13.75 = ☐   ⑮ 18.02 = ☐

⑯ 18.025 = ☐   ⑰ 14.866 = ☐   ⑱ 9.105 = ☐

Tony has run $\frac{3}{4}$ km. It is equal to 0.75 km.

1st ▶ Find a fraction equivalent to $\frac{3}{4}$ with a denominator of 10, 100 or 1000, e.g.

$$\frac{3}{4} = \frac{3 \times 25}{4 \times 25} = \frac{75}{100}$$

2nd ▶ Write as a decimal number.

$$\frac{75}{100} = 0.75$$

Find an equivalent fraction with denominator of 10, 100 or 1000. Then write as a decimal number.

⑲ $\frac{1}{4}$ = $\frac{}{100}$ = ☐

⑳ $\frac{6}{50}$ = $\frac{}{100}$ = ☐

Multiply the denominator and the numerator by the same number.

㉑ $\dfrac{5}{8}$ = ☐

㉒ $\dfrac{7}{20}$ = ☐

㉓ $\dfrac{9}{25}$ = ☐

㉔ $1\dfrac{1}{5}$ = ☐

㉕ $2\dfrac{6}{40}$ = ☐

㉖ $12\dfrac{24}{125}$ = ☐

<u>Change fractions into decimals</u>:
Divide the numerator by the denominator;
add zeros to the dividend when necessary.

e.g. $\dfrac{3}{7}$ = 0.43 (rounded to the nearest hundredth)

```
     0.4 2 8
7 ) 3.0 0 0
    2 8
    ‾‾‾
      2 0
      1 4
      ‾‾‾
        6 0
        5 6
        ‾‾‾
          4
```

round up

0.42   0.43
        0.428

Change all the signs on Tony's running course into decimals. Round to the nearest hundredth.

㉗

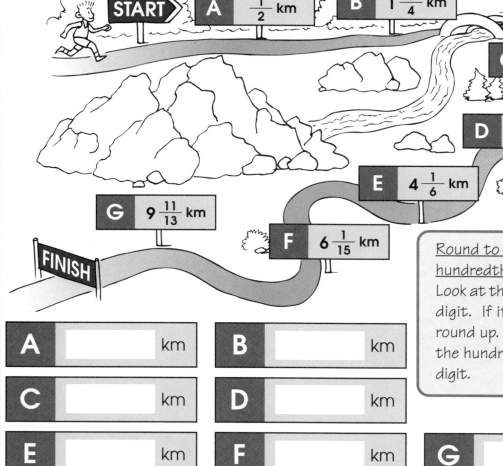

<u>Round to the nearest hundredth</u> :
Look at the thousandths digit. If it is 5 or more, round up. Add 1 to the hundredths digit.

A ☐ km   B ☐ km

C ☐ km   D ☐ km

E ☐ km   F ☐ km   G ☐ km

Multiplying decimals

e.g. $0.25 \times 0.5 = 0.125$

$$
\begin{array}{r}
0.2\,5 \\
\times \quad 0.5 \\
\hline
0.1\,2\,5
\end{array}
$$

0.25 — 2 decimal places

0.5 — 1 decimal place

0.125 — 2 + 1 = 3, 3 decimal places

1st Align the right-hand digits.

2nd Multiply as with whole numbers.

3rd Count the number of decimal places in the question.

4th Place the decimal point in the product.

Put the decimal point in the right place.

㉘
$$
\begin{array}{r}
1.6 \\
\times \quad 1.3 \\
\hline
2\,0\,8
\end{array}
$$

㉙
$$
\begin{array}{r}
2.1 \\
\times \quad 3.0 \\
\hline
6\,3\,0
\end{array}
$$

㉚
$$
\begin{array}{r}
0.9\,3 \\
\times \quad 1.2 \\
\hline
1\,1\,1\,6
\end{array}
$$

㉛
$$
\begin{array}{r}
1.5\,0 \\
\times \quad 0.8\,1 \\
\hline
1\,2\,1\,5\,0
\end{array}
$$

Find the answers.

㉜
$$
\begin{array}{r}
1.3 \\
\times \quad 1.9 \\
\hline
\end{array}
$$

㉝
$$
\begin{array}{r}
3.0\,6 \\
\times \quad 1.4 \\
\hline
\end{array}
$$

㉞
$$
\begin{array}{r}
0.0\,6 \\
\times \quad 0.1\,2 \\
\hline
\end{array}
$$

Place the decimal point in the product. Insert zero(s) as needed.

㉟ $0.62 \times 1.40 =$ _____

㊱ $4.8 \times 0.31 =$ _____

㊲ $2.5 \times 0.3 =$ _____

㊳ $1.62 \times 1.30 =$ _____

㊴ $1.2 \times 1.03 =$ _____

㊵ $1.45 \times 0.42 =$ _____

You can divide as with whole numbers. Remember to place a decimal point in the quotient above the one in the dividend.

To divide 2.85 by 5, follow these steps:

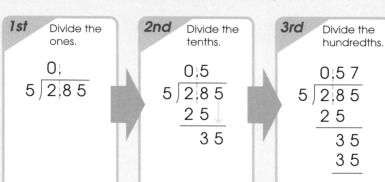

1st Divide the ones.

$$\begin{array}{r} 0. \\ 5\overline{\smash)2.85} \end{array}$$

2nd Divide the tenths.

$$\begin{array}{r} 0.5 \\ 5\overline{\smash)2.85} \\ 2\,5 \\ \hline 3\,5 \end{array}$$

3rd Divide the hundredths.

$$\begin{array}{r} 0.57 \\ 5\overline{\smash)2.85} \\ 2\,5 \\ \hline 3\,5 \\ 3\,5 \\ \hline \end{array}$$

Try these.

㊶

$$\begin{array}{r} . \\ 6\overline{\smash)8.82} \\ 8 \\ \hline 2 \\ \hline \end{array}$$

㊷

$$\begin{array}{r} . \\ 18\overline{\smash)1.998} \\ 9 \\ \hline 8 \\ \hline \end{array}$$

㊸

$$\begin{array}{r} . \\ 7\overline{\smash)14.91} \\ 9 \\ \hline 1 \\ \hline \end{array}$$

㊹

$$12\overline{\smash)5.52}$$

㊺

$$8\overline{\smash)27.76}$$

㊻

$$9\overline{\smash)32.85}$$

㊼ 38.57 ÷ 7 = _____

㊽ 17.08 ÷ 14 = _____

㊾ 4.95 ÷ 11 = _____

㊿ 24.48 ÷ 18 = _____

51. $2.55 \div 3 = $ _____

52. $16.45 \div 5 = $ _____

53. $10.92 \div 4 = $ _____

Don't forget to put a decimal point in the quotient above the one in the dividend.

54. $74.64 \div 6 = $ _____   55. $50.24 \div 16 = $ _____

Find the answers.

56. Tony bought 7 sandwiches for $18.13. How much did each sandwich cost?

$18.13 \div 7 = $ _____   Each sandwich cost $ _____ .

57. If candy bars are 6 for $3.78. How much is one candy bar?

_____ $\div$ _____ = _____   One candy bar is $ _____ .

58. Tony shared $8.62 with Dave. How much did each person get?

_____ $\div$ _____ = _____   Each person got $ _____ .

ACTIVITY

Tony must go in the direction of the smaller number. Help him reach the finish line. Colour the path.

0.7 $\frac{15}{10}$ 0.45

$\frac{3}{4}$ $\frac{4}{9}$ 0.3 $\frac{8}{60}$

$\frac{1}{4}$ 0.6 $\frac{1}{5}$

0.7   0.9 $\frac{3}{12}$

$\frac{1}{5}$ 1.2   FINISH

0.25 $1\frac{2}{5}$ $\frac{8}{10}$

13 More about Simple Equations

WORDS TO LEARN

Equation - a number sentence with an equal sign

e.g. $9 + 7 = 16$, $2y + 5 = 12$

Read what Dave says. Then help him solve the problems.

The 📦 weighs 50g.

Each ✏️ weighs 2g.

How many ✏️ are there?

① $50 + 2 \times k = 90$

k = number of ✏️

$50 + 2 \times k - \underline{} = 90 - \underline{}$

$2 \times k = \underline{}$

$2 \times k \div \underline{} = \underline{} \div \underline{}$

$k = \underline{}$

There are ___ ✏️ in the box.

To solve an equation, undo addition or subtraction first.

Try these.

② $3 \times p + 12 = 48$

$3 \times p + 12 - \underline{} = 48 - \underline{}$

$3 \times p = \underline{}$

$3 \times p \div \underline{} = \underline{} \div \underline{}$

$p = \underline{}$

③ $9 \times q - 16 = 29$

$9 \times q - 16 + \underline{} = 29 + \underline{}$

$9 \times q = \underline{}$

$9 \times q \div \underline{} = \underline{} \div \underline{}$

$q = \underline{}$

④ $m \div 4 + 13 = 19$

$m \div 4 + 13 - \underline{} = 19 - \underline{}$

$m \div 4 = \underline{}$

$m \div 4 \times \underline{} = \underline{} \times \underline{}$

$m = \underline{}$

⑤ $n \div 5 - 12 = 8$

$n \div 5 - 12 + \underline{} = 8 + \underline{}$

$n \div 5 = \underline{}$

$n \div 5 \times \underline{} = \underline{} \times \underline{}$

$n = \underline{}$

Write and solve the equations.

⑥

The difference between $2y$ and 9 is 3.

$2y - \boxed{} = \boxed{}$ $\qquad y = \boxed{}$

⑦

$4m$ divided by 2 is 6.

$\boxed{} \div \boxed{} = \boxed{}$ $\qquad m = \boxed{}$

⑧

The sum of $2p$ and 5 is 7.

$\boxed{} + \boxed{} = \boxed{}$ $\qquad p = \boxed{}$

ACTIVITY

Help Dave find the weight of his toys.

1.
a. _____ g
b. _____ g

2.
a. _____ g
b. _____ g

14 Percent

Percent (%) - means a part of 100 or "out of 100"

e.g. Dave got 86 out of 100 on his test. That means he got 86% on his test.

1 = 100%
30 out of 100 are shaded.

As a fraction:
$\frac{30}{100}$

As a percent
30%

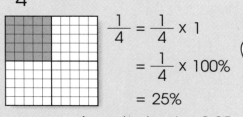

$\frac{1}{4}$ is shaded.

$\frac{1}{4} = \frac{1}{4} \times 1$

$= \frac{1}{4} \times 100\%$

$= 25\%$

As a decimal : 0.25

Write the shaded part of each 100-square as a fraction, a decimal and a percent.

①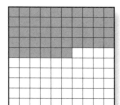

Fraction : _____

Decimal : _____

Percent : _____%

②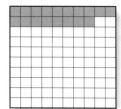

Fraction : _____

Decimal : _____

Percent : _____%

Rewrite as percent.

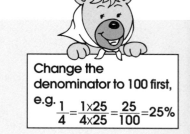

③ $\frac{13}{100}$ = _____

④ $\frac{9}{100}$ = _____

⑤ $\frac{8}{10}$ = _____

⑥ $\frac{7}{20}$ = _____

Change the denominator to 100 first,

e.g. $\frac{1}{4} = \frac{1 \times 25}{4 \times 25} = \frac{25}{100} = 25\%$

⑦ $\frac{3}{4}$ = _____

⑧ $\frac{8}{25}$ = _____

⑨ $\frac{1}{2}$ = _____

Write as fractions in simplest form.

⑩ 38% = ——————

⑪ 60% = ——————

⑫ 8% = ——————

⑬ 4% = ——————

⑭ 135% = ——————

⑮ 285% = ——————

Steve got 8 out of 10 questions correct on his math test.
The grade he got is
$$\frac{8}{10} = \frac{80}{100} = 80\%$$

Math Test
Student: Steve $\frac{8}{10}$
1. ✔   6. ✔
2. ✔   7. ✔
3. ✔   8. ✔
4. ✘   9. ✔
5. ✔   10. ✘

Change to fractions with 100 as the denominator first.

Follow Dave's method to grade the children's tests.

⑯
Science Test
Student: Steve $\frac{20}{25}$

$\frac{20}{25} = \frac{\boxed{}}{100}$

$= \boxed{}$ %

⑰
History Test
Student: Helen $\frac{38}{50}$

$\frac{38}{50} = \boxed{}$

$= \boxed{}$ %

⑱
Geography Test
Student: Elaine $\frac{14}{20}$

$\frac{14}{20} = \boxed{}$

$= \boxed{}$ %

Tick ✔ the correct answers and give a grade to Dave's math test.

⑲   Dave   **Math Test**

a. $\frac{4}{5} = 80\%$ b. $\frac{5}{25} = 40\%$ c. $\frac{1}{2} = 40\%$ d. $\frac{3}{5} = 60\%$

e. $\frac{4}{8} = 50\%$ f. $\frac{7}{20} = 35\%$ g. $\frac{1}{10} = 15\%$

h. $\frac{4}{25} = 16\%$ i. $\frac{3}{12} = 25\%$ j. $\frac{1}{5} = 20\%$

Grade:

$\frac{}{10}$

$= \underline{}$ %

Use the box graph to fill in the blanks.

GRADE 5 MATH CONTEST

Fractions of Students by Scores

Over 80 marks

Between 60 and 80 marks

Under 60 marks

⑳ _____ % of the students got marks between 60 and 80.

㉑ _____ % of the students got more than 80 marks.

㉒ _____ % of the students got less than 60 marks.

㉓ There were 100 students.

_____ students got more than 80 marks.

㉔ _____ students got marks between 60 and 80.

㉕ _____ students got less than 60 marks.

Decimals are like percents.

e.g.

$$0.5 = \frac{5}{10} = \frac{50}{100} = 50\%$$

$$1.25 = 1\frac{25}{100} = \frac{125}{100} = 125\%$$

1 means 100%.

Finish the chart.

㉖

Decimal	0.16			1.2	
Percent		45 %			134%
Fraction (in simplest form)			$\frac{1}{4}$		

Solve the problems.

㉗ 60% of the students in Steve's class are boys. What % are girls?

1 – _____ %

= _____ % – _____ %

= _____ %

_____ % are girls.

1 = 100%

㉘ In Steve's class, 30% of the students have blonde hair, 25% black hair and the rest brown hair. What % have brown hair?

_____

= _____

= _____

_____ % have brown hair.

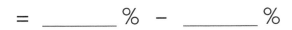

ACTIVITY

Study the bar graph and answer the questions.

100 students were asked about their favourite sports.

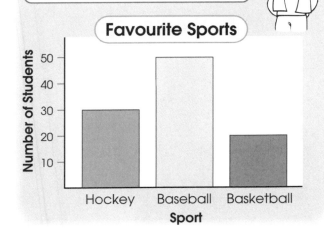

Favourite Sports

1. What kind of sport was the most popular?

   _____

2. What percent of students preferred:

   a. hockey? _____ %

   b. baseball? _____ %

   c. basketball? _____ %

More about Time

WORDS TO LEARN

Twelve-hour clock	– using a.m. for time between midnight and 12 noon, and p.m. for time between 12 noon and midnight
Twenty-four-hour clock	– using 01 - 24 to show hours of a day

Read what Steve says. Then write the times using the 24 h clock.

To avoid using a.m. or p.m., we can use the 24 h clock.

10:30 a.m. = 10:30

10:30 p.m. = 22:30

These numbers are used for p.m.

These numbers are used for a.m.

After noon, the 24h clock continues counting, e.g.
1:00 p.m. = 13:00

① 4:30 a.m. _____   ② 11:45 p.m. _____

③ 6:15 p.m. _____   ④ 9:20 p.m. _____

Write these times using a.m. or p.m.

⑤ 15:35 _____   ⑥ 09:28 _____

⑦ 21:19 _____   ⑧ 13:06 _____

⑨ 06:55 _____   ⑩ 2 h before 14:05 _____

⑪ 1 h after 19:25 _____   ⑫ 10 min before 09:07 _____

⑬ 3 h before 16:40 _____   ⑭ 45 min after 07:15 _____

128   COMPLETE MATHSMART (GRADE 5)

Dave noted down the times he reached some spots along the trail. Read what he says and answer his questions.

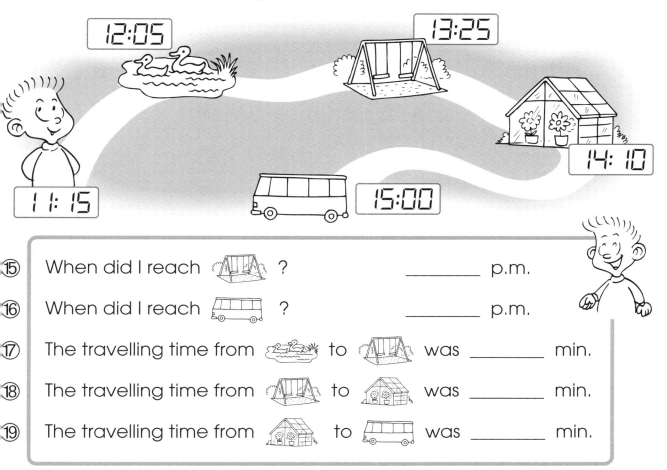

15. When did I reach ⛓️ ? _____ p.m.

16. When did I reach 🚌 ? _____ p.m.

17. The travelling time from 🦆 to ⛓️ was _____ min.

18. The travelling time from ⛓️ to 🏠 was _____ min.

19. The travelling time from 🏠 to 🚌 was _____ min.

ACTIVITY

Put the pictures in order from A to E to show what Dave did after school.

5 minutes past 5.

A quarter to five.

16 Circles

Circumference - the distance around a circle

Centre - the middle point of a circle

Diameter - a line segment joining two points on a circle and passing through the centre

Radius - a line segment joining the centre of a circle to a point on the circle

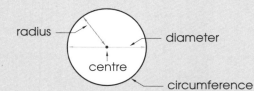

Write centre, circumference, diameter and radius.

①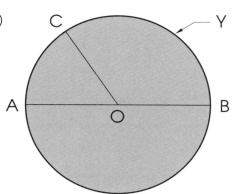

a. Line AOB : _____

b. Line OC : _____

c. Y : _____

d. O : _____

Measure and write the answers.

② Line AOB = [   ] cm

③ Line OC = [   ] cm

④ Line OD = [   ] cm

⑤ Line EF = [   ] cm

⑥ Line AOB = Line OC x [   ]

⑦ Line [   ] is the diameter.

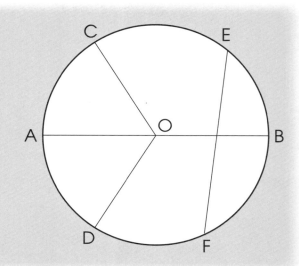

I can find the diameter of a toonie in this way.

1st Draw a circle around a toonie on a piece of paper.

2nd Use a ruler to find the longest distance from side to side of the circle. That is the diameter.

I can find the circumference in this way.

1st Make a roll of toonies for easy rolling.

2nd Make a mark on the toonie and roll one full turn on a tape or ruler.

Circumference

Follow Dave's methods to find the circumference and the diameter of a toonie. Tick ✔ the right boxes.

⑧ The approximate diameter is ☐ 3 cm ☐ 4 cm ☐ 5 cm.

⑨ The approximate circumference is ☐ 7 cm ☐ 9 cm ☐ 11 cm.

⑩ The circumference is approximately ☐ 2 ☐ 3 ☐ 4 times bigger than the diameter.

ACTIVITY

Draw and think.

1. Try the methods to draw circles.

Thumb pin   String

A pair of compasses

2. Think and tick ✔ the right answers.

a. How many diameters can you draw in a circle?

☐ 1   ☐ 2   ☐ many

b. When the radius is longer, how will the circle be?

☐ the same   ☐ bigger   ☐ smaller

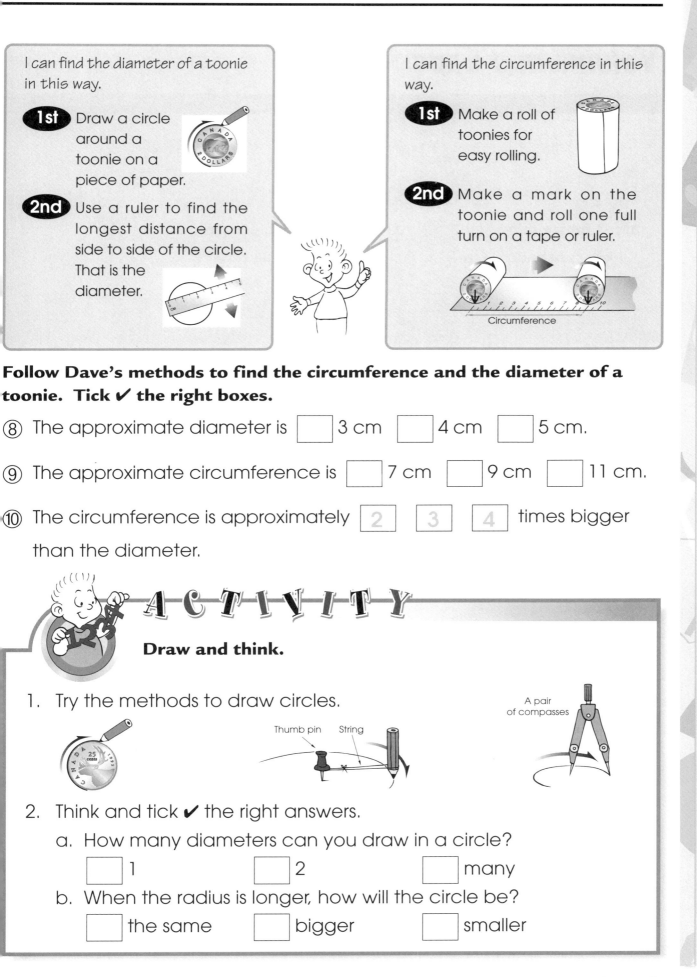

17 Volume and Capacity

WORDS TO LEARN

Capacity	-	the greatest amount of liquid a container can hold
Volume	-	the amount of space an object takes up
Cube	-	a block with 6 equal square faces
Centimetre cube	-	a cube with sides of 1 cm each
Cubic centimetre (cm³)	-	a unit for measuring volume

e.g. a block with 10 layers of

10 x 10 centimetre cubes,

its volume

= 10 cm x 10 cm x 10 cm

= 1000 cm³

Millilitre (mL) - a unit for measuring capacity

1 mL = 1 cm³, 1 L = 1000 mL

Find the volume of each block built by Dave with centimetre cubes.

①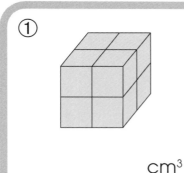

_____ cm³

②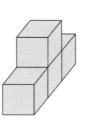

_____ cm³

③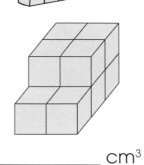

_____ cm³

④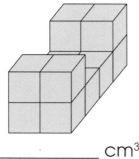

_____ cm³

⑤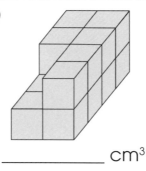

_____ cm³

Remember to count the hidden cubes.

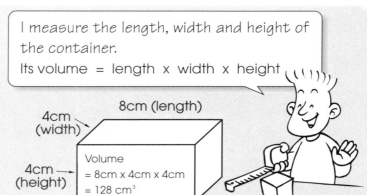

This container holds 128 centimetre cubes. Its volume is 128 cm³.

I measure the length, width and height of the container.

Its volume = length × width × height

8cm (length)
4cm (width)
4cm (height)

Volume
= 8cm × 4cm × 4cm
= 128 cm³

Follow Tony's method to find the volume of each wood block.

⑥

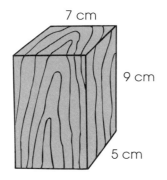

12 cm
4 cm
6 cm

a. Length = _____ cm

b. Width = _____ cm

c. Height = _____ cm

d. Volume = _____ X _____ X _____ cm³

= _____ cm³

⑦

7 cm
9 cm
5 cm

a. Length = _____ cm

b. Width = _____ cm

c. Height = _____ cm

d. Volume = _____ X _____ X _____ cm³

= _____ cm³

Help Dave find the volumes.

⑧

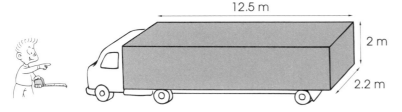

12.5 m
2 m
2.2 m

We use cubic metres (m³) as the unit for a large volume.

The volume of the container

= _____ X _____ X _____ m³ = _____ m³

⑨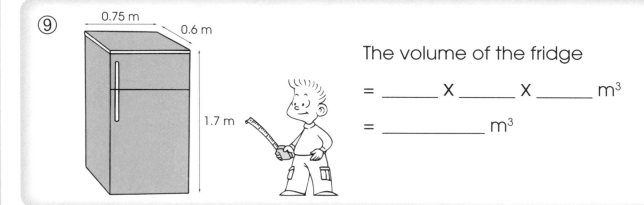

0.75 m

0.6 m

1.7 m

The volume of the fridge

= _____ X _____ X _____ m³

= _____ m³

I can find the volume of an irregular object, e.g. a stone.

1st Pour 1.5 L of water into a 2-Litre container.

2nd Put the stone into the container and mark the new water level. (e.g. 2 L)

3rd The volume of the stone = the amount of water displaced
= 2 L – 1.5 L
= 0.5 L or 500 mL (1L = 1000mL)
= 500 x 1cm³ (1mL =1cm³)
= 500 cm³

Help Dave find the volume of his toys.

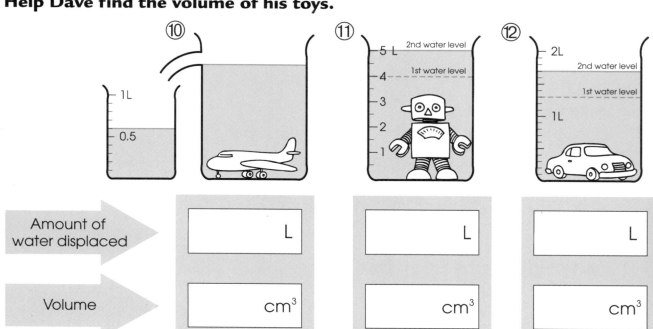

⑩

1 L

0.5

⑪ 5 L — 2nd water level
4 — 1st water level
3
2
1

⑫ 2L
2nd water level
1st water level
1 L

| Amount of water displaced | | L | | L | | L |
| Volume | | cm³ | | cm³ | | cm³ |

Help Dave find the capacity of his aquariums.

⑬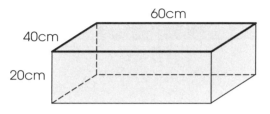

Capacity = _____ x _____ x _____

= _____ mL

⑭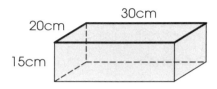

Capacity = _____ x _____ x _____

= _____ mL

Solve the problems.

⑮ How much water is there in the aquarium?

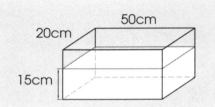

_____ mL

⑯ How many bottles are needed to hold the water in the tank?

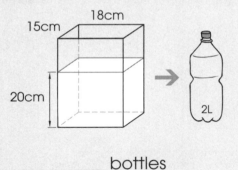

_____ bottles

⑰ How many bottles of water can the tank hold?

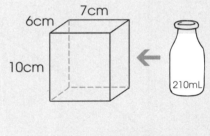

_____ bottles

ACTIVITY

Find the capacity and the volume of the containers.

1.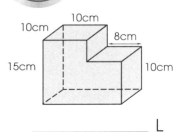

_____ L

2.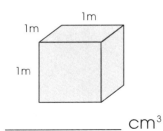

_____ cm³

1m	=	100cm
1cm³	=	1mL
1mL	=	0.001L
1cm³	=	0.001L

18 Line Graphs

Look at the line graph which shows Dave's savings. Do the questions.

I can save $4.00 a week.

I can save $32.00 by week 8.

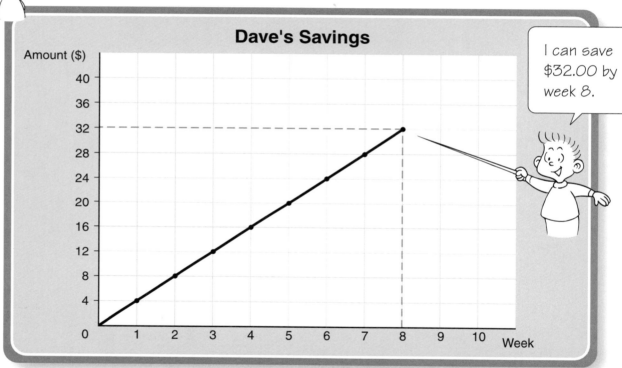

Dave's Savings

① By which week can Dave save $12? Week _____

② By which week can Dave save $24? Week _____

③ How much can he save by week 5? $ _____

④ How much can he save by week 7? $ _____

⑤ Follow the trend to find how much he can save by week 10. $ _____

Extend the straight line on the graph to week 10.

Tony has saved $50. He will spend $5 a week. Finish the table and draw a
line graph to show how he spends his savings. Then answer the questions.

⑥

Week	1	2	3	4	5	6	7
Money Left ($)	45			30			

⑦

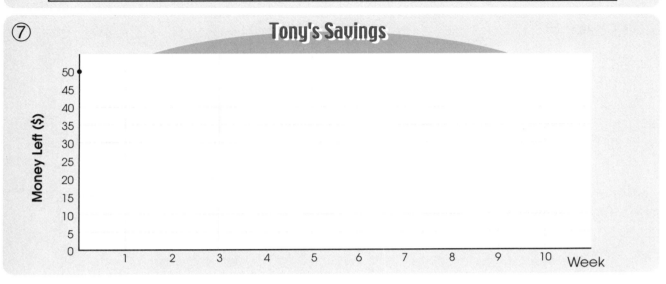

Tony's Savings

⑧ By which week will Tony have $40 left?   Week _____

⑨ By which week will Tony have $25 left?   Week _____

⑩ How much money will he have by week 3? $ _____

⑪ Follow the trend to find by which week he would
   spend all his savings.   Week _____

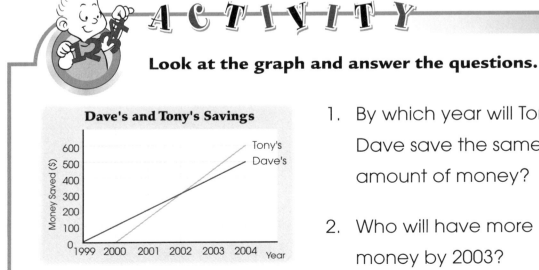

ACTIVITY

Look at the graph and answer the questions.

Dave's and Tony's Savings

1. By which year will Tony and
   Dave save the same
   amount of money?

2. Who will have more
   money by 2003?

Transformations and Coordinates

WORDS TO LEARN

Transformation	-	mapping of an object onto its image: translation, rotation or reflection	
Translation	-	sliding each point of a shape in the same direction and distance	
Rotation	-	turning the points of a shape about a fixed point	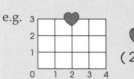
Reflection	-	flipping the points of a shape over a line	
Coordinates	-	an ordered pair of numbers used to locate a point on the grid	

What motion is shown in each set of pictures? Write translation, reflection or rotation.

① Before   After

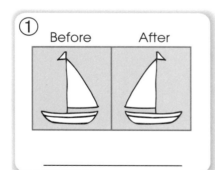

_____

② Before   After

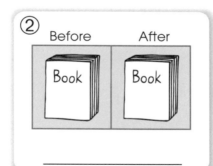

_____

③ Before   After

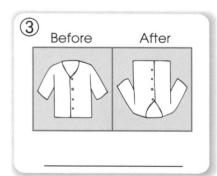

_____

④ Before   After

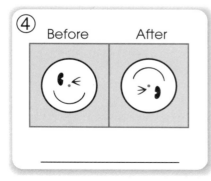

_____

⑤ Before   After

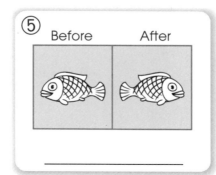

_____

⑥ Before   After

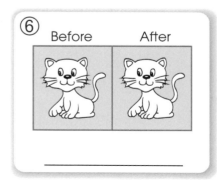

_____

Follow Dave's method to draw the slid, flipped or turned images. Then write the ordered pair of the transformed letters.

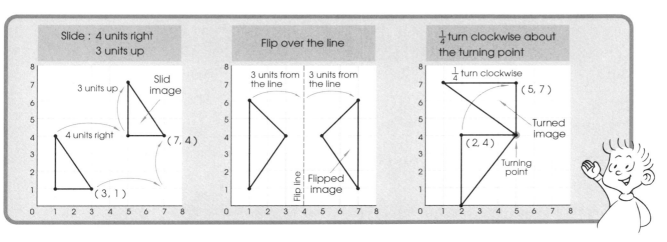

⑦ Slide : 4 units left
2 units down

⑧ Flip over the line

⑨ $\frac{1}{4}$ turn clockwise about the turning point

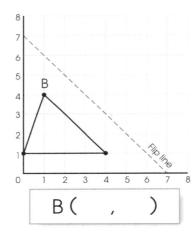

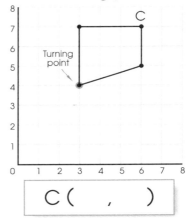

A (,)

B (,)

C (,)

ACTIVITY

Find the ordered pairs.

1. The slid image of (1, 1) is _____ .

2. The flipped image of (1, 1) is _____ .

3. The $\frac{1}{2}$ turned image of (1, 1) is _____ .

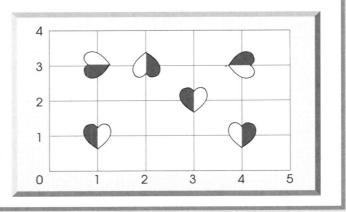

COMPLETE MATHSMART (GRADE 5)   139

20 Money

Change - the difference between the price and the amount given in payment

Write the missing numbers on the sales receipts.

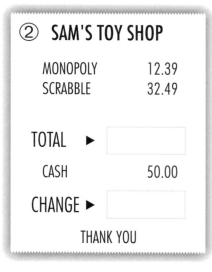

① SAM'S TOY SHOP

MONOPOLY	12.39
CLUE	27.65
TOTAL ▶	
CASH	45.00
CHANGE ▶	

THANK YOU

I paid $45.

② SAM'S TOY SHOP

MONOPOLY	12.39
SCRABBLE	32.49
TOTAL ▶	
CASH	50.00
CHANGE ▶	

THANK YOU

③ SAM'S TOY SHOP

CLUE	27.65
PUZZLE	15.97
SCRABBLE	32.49
TOTAL ▶	
CASH	
CHANGE ▶	13.89

THANK YOU

④ SAM'S TOY SHOP

MONOPOLY	12.39
PUZZLE	15.97
CLUE	27.65
TOTAL ▶	
CASH	
CHANGE ▶	13.99

THANK YOU

Solve the problems.

⑤ How much do 5 boxes of Monopoly cost? $_____

⑥ How much do 2 boxes of Puzzle and 4 boxes
of Clue cost? $_____

The children are playing Monopoly. See how much toy money they have.
Write the amounts and circle the right child.

⑦ $ _____

⑧ $ _____

⑨ $ _____

⑩ Circle the child who has the most toy money.

Write the number of each coin or bill needed to trade the bills on the left.

		10	5	CANADA 2 DOLLARS	CANADA DOLLAR	CANADA 25 cents
⑪	100	10				
⑫	50					

 ## 𝒜 𝒞 𝒯 𝐼 𝒱 𝐼 𝒯 𝒴

Read what Dave says and answer the question.

I spent $\frac{1}{2}$ of my money on candies. Then I gave $\frac{1}{2}$ of what was left to Steve. Now I have $2. How much did I have at first?

Dave had $ _____ at first.

21 Probability

Probability - the chance that something will happen

Outcome - the result of an experiment

Help Dave answer Uncle Ray's questions. Tick ✔ the right boxes.

① On which colour is the spinner most likely to stop?

☐ Blue   ☐ Yellow   ☐ Red

② On which colour is the spinner least likely to stop?

☐ Blue   ☐ Yellow   ☐ Red

③ Does red have a better chance than blue?

☐ Yes   ☐ No

④ How best can you describe the chance of the spinner stopping on yellow?

☐ maybe   ☐ likely   ☐ certain

⑤ If the spinner is spun 100 times, on which colour will the spinner most often stop?

☐ Blue   ☐ Yellow   ☐ Red

⑥ If the spinner is spun 1000 times, on which colour will the spinner least often stop?

☐ Blue   ☐ Yellow   ☐ Red

Help Dave write the fraction of the times each outcome occurs.

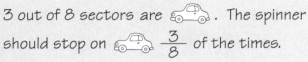 3 out of 8 sectors are . The spinner should stop on $\frac{3}{8}$ of the times.

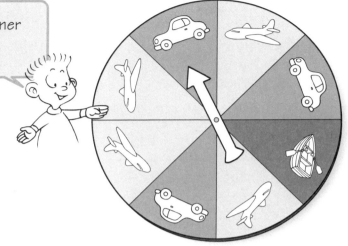

Outcome	Fraction of times the spinner stops on
	$\frac{3}{8}$
⑦	
⑧	

Look at the above spinner and circle the right answers.

⑨ Which of the outcomes is most likely?

⑩ Which of the outcomes is least likely?

⑪ What is the chance of getting or ? $\frac{3}{8}$ $\frac{4}{8}$ $\frac{7}{8}$

⑫ What is the chance of getting or ? $\frac{5}{8}$ $\frac{4}{8}$ $\frac{1}{8}$

ACTIVITY

Colour the sectors of the wheel to match the probability of the spinner stopping on each colour.

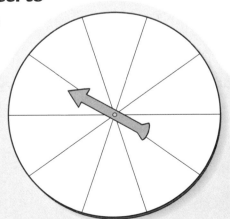

Yellow	Red
0.3	0.4

Blue	Green
0.2	0.1

Complete the tables. (8 marks)

① 2 children divide a box of candies with each getting 12. How many candies will each one get if the number of children changes?

Number of children	2	3	4	6	8
Number of candies	12				

② Uncle Ray works 4 hours a day to finish his project in 12 days. How many days are needed if he works for a different number of hours a day?

Number of hours	2	3	4		
Number of days			12	6	4

Write as decimal numbers. (4 marks)

③ 14 and 267 thousandths

_____

④ 5 and 42 hundredths

_____

⑤ 10 and 25 thousandths

_____

⑥ 2 thousandths

_____

Write as decimal numbers and round to the nearest hundredth. (4 marks)

⑦ $\dfrac{6}{7}$

⑧ $1\dfrac{2}{5}$

⑨ $3\dfrac{5}{6}$

⑩ $2\dfrac{5}{9}$

Find the answers. (18 marks)

⑪
$$\begin{array}{r} 1.6 \\ \times \quad 2.3 \\ \hline \end{array}$$

⑫
$$\begin{array}{r} 3.1\,9 \\ \times \quad 0.4\,5 \\ \hline \end{array}$$

⑬
$$\begin{array}{r} 0.6\,2 \\ \times \quad 0.0\,3 \\ \hline \end{array}$$

⑭ $1.42 \times 0.3 = $ _____

⑮ $3.59 \times 0.04 = $ _____

⑯ $12.36 \div 0.06 = $ _____

⑰ $4.23 \div 0.3 = $ _____

⑱ $5.64 \div 0.12 = $ _____

⑲ $13.5 \div 0.15 = $ _____

Solve the equations. (12 marks)

⑳ $2 \times q + 6 = 10$

$q = $ _____

㉑ $5 \times k - 2 = 18$

$k = $ _____

㉒ $3 \times p + 1 = 10$

$p = $ _____

㉓ $m \div 4 + 3 = 5$

$m = $ _____

Fill in the blanks with centre, circumference, diameter or radius. (4 marks)

㉔ Line POQ : _____

㉕ O : _____

㉖ Line OS : _____

㉗ Y : _____

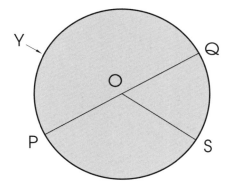

Measure and complete the table. (4 marks)

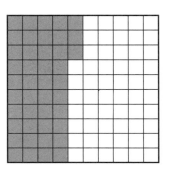

A

B

Circle	Radius (cm)	Diameter (cm)
㉘ A		
㉙ B		

Write the shaded part of each 100-square as a fraction, a decimal and a percent. (6 marks)

㉚

Fraction : _____

Decimal : _____

Percent : _____

㉛

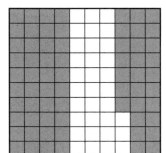

Fraction : _____

Decimal : _____

Percent : _____

Look at the spinner and answer the questions. (3 marks)

㉜ What fraction of the spins will be ?

[   ]

㉝ What fraction of the spins will be 🍓 ?

[   ]

㉞ What fraction of the spins will be 🍇 ?

[   ]

Study the box graph and fill in the blanks. (5 marks)

㉟ [   ] % of the students are under 125 cm in height.

㊱ [   ] % of the students are between 126 - 144 cm in height.

㊲ [   ] % of the students are over 145 cm in height.

㊳ If there were 100 students, [   ] students would be under 125 cm in height.

㊴ If there were 200 students, [   ] students would be over 145 cm in height.

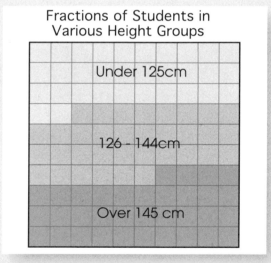

Fractions of Students in Various Height Groups

Under 125cm

126 - 144cm

Over 145 cm

Final Test

Write the show times in a.m. or p.m. and answer the questions. **(6 marks)**

MEGA Theatre

Movie	Time
Monster Dance	10 : 30
Paper Moon	11 : 45
Rumble	14 : 35
Paper Moon	16 : 40
Monster Dance	18 : 30
The Journey	20 : 35
The Journey	22 : 35

㊵ When is the first show of Monster Dance?

____

㊶ When is the second show of Paper Moon?

____

㊷ Which movie is shown at 8:35 p.m.?

____

㊸ Which movie is shown at 2:35 p.m.?

____

㊹ Rumble lasts 1 hour and 32 minutes. When does it end?

____

㊺ The Journey ends at 22:03. How long does it last?

__________ minutes

Tickets

Adult	**$7.25** each
Children	**$3.95** each

Solve the problems. **(4 marks)**

㊻ Dave pays $50 to buy 1 adult and 2 children's tickets.
How much is the change? $__________

㊼ Steve had $49.69. He bought 2 adult and 1 children's ticket. How much does he have now? $__________

Look at the line graph. Answer the questions. (4 marks)

(48) How much do 10 special tickets cost? $ ______

(49) How much do 40 special tickets cost? $ ______

(50) How much does each special ticket cost? $ ______

(51) How many special tickets can be bought for $125? ______

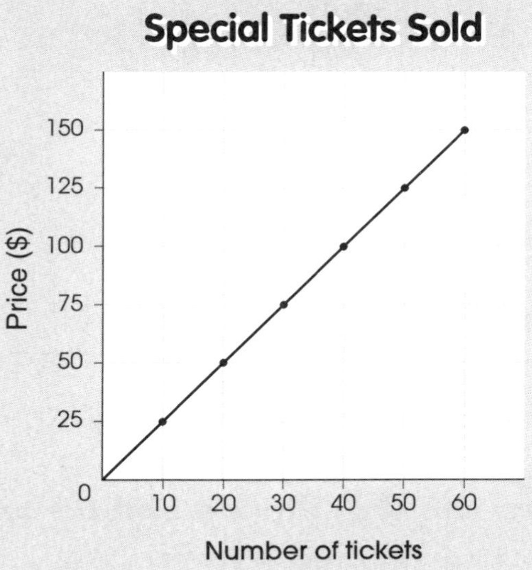
Special Tickets Sold
Price ($)
150
125
100
75
50
25
0
10
20
30
40
50
60
Number of tickets

Find the volume of the blocks. Each cube is 1 cm^3. (2 marks)

(52)

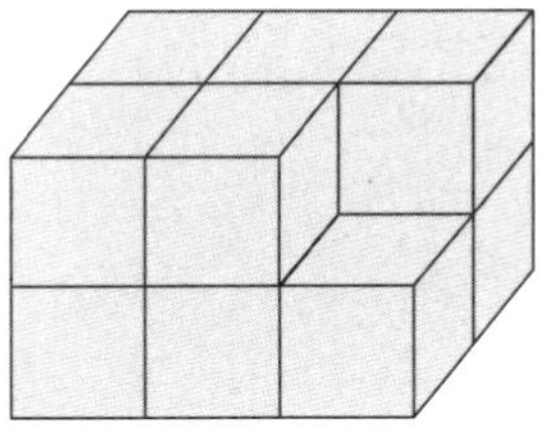

Volume = ________ cm^3

(53)

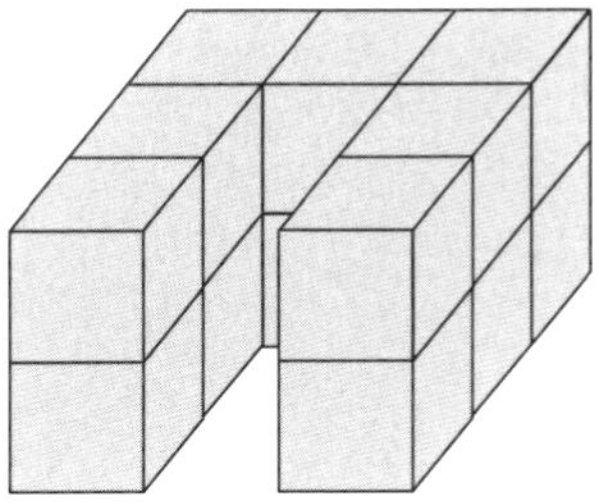

Volume = ________ cm^3

Find the volume of the blocks. (4 marks)

(54)

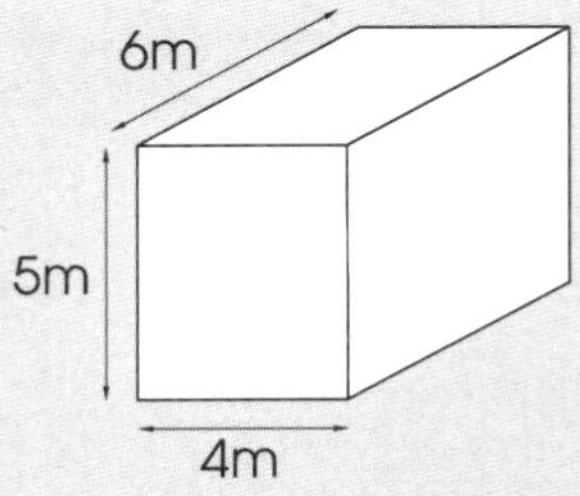
6m
5m
4m

Volume = ________ m^3

(55)

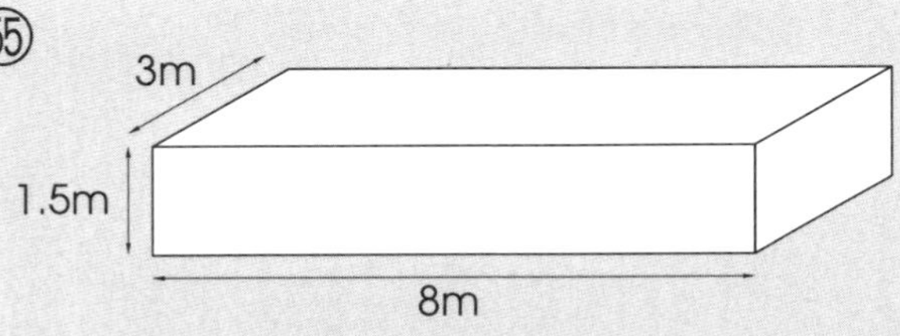
3m
1.5m
8m

Volume = ________ m^3

Write the capacity of each container in millilitres. (3 marks)

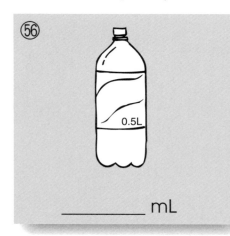

56 0.5L

_____ mL

57 1.2L

_____ mL

58 0.75L

_____ mL

Draw the slid, flipped and turned images. Then write the ordered pair of the transformed letters. (9 marks)

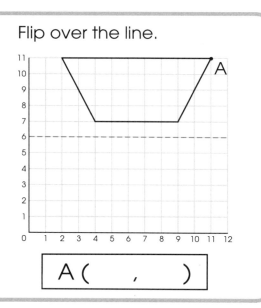

59 Flip over the line.

A (,   )

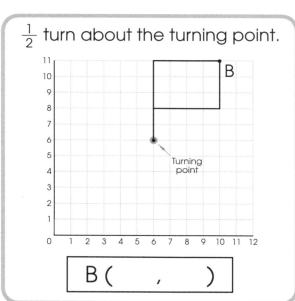

60 $\frac{1}{2}$ turn about the turning point.

Turning point

B (,   )

61 Slide 12 units right, 4 units up.

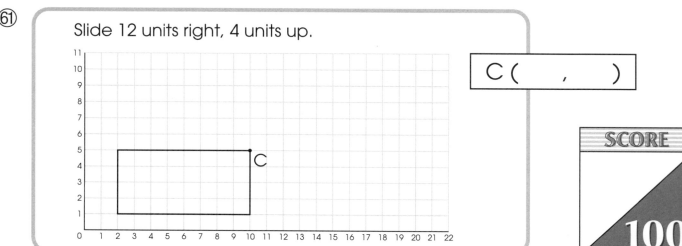

C (,   )

SCORE

100

Section III

Overview

In the previous section, number skills were developed using whole numbers, fractions and decimals. In this section, these skills are applied in order to solve word problems.

Students learn to recognize patterns and to use these to solve problems. Careful reading is required and many solutions involve two steps.

Answers are written in full sentences using appropriate units.

Multiplication and Division of Whole Numbers

EXAMPLE

Gary ate 2 cookies each day per week and drank 28 glasses of milk per week. How many cookies and how much milk would he consume in 3 weeks?

Cookies Gary ate in 1 day : 2

Cookies he would eat in 3 weeks : $2 \times 7 \times 3 = 42$

Milk Gary drank in 1 week : 28

Milk he would drink in 3 weeks : $28 \times 3 = 84$

Answer : Gary would consume 42 cookies and 84 glasses of milk in 3 weeks.

Solve the problems. Show your work.

Frank's class has 28 pupils. There are 21 girls and 7 boys. Each pupil is given 3 pencils and 5 books at the beginning of the year. There are 2 extra chairs in the room.

① How many pencils are given out at the beginning of the year?

Answer : _____ pencils are given out at the beginning of the year.

② How many more books than pencils are given out at the beginning of the year?

Answer : _____

③ If all the chairs in the room were stacked in piles of 5 for cleaning, how many stacks would there be?

Answer : _____

④ If the girls used 2 pencils each by the end of November, how many pencils belonging to girls would there be in the classroom?

Answer : _____

⑤ For a special activity, the chairs that were being used by pupils in the classroom were to be put in rows of 7. How many rows would there be?

Answer : _____

Donny moved into a new house with French doors. Each of these doors had 8 panes of glass. When Donny counted the doors, he found that there were 9 in all. There were also 19 windows with 2 panes of glass in each. The glass was all dirty from construction, and a cleaning company said that they would clean the windows for $5.00 each pane and the doors for $3.00 every 2 panes.

⑥ How many panes of glass are there in the doors?

Answer : _____

⑦ How many panes of glass are there in the windows?

Answer : _____

⑧ How much would it cost to clean the panes of glass in the doors?

Answer : _____

⑨ How much would it cost to clean all the glass in the house?

Answer : _____

Sally was counting her collection of old coins. She had 34 pennies, 9 nickels, 31 dimes and 19 quarters.

⑩ Sally was told that her pennies were worth 11 cents each. What was the value of Sally's pennies?

Answer : _____

⑪ Sally was told that her collection of nickels was worth 135¢. How much was each nickel worth?

Answer : _____

⑫ Her dimes were only worth 14 cents each. What was the value of her collection of dimes?

Answer : _____

⑬ Sally had 5 valuable quarters. They were worth 116¢ each. The rest were worth 76¢ each. What was the value of her quarters?

Answer : _____

⑭ What was the value of her collection?

Answer : _____

⑮ Would it be a good idea to sell her entire collection for 25 cents for each coin?

Answer : _____

September is the first month of school. Wanda's class had homework assigned every day of the month. The homework took 2 hours to complete every night including weekends. All 17 girls in the class thought that this was too much. They only wanted to do 25 hours of homework every 15 days.

⑯ How many hours did Wanda spend on doing homework in September?

Answer : _____

⑰ How many hours did all the girls spend on doing homework in September?

Answer : _____

⑱ If there were 20 school days in September, how many hours of homework would be assigned each school day?

Answer : _____

⑲ If the teacher reduced the amount of homework as the girls requested, how many hours of homework would Wanda have to do in September?

Answer : _____

⑳ How many hours of homework would all the girls have to do in September then?

Answer : _____

Lisa makes 4 phone calls a day to her friends. The telephone company charges for telephone calls at a rate of 2 for $3.00. Each week, Lisa tries to keep track of the amount of money she spends on calling her friends.

㉑ How much does Lisa spend each week on phone calls?

Answer : _____

㉒ How many phone calls would she make in January?

Answer : _____

㉓   How much would her phone calls cost in October?

Answer : _____

㉔   If each day, each call was to a different friend, how much could she save each day by sending them a letter, if a stamp costs 46 cents?

Answer : _____

㉕   Another phone company is offering a rate of 4 calls for $5.00. How much would she save each week by switching companies?

Answer : _____

There are 936 paperbacks and 882 hardcover books in a small library. It takes 36 seconds to dust each book. They are stored on shelves with 26 paperbacks or 21 hardcover books on each shelf.

㉖   How long does it take to dust all the paperback books?

Answer : _____

㉗   How long does it take to dust all the hardcover books?

Answer : _____

㉘   How many shelves of paperback books will there be in the library?

Answer : _____

㉙   How many shelves of hardcover books will there be in the library?

Answer : _____

㉚   If Uncle Bill uses 6 boxes to store the paperback and hardcover books, how many books are in each box?

Answer : _____

Allan is taking stock of the items in his kitchen. He has 1242 grams of raisins, 1896 grams of peanuts, 4 bags of 63 figs each, 5 bags of 32 apricots each, and 486 cookies.

㉛ Allan divides his raisins into 6 bags. How many grams of raisins are there in each bag?

Answer : _____

㉜ Allan divides his peanuts into 8 servings. How many grams of peanuts are there in each serving?

Answer : _____

㉝ If each fig weighs 15 g, how heavy do Allan's figs weigh?

Answer : _____

㉞ Allan and his sister each eat 4 apricots after lunch every day. How long will Allan's apricots last?

Answer : _____

㉟ If Allan shares his cookies with 5 of his friends, how many cookies does each person get?

Answer : _____

㊱ Allan wants to put his cookies in bags of 5 or in bags of 7. Which way will there be more cookies left over?

Answer : _____

㊲ If Allan divides his figs into 3 bags, how many more figs does each bag hold than before?

Answer : _____

㊳ If Allan divides his peanuts into small bags each holding 25 grams, how many bags does he need to hold all the peanuts?

Answer : _____

㊴ If every 18 grams of raisins costs 12 cents, how much do Allan's raisins cost?

Answer : _____

- **Question 39 is a 2-step problem. First, find how many portions of 18 grams each there are in 1242 grams of raisins. Then multiply the number of portions by the cost.**

Read this first.

Solve the problems. Show your work.

⓽ Karen was collecting pebbles on the beach. After a couple of hours, she collected 308 pebbles. Karen wanted to take them home, but couldn't carry all those pebbles at once. She was going to be at the beach for 4 days. How many pebbles would she have to carry each day?

Answer : _____

㊶ Larry had 17 CDs. He played them 4 times each on average in a month. If each CD was 1 hour long, how much time would he spend in a year listening to the CDs?

Answer : _____

㊷ Don's dad had 1648 books. If he could fit 24 books on each shelf, how many shelves would he need?

Answer : _____

㊸ Peter was planting pansies in his garden. The pansies were planted in rows of 35. There were 23 rows across the garden. How many plants did Peter need?

Answer : _____

㊹ Peter uses about 45 L of water each day to water his plants. How much water will Peter use in a month of 31 days?

Answer : _____

CHALLENGE

The number of ants in Quincey's garden seems to double each day. Quincey saw 100 ants on Monday, how many ants might there be on Thursday?

Answer : _____

Operations with Whole Numbers

EXAMPLE

Two students were comparing their marks. Sylvia had 80 and Tim had half of Sylvia's mark plus 10. What was Tim's mark?

Tim's mark: $80 \div 2 + 10 = 40 + 10 = 50$

Answer: Tim's mark was 50.

Use the table below to solve the problems. Show your work.

A group of friends were playing a game. They threw a ball as far as they could in the park, and measured the distances. The person who threw the ball third farthest won 1 point, second farthest, 3 points and farthest, 5 points.

Name	Mario	Sandy	Danny	Jimmy	Dolores
Distance (m)	12	18	14	19	16

① How much farther did Jimmy throw than Sandy?

Answer: Jimmy threw _____ farther than Sandy.

② How far did everyone throw altogether?

Answer: _____

③ If Mario and Jimmy formed a team against Sandy and Dolores, which team threw the ball farther?

④ If Danny got to double his distance because he had no one on his team, how much farther did the winning team throw than Danny did?

Answer: _____

⑤ The friends thought of a new game. They got to multiply their distance by their score. Who got the highest number? What is the number?

Answer: _____

Answer: _____

Solve the problems. Show your work.

⑥ How many days are there in a leap year?

Answer: _____

⑦ If there were 56 marbles in a bag, how many marbles would Frank have if he bought 6 bags?

Answer: _____

⑧ A theatre has 47 seats in each row. How many people would fill 12 rows?

Answer: _____

⑨ Bill's father buys paper in 250 sheet packages. If he wants to print 1371 pages, how many packages of paper must he buy?

Answer: _____

⑩ George can ride his bike around a park in 4 minutes. How many times can he ride his bike around the park in 1 hour 20 minutes?

Answer: _____

⑪ Sally collects stamps. She has 482 stamps in her first album, 561 in her second one, and 398 in her third one. How many stamps does she have in all?

Answer: _____

⑫ A jacket costs $75.00. A pair of jeans costs $34.00. If John bought 2 jackets and 3 pairs of jeans, how much should he pay?

Answer: _____

Lorraine was helping out in a lumber yard. There were 2352 pieces of pine, 598 pieces of oak and 28 pieces of maple. Each piece of lumber was 2 metres long.

⑬ How many pieces of lumber did they have in all?

Answer:

⑭ How many more pieces of pine did they have than maple?

Answer:

⑮ How many more pieces of pine did they have than oak ?

Answer:

⑯ How many metres of lumber did they have at the lumber yard?

Answer:

⑰ If they sold 269 pieces of oak on Wednesday, how many metres of oak did they have left to sell?

Answer:

⑱ If they sold 1568 metres of pine per day, how many days would it take to sell all their pine pieces?

Answer:

⑲ If there are 414 metres of oak left over, how many pieces of oak were sold?

Answer:

Solve these problems in your head and write the statements.

⑳ Jean works part-time at the mall. She works 2 hours a day for $9.00 an hour. How much did she earn in a five-day week?

Answer: _____

• The product of multiplication will be the same no matter what order the numbers are in.

Read this first.

e.g. 4 x 17 x 5 = 17 x 4 x 5
= 17 x 20
= 340

㉑ Tim started his homework at 4:00 p.m. It took him 25 minutes to finish his Math, 17 minutes for his Social Studies and 28 minutes to read the next part of his English book. When did he finish his homework?

Answer: _____

㉓ It takes Sandy 20 minutes to walk to school and 14 minutes to run to school. How much time could she save each week, if she ran to school and ran home each day instead of walking?

Answer: _____

㉒ Mario wanted two CDs. The first one was on sale for $15.00 and the other's regular price was $18.00. If all the prices included taxes and Mario had a twenty-dollar bill, a ten-dollar bill and a five-dollar bill, could he afford the two CDs?

㉔ Brian collects baseball cards. He read in a collector's magazine that one of his rare cards should double in price every seven years. How many times should its present value be worth in 21 years?

Answer: _____

Answer: _____

CHALLENGE

① George was born in a leap year. If George is 11 years old this year, how many days old is he?

Answer: _____

② A small company bills one of their clients $158 920.00 each quarter. How much money would the client pay them for 9 months' work?

Answer: _____

EXAMPLE

Sally walks $\frac{2}{3}$ of a block to school. Kari walks $\frac{3}{4}$ of a block. Who walks the farther? *(Hint: The L.C.M. of 3 and 4 is 12.)*

Sally walks: $\frac{2}{3} = \frac{2 \times 4}{3 \times 4} = \frac{8}{12}$ Kari walks: $\frac{3}{4} = \frac{3 \times 3}{4 \times 3} = \frac{9}{12}$

Answer: Kari walks farther.

Solve the problems. Show your work.

① Peter and Joe were comparing hat sizes. Peter's hat was $6\frac{1}{2}$ and Joe's hat was $6\frac{3}{8}$. Who had the larger hat size?

Answer: _____ had the larger hat size. _____

② If Mary spent $\frac{1}{2}$ hour reading a History chapter and Jill spent 42 minutes, who read the chapter faster?

Answer: _____

③ Douglas had 1 quarter, 1 dime, and 3 pennies. Jill had 1 dime, 6 nickels, and 1 penny. Who had the larger fraction of a dollar?

Answer: _____

④ Mary's mother served $\frac{2}{7}$ of a cake and kept $\frac{1}{4}$ of it. Did she save more cake than she serve?

Answer: _____

⑤ Henry and Ann each had a chocolate bar of the same size. Henry ate $\frac{1}{3}$ of his bar and Ann ate $\frac{2}{5}$ of her bar. Who ate less?

Answer: _____

The young people on Single Street wanted to raise money for charity. They decided that any time any member of their family raised their voice, they would have to put one coin in a special box. The louder the voice, the larger the coin. At the end of the month, they would meet and put all their coins together.

⑥ Patricia had 63 pennies. What fraction of a dollar did she have?

Answer: _____

⑦ Dolores brought in a dollar and 7 quarters. What fraction of a dollar did she have?

Answer: _____

⑧ Milly had 1 quarter, 4 dimes and 12 nickels. What fraction of a dollar did she have?

Answer: _____

⑨ Gerry had 7 quarters, 2 dimes and 6 nickels. What fraction of a dollar did he have?

Answer: _____

⑩ Who raised the most money for charity?

Answer: _____

⑪ How much money did they raise for charity in all?

Answer: _____

Sam has 147 trading cards, Hindy 216, Kelly 98, and Oliver 166. They went to a trading card show where an expert told them that Sam had 21 valuable cards, Hindy 54, Kelly 28 and Oliver 2.

① Who had the largest fraction of valuable cards in his or her collection?

Answer: _____

② Who had the second smallest fraction of valuable cards in his or her collection?

Answer: _____

③ List the people from the one with the largest fraction of valuable cards to the one with the smallest.

Answer: _____

Addition and Subtraction of Fractions

EXAMPLE

Frank had $\frac{1}{5}$ of a bag of marbles, Jerry has $\frac{3}{5}$ of a bag of marbles and Kelly has $\frac{4}{5}$ of a bag of marbles. Yesterday they lost $\frac{2}{5}$ of a bag playing at recess. How many marbles do they still have in all?

No. of marbles they have in all : $\frac{1}{5} + \frac{3}{5} + \frac{4}{5} = \frac{8}{5}$

After losing, they still have : $\frac{8}{5} - \frac{2}{5} = \frac{6}{5} = 1\frac{1}{5}$

Answer : They still have $1\frac{1}{5}$ bags of marbles in all.

Solve the problems. Show your work.

Ann, Dolores and Mario were working on a project together. Ann spent $1\frac{5}{6}$ hours, Dolores $1\frac{4}{6}$ hours and Mario $\frac{1}{6}$ of an hour working on it.

① How many hours did they spend in all working on the project?

Answer : They spent _____ hours in all.

② How many more hours did Dolores spend on the project than Mario?

Answer : _____

③ How many more hours did Ann and Dolores spend on the project than Mario?

Answer : _____

④ How many hours did Ann and Mario spend on the project in all?

Answer : _____

⑤ Compare the number of hours Dolores spent on the project with that spent by Ann and Mario together.

Answer : _____

⑥ How much more time would Mario have to spend to equal the time spent by Ann?

Answer : _____

Harry's class was collecting bottles for recycling. They put them in large plastic bags. Harry filled $\frac{3}{7}$ of a bag the first day, $\frac{5}{7}$ the second and $\frac{1}{7}$ the third. Barry filled $\frac{5}{7}$ of a bag the first day, $\frac{3}{7}$ the second and $\frac{2}{7}$ the third. Mary filled $\frac{6}{7}$ of a bag the first day, $\frac{6}{7}$ the second and 1 the third.

⑦ How many bags of bottles did Harry collect in all?

Answer : _____

⑧ How many bags of bottles did Barry collect in all?

Answer : _____

⑨ How many bags of bottles did Mary collect in all?

Answer : _____

⑩ Who collected the most bottles?

Answer : _____

⑪ How many bags of bottles did the children collect in all?

Answer : _____

⑫ How many more bags of bottles did Mary collect than Harry?

Answer : _____

⑬ How many more bags of bottles did Mary collect than Barry?

Answer : _____

⑭ How many more bags of bottles does Harry need to collect if he wants to have 2 bags?

Answer : _____

⑮ How many more bags of bottles does Barry need to collect if he wants to have 3 bags?

Answer : _____

⑯ How many more bags of bottles does Mary need to collect if she wants to have 5 bags?

Answer : _____

- **To subtract from a whole number, change the whole number into a mixed number, e.g.**

Read this first.

$5 = 4\frac{7}{7}$

Gary was looking at the breakfast cereals in his kitchen. He had $\frac{2}{5}$ of a box of corn flakes, $\frac{4}{5}$ of a box of bran flakes and $\frac{3}{5}$ of a box of rice flakes.

⑰ How much cereal did he have in all?

Answer : _____

⑱ How much more bran flakes did he have than corn flakes?

Answer : _____

⑲ How much more rice and corn flakes did he have than bran flakes?

Answer : _____

⑳ If Gary's mother used $\frac{1}{5}$ of a box of each type of cereal to make healthy cookies, how much cereal would be left?

Answer : _____

㉑ If Gary bought a box of granola and ate $\frac{1}{5}$ of it, how much cereal would he have altogether?

Answer : _____

Kim's class was running for charity. Kim ran $2\frac{7}{20}$ km. Lori ran $3\frac{19}{20}$ km. Freda ran $2\frac{11}{20}$ km. Toni ran 5 km.

㉒ How far did they run in all?

Answer : _____

㉓ How much farther did the person who ran the farthest run than the one who ran the shortest distance?

Answer : _____

㉔ If Kim and Freda ran as a team, how far did their team run?

Answer : _____

㉕ If Lori and Freda ran as a team, how far did they run in total?

Answer : _____

㉖ How much farther did Toni run than Lori?

Answer : _____

㉗ How much farther did Freda run than Kim?

Answer : _____

Yvon has a collection of magazines. $\frac{7}{19}$ of his collection is from 1980 to 1989, $\frac{9}{19}$ from 1970 to 1979, $\frac{1}{19}$ from before 1970 and the rest new.

㉘ What fraction of his magazines are new?

Answer : _____

㉙ What fraction of his magazines were printed between 1980 and the present?

Answer : _____

㉚ What fraction of his magazines were printed between 1970 and 1990?

Answer : _____

㉛ Yvon was told that magazines printed before 1980 should be stored in protective envelopes. What fraction of his magazines need this protection?

Answer : _____

㉜ What fraction of his magazines do not need protective envelopes?

Answer : _____

㉝ If Yvon gives $\frac{3}{8}$ of his collection of magazines to his friends, what fraction of his magazines are left?

Answer : _____

㉞ Yvon has 190 magazines. 113 of them are in English and the rest in French. What fraction of his magazines are in English?

Answer : _____

㉟ What fraction of his magazines are in French?

Answer : _____

CHALLENGE

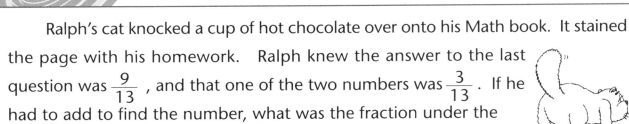

Ralph's cat knocked a cup of hot chocolate over onto his Math book. It stained the page with his homework. Ralph knew the answer to the last question was $\frac{9}{13}$, and that one of the two numbers was $\frac{3}{13}$. If he had to add to find the number, what was the fraction under the chocolate stain?

Answer : _____

Addition and Subtraction of Decimals

EXAMPLE

Frank's score on the English test was 79.8 and Jerry's was 92.3. How much higher was Jerry's score than Frank's?

Difference: 92.3 − 79.8 = 12.5

Answer : Jerry's score was 12.5 higher than Frank's.

Solve the problems. Show your work.

Franco was trying out a recipe. He needed 0.75 kg of egg-plant, 0.007 kg of salt, 1.28 kg of sliced raw onions, 0.95 kg of chopped tomato and 0.01 kg of parsley to add to the liquid ingredients.

① How much would the raw solid ingredients weigh?

Answer : The raw solid ingredients would weigh _____.

② Franco knew that he couldn't put more than 4 kg into a shopping bag before the handles broke. How much more weight could he add to his dry ingredients and still carry the bag by the handles?

Answer : _____

③ What weight of vegetables does this recipe require?

Answer : _____

④ What weight of herbs and spices does this recipe require?

Answer : _____

⑤ If Franco required 0.599 kg of liquid ingredients, how much would the entire dish weigh before cooking?

Answer : _____

Hortense received $7.50 each week for an allowance. She spent $3.49 for entertainment, $1.78 for snacks, $2.00 for transportation and saved the rest.

⑥ How much money did she save each week?

Answer : _____

⑦ How much money did she spend for entertainment and snacks each week?

Answer : _____

⑧ How much more money did she spend for entertainment than transportation each week?

Answer : _____

⑨ If she got a $0.68 raise in allowance on the condition that she save it all, how much would she save each week?

Answer : _____

• **Align the decimal points when you add or subtract the decimal numbers,**

e.g. 1.78 + 2.00

```
  1. 78
+ 2. 00
```
align

Read this first.

⑩ If she needed $2.23 for snacks one week and wanted to take that money from her entertainment budget, how much would she have left for entertainment that week?

Answer : _____

CHALLENGE

① If Kim had completed 1.78 km of a 5.78 km trip and wanted to travel 1.97 km before stopping for the day, how much farther would he have to go?

Answer : _____

② Harriette made deposits of $5.78 and $1.99, and withdrawals of $3.14 and $2.67 from her bank account. If the bank charged her $0.15 per transaction and her initial balance was $15.02, what was her final balance?

Answer : _____

Multiplication and Division of Decimals

EXAMPLE

Every day for one week, Gary ate 2 cookies, each weighing 27.8 grams. He also drank 10.5 litres of milk that week. How many grams of cookies and litres of milk did he consume each day?

Cookies Gary ate each day : $2 \times 27.8 = 55.6$

Milk Gary drank each day : $10.5 \div 7 = 1.5$

Answer : Gary ate 55.6 grams of cookies and drank 1.5 litres of milk each day.

Solve the problems. Show your work.

Eddie was saving for a special game, which cost $75.60. He was planning on saving $5.75 per month for a year. His father suggested that he save $6.45 per month instead, but Eddie wasn't sure if he could afford that.

① Would Eddie save up enough money to buy the game by putting aside $5.75 per month for a year?

Answer : Eddie _____ save up enough money to buy the game.

② If he couldn't save the money within the year, how much would he be short of?

Answer : _____

③ Would his father's suggestion allow him to buy the game on time?

Answer : _____

④ How much extra would he have to save each month above the $5.75 a month to buy the game in a year?

Answer : _____

⑤ If the game went on sale for $59.88, how much less than $5.75 would he have to save each month to buy the game in a year?

Answer : _____

Jenny was building a project out of wood. She needed 2.16 metres of pine, 0.3 metres of oak and 2.4 metres of walnut. Pine was $2.00 a metre, oak was $4.70 a metre and walnut was $5.65 a metre.

⑥ How much would she spend for pine?

Answer : _____

⑦ How much would she spend for oak?

Answer : _____

⑧ How much would she spend for walnut?

Answer : _____

⑨ How much would she spend for wood altogether?

Answer : _____

⑩ If it cost $0.50 per metre for finishing the wood, what would be the total cost?

Answer : _____

⑪ What was the total cost for the wood plus finishing?

Answer : _____

⑫ If Jenny shared the total cost of the wood with 2 friends, how much would each person pay?

Answer : _____

⑬ If Jenny cut the pine into 3 equal parts, how long was each part?

Answer : _____

⑭ If Jenny cut off 0.04 metres of the walnut and divided the rest into 4 equal parts, how long was each part?

Answer : _____

⑮ How many metres of pine can you buy for $16.50?

Answer : _____

• **For decimals,** ◀— **Read this first.** multiply or divide as with whole numbers, but remember the rule for placing the decimal point in the product or quotient.

Oliver travelled the following distances on his vacation. Read the table and solve the problems. Show your work.

Day	1	2	3	4	5
Distance travelled (km)	271	305	652	186	395
Cost (per km)	$0.04	$0.06	$0.05	$0.05	$0.04

⑯ What was the travel cost on Day 2?

Answer : _____

⑰ What was the difference in travel cost between Day 1 and Day 4?

Answer : _____

⑱ On which day was his travel cost the lowest? What was the cost?

Answer : _____

⑲ On which day was his travel cost the highest? What was the cost?

Answer : _____

⑳ If Oliver had budgeted $12.00 per day for travel costs, would Day 5 have exceeded his budget?

Answer : _____

㉑ Which days exceeded Oliver's travel budget?

Answer : _____

㉒ If the travel cost on Day 6 was $4.12 and the distance travelled was 10 km, what would be the cost per km?

Answer : _____

㉓ The travel cost on Day 7 was also $4.12 but the distance travelled was 100 km because Oliver used some gas coupons. What would be the cost per km?

Answer : _____

A quick way to do division in Questions 22 & 23 :   **Read this first.**

- *Divided by 10 : move the decimal point 1 place to the left, e.g. 7.96 ÷ 10 = 0.796*

- *Divided by 100 : move the decimal point 2 places to the left, e.g. 7.96 ÷ 100 = 0.0796*

Solve the problems. Show your work.

㉔ Matthew paid $8.76 to buy 4 boxes of juice. How much does each box of juice cost?

Answer : _____

㉕ The capacity of a box of juice is 1.25 L. If the box of juice can fill up 5 glasses, what is the capacity of each glass?

Answer : _____

㉖ How much juice is there in 7 boxes?

Answer : _____

㉗ Which size is the better buy, regular size distilled water 2 L for $1.38 or jumbo size 10 L for $5.90?

Answer : _____

㉘ How much should Matthew pay for buying 8 bottles of regular size distilled water?

Answer : _____

㉙ If Matthew drinks 1.75 L of water a day, how much water will he drink in a week?

Answer : _____

Darlene is going to paint a wall 16.8 m long and 2.4 m high. If 1L of paint covers 32 square metres, how much paint will she need for 2 coats of paint for the wall?

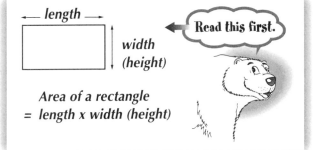

length

width (height)

Read this first.

Area of a rectangle
= length x width (height)

Answer : _____

Solve the problems. Show your work.

Last Sunday, Mr Stanley held a Food Fair at Asna Park. His bakery baked different kinds of food for the Food Fair. Mr Stanley decided to donate half of the money collected to the Children's Hospital.

① There were 9 groups of girls and 12 groups of boys helping out at the fair. Each group had 4 people. How many helpers were there?

Answer : _____

② The baker, Mrs White, baked 64 cakes. If each cake was cut into 8 pieces, how many pieces of cake did Mrs White make?

Answer : _____

③ Each piece of cake was sold for $0.75. How much did a whole cake cost?

Answer : _____

④ If it cost $2.16 to bake each cake, what would be the total cost for baking all the cakes?

Answer : _____

⑤ There were 1064 chocolate doughnuts and 898 honey doughnuts. How many doughnuts were there in all?

Answer : _____

⑥ The chocolate doughnuts were sold in packages of 4. How many packages of chocolate doughnuts were there?

Answer : _____

⑦ At the end of the fair, 159 honey doughnuts were left. How many honey doughnuts had been sold?

Answer : _____

⑧ Gary bought 8 honey doughnuts for $5.04. How much did 1 honey doughnut cost?

Answer : _____

⑨ Each tray had 4 rows of 6 cookies. There were 15 trays altogether. How many cookies were there?

Answer : _____

⑩ 218 cookies were sold. How many cookies were left?

Answer : _____

⑪ The weight of a bag of 5 cookies was 486.5 grams. How much did 1 cookie weigh?

Answer : _____

⑫ Gary bought $\frac{1}{8}$ of a cake and Sally bought $\frac{5}{8}$ of the same cake. How much of the cake did they buy in all?

Answer : _____

⑬ How much more of the cake did Sally buy than Gary?

Answer : _____

⑭ Jill paid $4.16 for the cake. What was her change from a $10 bill?

Answer : _____

⑮ A bag of 5 bagels costs $1.30 and a bag of 8 bagels costs $1.76. Which bag is a better buy?

Answer : _____

⑯ Each stall collected $459.00. There were 8 stalls at the Food Fair. How much money did the stalls collect in all?

Answer : _____

⑰ How much money did Mr Stanley donate to the Children's Hospital?

Answer : _____

⑱ The total cost for organizing the fair was $1285.00. Did Mr Stanley make a profit after the donation?

Answer : _____

⑲ How much did Mr Stanley gain or lose?

Answer : _____

Inger's family want to redecorate their home. There are 4 bedrooms, 1 living room, 1 kitchen and 3 bathrooms in the house.

⑳ If each bedroom needs 3.48 L of paint, how many litres of paint are needed for all the bedrooms?

Answer : _____

㉑ A can of paint is 4 L. How many cans of paint does Inger need for all the bedrooms?

Answer : _____

㉒ Each bathroom needs $1\frac{3}{5}$ boxes of tiles. How many boxes of tiles are needed to cover all the bathrooms?

Answer : _____

㉓ If the tiles have to be bought in full boxes, how many boxes does Inger need to buy?

Answer : _____

㉔ If there are 100 tiles in each box, how many boxes of tiles will be left over?

Answer : _____

㉕ For the living room, they want to buy a couch for $798.65 and a rug for $268.47. How much do they spend in all to furnish the living room?

Answer : _____

㉖ Inger wants to buy 6 chairs and 1 dining table. Store A charges $102.00 each for the chairs and store B charges $621.00 for 6 chairs. Which store offers a better buy?

Answer : _____

㉗ The dining table is priced at $1295.00. How much will Inger pay for the dining table and 6 chairs at the lowest price?

Answer : _____

Circle the correct answer in each problem.

28. Mary drank $\frac{3}{7}$ of a bottle of milk. Kevin drank $\frac{5}{7}$ of a bottle and Lori drank an entire bottle. How many bottles of milk did they drink in all?

   A. $\frac{8}{7}$ B. $2\frac{1}{7}$ C. $2\frac{3}{7}$ D. None of the above

29. Peter spent $1.68 for lunch. If he brought 1 loonie, 2 quarters and 4 dimes to school, how much would he have after lunch?

   A. $2.20   B. $0.32   C. $0.22   D. $0.02

30. Billy went shopping with 3 of his friends. Each of them bought 4 shirts. How many shirts did they buy altogether?

   A. 4   B. 8   C. 12   D. 16

31. Jim and Jane want to buy a gift for their parents and share the cost equally. The price of the gift is $44.00. If they have a $5 off coupon, how much does each person pay?

   A. $19.50   B. $19.05   C. $24.50   D. $24.05

32. Each cake costs $8.00. If Kim paid for 3 cakes with 2 $20 bills, how much change would he get?

   A. $4.00   B. $8.00   C. $16.00   D. $24.00

33. A pail of water weighs $1\frac{4}{5}$ kg. A pail of sand weighs $\frac{3}{5}$ kg heavier. How heavy is a pail of sand?

   A. $2\frac{2}{5}$ kg   B. $2\frac{1}{5}$ kg   C. $1\frac{2}{5}$ kg   D. $1\frac{1}{5}$ kg

34. How heavy are the pail of water and the pail of sand together?

   A. $2\frac{2}{5}$ kg   B. 3 kg   C. $3\frac{3}{5}$ kg   D. $4\frac{1}{5}$ kg

35. Ray bought 24 packets of gum each containing 12 pieces. Ray gave his 18 classmates 4 pieces each. How many pieces of gum were left over?

   A. 206   B. 264   C. 216   D. 240

36. How many packets of gum were left over?

   A. 18   B. 22   C. 16   D. 20

Operations with Decimals

EXAMPLE

Terry wants to make a table 1.2 metres long and 0.6 metre wide. He wants to attach a rare wood edging around the table top. How many square metres would he need for the table top? How many metres of rare wood would he need for the edging?

Area of the table top : 1.2 × 0.6 = 0.72

Perimeter of the table top : (1.2 + 0.6) × 2 = 3.6

Answer : Terry would need 0.72 m² of wood for the table top and 3.6 m rare wood for the edging.

Solve the problems. Show your work.

The Orange and Black Department Store is having a sale. The prices shown below are taxes included.

① What would be the cost of 3 shirts and 1 CD?

   Answer : The cost would be _____ .

② What is the amount Joan would save if she bought 5 CDs on sale?

   Answer : _____

③ Can Mr Ray buy a shirt and a 17" colour TV with $230.00?

   Answer : _____

④ Jenny bought 2 pairs of running shoes. What was her change from $150.00?

   Answer : _____

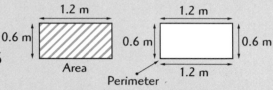

Shirt
$14.95
$12.37

17" Colour TV
$299.95
$227.36

Selected CDs
$19.99
$14.62

Ball Point Pens
$0.3 each
2 for **$0.59**

Running Shoes
$86.33
$67.99

Hi-Lighter
$0.99
$0.79

⑤ Mr Winter bought a shirt, a CD and a pair of running shoes. What is the average price of these 3 items?

   Answer : _____

Mary and Sally went shopping on Wednesday. They spent $5.88 for apples, $3.35 for lettuce, $4.32 for carrots and $8.37 for candies.

⑥ How much did they spend in all?

Answer : _____

⑦ How much change should they receive from a $50 bill?

Answer : _____

⑧ Mary and Sally shared the bill. How much should each person pay?

Answer : _____

⑨ The store offers a special discount every Tuesday. Customers get $1.05 off every $10.00 spent. How much would Mary and Sally have paid by shopping one day earlier?

Answer : _____

⑩ The apples weighed 6 kg. What was the cost of 1 kg of apples?

Answer : _____

⑪ The candies weighed 3 kg. What was the cost of 1kg of candies?

Answer : _____

⑫ They bought 5 heads of lettuce. What was the cost of 1 head of lettuce?

Answer : _____

⑬ A 5-pound bag of potatoes costs $6.45. An 8-pound bag of potatoes costs $9.28. Which bag is a better buy?

• *To compare the prices of 2 items, find the price per unit first.*

Read this first.

Answer : _____

Use the map to solve the problems. Show your work.

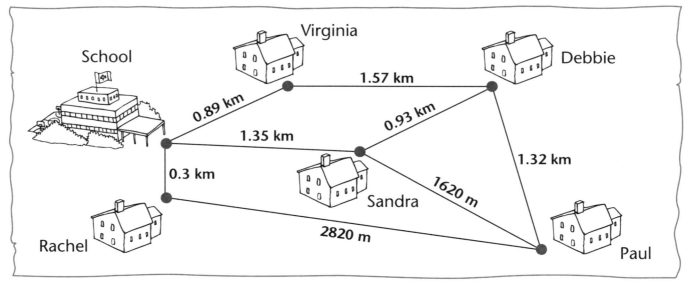

⑭ Who lives the closest to the school? What is the distance in metres?

Answer : _____

⑮ What is the distance in kilometres between Sandra's house and Paul's house?

Answer : _____

⑯ How far is it from Debbie's house to the school if she walks by Virginia's house?

Answer : _____

⑰ What is the shortest distance in metres from Debbie's house to the school?

Answer : _____

⑱ What is the shortest distance in kilometres from Rachel's house to Debbie's house?

Answer : _____

⑲ Yesterday Sandra walked to school in 5 minutes. What was the average distance she walked per minute?

Answer : _____

⑳ Debbie went from home to school passing Virginia's house in 6 minutes. What was the average distance she travelled per minute?

Answer : _____

㉑ Rachel went from home to Debbie's house passing Paul's house in 9 minutes. What was the average distance she travelled per minute?

Answer : _____

㉒ If Sandra shuttles between her house and school 4 times a day, how many kilometres will she travel in 5 days?

Answer : _____

㉓ Virginia and Sandra decide to meet at the school and walk over to Rachel's house together. How far do they walk in total?

Answer : _____

㉔ On a map, each centimetre represents 0.3 km. What is the actual distance if it is 2.5 cm on the map?

Answer : _____

CHALLENGE

Mr Headley's class was going to see a play. Each student ticket costs $3.75 and each adult ticket costs $6.90, taxes included. If 30 or more students attended, the theatre would give them $12.60 off and a free ticket for the teacher.

① If 25 students attended, how much would the students and Mr Headley have to pay in total?

Answer : _____

② If 35 students attended, how much would the students and Mr Headley have to pay in total?

Answer : _____

Two-Step Problems

EXAMPLE

Mark bought 3 packages of trading cards for $0.99 each. He paid with a $5 bill. What was his change?

Cost of 3 packages of cards : 0.99 × 3 = 2.97

Change : 5.00 − 2.97 = 2.03

Answer : His change was $2.03.

Solve the problems. Show your work.

The theatre has 26 rows of seats with 48 seats in each row. Tickets are $4.50 for adults and $3.00 for children. On Tuesdays, the $2.00 box of popcorn is free with the purchase of 1 adult and 1 children's ticket.

① If 952 people attended a show, how many empty seats were there?

Answer : There were _____ empty seats.

② Yesterday the theatre sold 462 adult tickets and the total amount from ticket sales was $2475.00. How many children's tickets were sold?

Answer : _____

③ If the entire theatre was filled with children and each bought a popcorn, how much money would be collected for that show?

Answer : _____

④ If the entire theatre was filled with adults and each bought a popcorn, how much money would be collected for that show?

Answer : _____

⑤ If Mrs Harris brought 4 children to the theatre on Tuesday, and bought each child a popcorn, how much would she pay in all?

Answer : _____

There was a sale at Smirdley's Discount Department Store. All shirts were on sale for 2 for $9.00. All blouses were on sale for 3 for $18.00. All dresses were on sale for $19.00 each. All trousers were on sale for $14.00 each. The store decided to give a $4.00 discount for every 6 items bought. All the prices included taxes.

⑥ Peter bought 2 shirts and 1 pair of trousers. How much would he pay for his purchases?

Answer : _____

⑦ Miranda bought 6 blouses and 1 dress. She paid with a $100 bill. How much change would she get?

Answer : _____

⑧ Jerome's mother bought 4 shirts and 3 blouses for her children. She had a twenty-dollar bill and a ten-dollar bill in her wallet and the rest of her money loose in her purse. How much money would she need from her purse?

Answer : _____

⑨ Wayne bought 2 pairs of trousers and 4 shirts. How much would he pay for his purchases?

Answer : _____

⑩ Mrs Von bought 9 blouses and 3 pairs of trousers. How much would she pay for her purchases?

Answer : _____

⑪ Frances wanted to buy 4 dresses. She had saved up $50.00 for her clothing and would borrow the rest from her father. How much would she need to borrow from her father?

Answer : _____

⑫ What was the price difference between 6 blouses and 4 dresses?

Answer : _____

⑬ Amy paid $71.00 for buying a pair of trousers and some dresses. How many dresses did she buy?

Answer : _____

⑭ There were 128 blue shirts and 224 white shirts. If the salesman put them in packages of 4, how many packages of 4 did he make?

Answer : _____

⑮ If the salesman put them in packages of 3, how many packages of 3 did he make?

Answer : _____

A radio station plays music and ads according to a formula. Every half hour, they play 8 minutes of ads, 16 minutes of music and the rest is talk. The station broadcasts 16 hours a day.

⑯ How much talk will there be every hour?

Answer : _____

⑰ If an ad costs $120 per 30 seconds, how much will the station earn per hour?

Answer : _____

⑱ If the average song is 4 minutes long, how many songs can be played between 4:00 p.m. and 9:00 p.m.?

Answer : _____

⑲ How many minutes of non-ad time will there be in a day?

Answer : _____

⑳ If a disc Jockey speaks at a rate of 12 words every 10 seconds, how many words will he say in each hour's talk time?

Answer : _____

Anna received a chain letter, telling her to make 4 copies of it and send them to 4 friends. Each of her friends was to do the same, and so on. Stamps cost $0.46 each.

㉑ Anna had no stamps at home and had to buy them to send her letters. How much change would she get from a $5 bill?

Answer : _____

㉒ If Anna sent out her letters and each of her friends sent out their letters, how much would have been spent in postage by all of them?

Answer : _____

㉓ If Anna's chain was 3 friends long, how many people were involved in the chain?

Answer : _____

㉔ If Anna's chain was 3 friends long, and everybody did as they were requested, how much would they all pay for postage?

Answer : _____

㉕ If it took 6 minutes to copy the letter and 2 minutes to fold and put it in an envelope, how much time would be spent by Anna and her 4 friends in doing this?

Answer : _____

CHALLENGE

① Ellen reads 38 pages each night before going to sleep and 29 pages each morning before breakfast. If she was reading a 249-page book, and started it on a Monday afternoon, how many pages would she have left to read on Thursday at noon?

Answer : _____

② A television set is on sale for $2120.50. It can also be bought for 24 payments of $92.60 each. How much more does Wayne pay by purchasing it on the instalment plan?

Answer : _____

UNIT 9 Patterns

EXAMPLE

Gary entered a contest. The skill-testing question was:

Take a number. Multiply it by 8. Subtract 6. Divide by 2. Add 15. Divide by 4. Subtract 3. What pattern did you find in Gary's number and the answer?

If Gary chose 14 as his number:

$14 \times 8 = 112$ ➡ $112 - 6 = 106$ ➡ $106 \div 2 = 53$ ➡ $53 + 15 = 68$ ➡

$68 \div 4 = 17$ ➡ $17 - 3 = 14$

Answer : Gary's number and the answer are the same.

Solve the problems. Show your work.

Dorothy and Gladys are playing a pattern game. Dorothy would think of a pattern like "add 2 and multiply by 3" and keep it secret. Gladys would say a number like "2" and Dorothy would answer "12". Gladys would have to guess the pattern.

① If Gladys said "4", what would Dorothy answer?

Answer : Dorothy would answer _____ .

② If Gladys said "6", what would Dorothy answer?

Answer : _____

③ If Gladys said "5.5", what would Dorothy answer?

Answer : _____

④ Gladys wanted a turn to think of a pattern. When Dorothy said "4", she would answer "14". Which of the following is Gladys' pattern?

    A.   Divide by 2. Add 10.

    B.   Multiply by 6. Subtract 10.

    C.   Subtract 3. Multiply by 10.

    D.   Add 8. Divide by 2.

Answer : _____

⑤ If Dorothy said "2.4", what would Gladys answer?

Answer : _____

Billy was practising shooting hoops. He kept track of the number of baskets he scored each day he played.

Day	1st	2nd	3rd	4th	5th
Number of Baskets	1	3	5	7	9

⑥ Was Billy improving as the week progressed?

Answer : _____

⑦ There was a pattern in his improvement. Look at the data and write out the pattern in words.

Answer : _____

⑧ Following the pattern, how many baskets would Billy score on the 6th day?

Answer : _____

⑨ On which day would Billy score 19 baskets?

Answer : _____

⑩ What was the total number of baskets Billy scored in the first 2 days?

Answer : _____

⑪ What was the total number of baskets Billy scored in the first 3 days?

Answer : _____

⑫ What was the total number of baskets Billy scored in the first 4 days?

Answer : _____

⑬ What was the total number of baskets Billy scored in the first 5 days?

Answer : _____

⑭ If this pattern were to continue, what would be the total number of baskets Billy scored in the first 9 days?

Answer : _____

⑮ If this pattern were to continue, how many days would Billy take to get 121 baskets in all?

Answer : _____

Sandy and Andy were on a long walk. To make sure that they did not get bored, they made up some problems for each other to solve.

⑯ Sandy gave Andy this list of number : 1, 3, 9, 27, ... She asked Andy to tell her the pattern and the next 2 numbers.

Answer : _____

⑰ Andy wanted to stump Sandy. He used this list of numbers : 1, 1.9, 2.8, 3.7, ... What is the pattern? What are the next 2 numbers?

Answer : _____

⑱ Sandy wanted to find a series that Andy could not figure out. She asked him to try this one : a, c, f, j, ... What is the pattern? What are the next 2 letters?

Answer : _____

⑲ Andy was in trouble. He could not stump Sandy. So he tried this one : 3, 6, 10, 15,... What is the pattern? What are the next 2 numbers?

Answer : _____

⑳ Andy used this list of numbers : 1, 1, 2, 2, 2, 4, 3, 3, 6, ... to stump Sandy. What is the pattern? What are the next 6 numbers?

Answer : _____

㉑ Sandy had the last laugh. She said : 1, 2, 3, 5, 8, 13, 21, ... What is the pattern? What are the next 2 numbers?

Answer : _____

Solve the problems. Show your work.

㉒ Hortense's parents have strange ideas about allowances. They offered her $0.10 the first day and doubled that each day for a week or Hortense could receive $12.00 per week. Which was a better deal for Hortense's parents?

Answer : _____

㉓ Karen got only 52 in Math. The Math teacher, Mr Finley, said that if she worked hard to improve, he would double any improvement she made on the next test to reach a final mark. Karen got 58 on the next test. What score would Mr Finley give her?

Answer : _____

㉔ On Jerry's 12th birthday, he received a gift from his grandparents. It was a $25.00 bond that doubled in value every 10 years. What will the bond be worth when Jerry is 72 years old?

Answer : _____

Donald and Ronald invented a pattern machine. It had a door to put numbers in, 4 dials to set and a door to take numbers out. The first example would be : (5 + 12) × 3 = 51. Help them complete the table.

	Number in	1st Operation		2nd Operation		Number out
		Number	Operation	Number	Operation	
	5	12	Addition	3	Multiplication	51
①	8	4	Multiplication	8	Addition	
②	45	3	Division	7		8
③	1	17		9	Division	2

EXAMPLE

A magic rabbit jumps 1.6 metres with its first jump, and half that distance each jump after. The problem is that the magic rabbit cannot jump less than 0.3 of a metre. How many jumps can the magic rabbit take?

1st jump	2nd jump	3rd jump	4th jump
1.6	1.6 ÷ 2 → 0.8	0.8 ÷ 2 → 0.4	0.4 ÷ 2 → 0.2

But 0.2 < 0.3, so the magic rabbit can only take 3 jumps.

Answer : The magic rabbit can take 3 jumps.

Solve the problems. Show your work.

The price of a savings bond doubles every 10 years. Use this fact to complete the table.

①

Year	1940	1950	1960	1970	1980	1990	2000
Price ($)			250.00		1000.00		

② What would the price of the savings bond be in 2020?

Answer : _____

③ In which year would the price of the savings bond be $64 000.00?

Answer : _____

④ How many times more was the price of the bond in 1960 than that in 1940?

Answer : _____

⑤ How much would you have earned if you bought the bond in 1980 and sold it in 2020?

Answer : _____

Matthew buys trading cards each week. He buys as many as he can with the money left over after paying for everything else.

⑥ Complete the table to see what pattern you can find.

Week	1	2	3	4	5	6	7
No. of cards bought	5	6	8	5			
Money spent ($)	2.25	2.70	3.60		2.70		2.25
No. of cards in collection	5	11					

⑦ How many cards will Matthew buy in week 9?

Answer :

⑧ How much money will Matthew spend in week 10 on buying cards?

Answer :

⑨ How many cards will Matthew collect in the first 3 weeks?

Answer :

⑩ How many cards will Matthew collect in the first 6 weeks?

Answer :

⑪ How many cards will Matthew collect from week 1 to week 9?

Answer :

⑫ How many cards will Matthew collect from week 1 to week 30?

Answer :

⑬ If Matthew buys 5 cards in week 22, how many cards will he buy in week 23?

Answer :

⑭ How much money will Matthew spend in the first 3 weeks?

Answer :

⑮ How much money will Matthew spend in the first 6 weeks?

Answer :

Tony has 12 yellow marbles and 5 blue marbles. Each day Tony buys 2 yellow marbles and 3 blue marbles.

⑯ Help Tony complete the table.

Day	1st	2nd	3rd	4th	5th	6th
No. of yellow marbles	12					
No. of blue marbles	5					

⑰ How many yellow marbles does Tony have on the 7th day?

Answer : Tony has _____ yellow marbles on the 7th day. _____

⑱ How many blue marbles does Tony have on the 7th day?

Answer : _____

⑲ How many days does Tony take to have 32 yellow marbles?

Answer : _____

⑳ How many days does Tony take to have 32 blue marbles?

Answer : _____

㉑ How many days does Tony take to have the same number of yellow and blue marbles?

Answer : _____

㉒ How many marbles does Tony have in all in the first 6 days?

Answer : _____

㉓ What is the pattern of increase in the number of marbles?

Answer : _____

Mrs Faam's class is studying a table. The numbers in column or row follow a pattern.

㉔ Help them complete the table.

Column \ Row	1	2	3	4	5	6
1	0	0	0		0	
2	2	4		8		12
3				20		
4			18			36
5	8			32	40	
6	10	20	30			60

㉕ What is the pattern in column 3? What would the next 3 numbers be after 30?

Answer : _____

㉖ What is the pattern in row 3? What would the next 3 numbers be after 24?

Answer : _____

㉗ Which of the columns has the same pattern as that in row 6? What is the pattern?

Answer : _____

㉘ Joe has 10 cards. The number of cards that Joe collects increases by 10 each day. Which of the rows above can show the counting pattern of Joe's cards? How many cards will he have after 5 days?

Answer : _____

㉙ Raymond uses $8.00 every day. Which of the rows above can show the total amount of money he has spent? How much money will Raymond have spent after 4 days?

Answer : _____

The Johnson twins are setting up an agency to take care of dogs. Read the rate card. Then complete the table and answer the questions.

Simple care : $4.00 for the first hour; $5.00 per hour thereafter

Walking : $2.00 each time, plus $0.50 per km

Washing : 2 times total charges

Drying : Free with care over 3 hours; $2.00 otherwise

㉚ Simple care :

Hour(s)	1	2	3	4	5	6
Charge ($)						

㉛ Walking :

Distance(km)	1	2	3	4	5	6
Charge ($)						

㉜ Tina had the twins look after her dog, Dorfus, for 10 hours. What was the charge?

Answer : _____

㉝ Kevin asked the twins to look after his dog for 4 hours and take her for a 3 km walk. How much did the twins earn for the service?

Answer : _____

㉞ Lily wanted her poodle walked for 4 km and washed. What was her bill?

Answer : _____

㉟ Dolly's parents asked the twins to look after their dog for 8 hours. They wanted the dog washed and dried. What was their total bill?

Answer : _____

Keri and Harry were so impressed with the Johnson twins' business, they decided to start one of their own. They would look after cats. Use the following tables to complete their rate card and answer the questions.

Simple Care				
Hour(s)	1	2	3	4
Charge ($)	3.50	8.00	12.50	17.00

Feeding				
No. of meals	1	2	3	4
Charge ($)	5.00	10.00	15.00	20.00

㊱

Simple care : $_____ for the first hour;

$_____ per hour thereafter

Chasing cat : $12.00 per hour, plus $0.75 a km

Feeding cat : $_____ per meal

㊲ Ralph had a cat that was a little wild. His bill showed 3 hours' care and 1 hour and 6 km of chasing . What was his total bill?

Answer : _____

㊳ Mr and Mrs Quorley had a very well-behaved cat. They wanted it cared for 7 hours and fed two meals. What was their total bill?

Answer : _____

CHALLENGE

Willy and Billy set up a baby-sitting service. They charged $1.00 for the first hour and $1.50 per hour after that. If the children were under 3, there was a surcharge of $2.00 for the first hour.

Mr and Mrs Jones wanted them to babysit their two children for 5 hours. One was 2 years old and the other 4 years old. How much would their bill be?

Answer : _____

Solve the problems. Show your work.

This is a map of a section of Squaretown. Each block in Squaretown is 1.96 km² and each side of the block is 1.4 km. On this map, Allan lives at A. Bobby lives at B. Carol lives at C and Doris lives at D.

① What is the area bounded by Grand Ave. on the north, Bottom Ave. on the south, Mountain Blvd. on the west and Desert Blvd. on the east?

Answer : _____

② If Doris walks along Middle Ave. and then turns right on Mountain Blvd. to Allan's house, how far has she walked?

Answer : _____

③ If Bobby walks along Desert Blvd., and then turns left on Grand Ave. to Allan's house, how far has he walked?

Answer : _____

④ If both Allan and Carol walk to Doris' house by the shortest route, how far have they travelled in all?

Answer : _____

⑤ Carol was walking to Bobby's house by the shortest route. If she completed 1.86 km, how much farther would she have to walk?

Answer : _____

⑥ If Bobby walked to Doris' house in 5 minutes, how far did he travel in 1 minute?

Answer : _____

⑦ If Doris walked to Bobby's house in 4 minutes, how much farther did she walk in 1 minute than Bobby?

Answer : _____

Bobby was cycling along Desert Blvd. He kept track of the time he took to travel each block.

⑧ Complete the table.

No. of blocks	1	2	3	4	5	6
Distance travelled (km)	1.4	2.8				
Time (min)	3	6				

⑨ What is the pattern of the time taken by Bobby to travel each block?

Answer : _____

⑩ What is the pattern of the distance travelled by Bobby?

Answer : _____

⑪ How long would Bobby take to travel 8 blocks?

Answer : _____

⑫ If Bobby rode for 36 min, how many blocks would he pass?

Answer : _____

⑬ If Bobby passed 9 blocks, how many kilometres would he travel?

Answer : _____

⑭ If Bobby drank $\frac{1}{4}$ L of water every 15 minutes, how many litres of water would he have drunk after 75 minutes?

Answer : _____

⑮ If Bobby drank $1\frac{3}{4}$ L of water, for how long would he have travelled on his bike?

Answer : _____

SuperSave Department Store is having a sale and all the prices include taxes. They take $3.25 off purchases between $10.00 and $20.00, $7.15 off purchases between $20.01 and $40.00, and $15.50 off purchases $40.01 and over.

⑯ The price of a sweater is $29.45. How much do you have to pay?

Answer : _____

⑰ Jane paid $53.25 for a pair of jeans. What is its original price?

Answer : _____

⑱ Richard buys 3 packs of socks at $10.80 each. How much can he save?

Answer : _____

⑲ The regular price of a book is $15.99. If Jim buys 2 books, how much will he pay?

Answer : _____

⑳ Billy pays $50.00 for 2 CDs at $22.99 each. How much change will he get?

Answer : _____

㉑ Tina pays $60.00 for 1 pair of shoes at $59.99 and 1 pair of socks at $3.99. How much change will she get?

Answer : _____

㉒ A box of chocolates costs $19.87. If Gary has 1 $10 bill, 3 twoonies and 3 quarters, will he have enough money to buy a box of chocolates?

Answer : _____

㉓ There are 329 customers in the store. If 251 customers are female, how many male customers will there be?

Answer : _____

㉔ On average, each customer spends $5.00 in the store. How much money can be collected from 215 customers?

Answer : _____

㉕ Ray wants to buy either sweater A or sweater B. The price of sweater A is $34.87. The price of sweater B is $40.05. What is the price difference between sweater A and sweater B after the discount?

Answer : _____

㉖ Which sweater should Ray buy? Explain.

Answer : _____

Circle the correct answer in each problem.

Frank has invented a machine. If he drops a number in the top, a related number comes out from the side.

㉗ If you drop a 1 in the top, a 5 comes out from the side. A 2 produces an 8 and a 3 produces an 11. Which of the following is the machine's pattern?

A. Add 4   B.   Multiply by 3 and add 2

C. Add 2 and multiply by 3   D.   Multiply by 2 and add 3

㉘ If you drop a 4 in the top, what number will come out from the side?

A. 8   B.   11   C.   14   D.   18

㉙ Frank dreams of a machine that works on the same pattern, but turns 1 loonie into 5, 2 loonies into 8 and so on. How much money would he make if he dropped 7 loonies into his machine?

A. 23   B.   42   C.   17   D.   11

㉚ To make 29 loonies, how many loonies would Frank have to drop into the machine?

A. 8   B.   9   C.   25   D.   13

㉛ What pattern would Frank have to create for the machine to turn 2 twoonies into $17.00 and 3 twoonies into $27.00?

A. Add 3 and multiply by 3   B.   Multiply by 5 and add 3

C. Multiply by 4 and add 9   D.   Multiply by 5 and subtract 3

㉜ If the machine made $47.00, how many twoonies would Frank have dropped into the machine?

A. 7   B.   6   C.   5   D.   4

㉝ What pattern would Frank have to create for the machine to turn 6 nickels into $9.00 and 8 nickels into $10.00?

A. Multiply by 1.5   B.   Multiply by 10 and add 6

C. Multiply by 1.25 and add 1.5   D.   Add 4.2 and multiply by 2

There are 72 seats in the Virtual Reality Game Centre. Each adult ticket costs $6.49 and each children's ticket is $2.90 less than an adult ticket.

㉞ If all the seats were occupied by adults, how much money would the centre collect?

    A. $467.28   B. $487.28   C. $457.28   D. $367.28

㉟ If all the seats were occupied by children, how much money would the centre collect?

    A. $248.48   B. $258.48   C. $348.48   D. $358.48

㊱ If 46 seats were occupied by children and the rest by adults, how much money would the centre collect?

    A. $391.88   B. $398.78   C. $268.98   D. $333.88

㊲ Mrs Faam buys 8 tickets for $46.12. The number of children's tickets she intends to buy is fewer than 5, how many adult tickets does she buy?

    A. 4   B. 5   C. 6   D. 7

㊳ How many children's tickets does she buy?

    A. 1   B. 2   C. 3   D. 4

㊴ Game A lasts $6\frac{7}{12}$ minutes and Game B lasts $5\frac{11}{12}$ minutes. How long do these two games last?

    A. $11\frac{8}{12}$ minutes   B. $12\frac{6}{12}$ minutes

    C. $11\frac{18}{24}$ minutes   D. $13\frac{8}{12}$ minutes

㊵ By how many minutes is Game A longer than Game B?

    A. $1\frac{8}{12}$ B. $\frac{9}{12}$ C. $1\frac{3}{12}$ D. $\frac{8}{12}$

㊶ Joe played Game A twice. How long did he play Game A?

    A. $12\frac{1}{12}$ minutes B. $12\frac{14}{24}$ minutes C. $12\frac{7}{12}$ minutes D. $13\frac{2}{12}$ minutes

Section IV

Overview

In the previous section, problem-solving strategies were applied in the context of the four arithmetic operations and pattern recognition.

In this section, word problems involve finding perimeter, area, volume, speed and time. Geometry units include applications of coordinate systems and transformations. Statistics topics covered are the interpretation of circle graphs and line graphs. Students also practise solving problems involving mean and mode, and probability.

EXAMPLE

Mary buys 2 desk pads at $14.95 each and 5 binders at $2.97 each. If Mary gets a $2.18 discount on desk pads and a $1.48 discount on binders, how much will she spend in all?

Cost of desk pads : $(14.95 \times 2) - 2.18 = 27.72$

Cost of binders : $(2.97 \times 5) - 1.48 = 13.37$

Cost in all : $27.72 + 13.37 = 41.09$

Answer : Mary will spend $41.09 in all.

Solve the problems. Show your work.

Ben wants to make some money by doing odd jobs.

Excellent Service
Call Ben • 725-JOBS

Raking Leaves	$ 4.98
Sweeping Sidewalks	$ 2.84
Mowing Lawns	$12.49
Cleaning Garages	$20.18
Washing Cars	$ 5.39

* $4.50 off for 3 jobs or more at the same time.

① If Mrs Donovan hired Ben to rake her leaves and mow her lawn, what would her bill be?

Answer : Her bill would be _____ .

② If Mr Kell hired Ben to clean his garage and wash his car, what would his bill be?

Answer : _____

③ If Mr Ryan hired Ben to do all the jobs except car washing, what would his bill be?

Answer : _____

④ If Mr Ryan gave Ben a $100 bill, how much change would he get?

Answer : _____

⑤ Mrs Winter hired Ben to do 2 jobs and her bill was $23.02. Which 2 jobs did Ben do?

Answer : _____

⑥ If Mrs Winter gave Ben a $50 bill, how much change would she get?

Answer : _____

⑦   If Ben took 2 hours to clean a garage, how much money would he earn per hour?

Answer : _____

⑧   Ben decided to give a quarter of his earnings to charity. He earned $37.65 the first week, $35.94 the second and $31.53 the third. How much would he have after his donation?

Answer : _____

Edward's Emporium is having a year-end sale. There is a $1.50 rebate for every $10 spent. If a customer spends over $100.00, he or she gets an additional $0.30 off every $10. All prices include taxes.

⑨   Ann buys a blouse at $82.97. What is her change from a $100 bill?

Answer : _____

⑩   Tim buys a shirt at $120.45. What is his change from a $100 bill?

Answer : _____

⑪   Ray buys 3 sweaters at $16.99 each. How much rebate does he get? What is his change from a $50 bill?

Answer : _____

⑫   A pair of boots costs $92.85. If Sally wants to buy 2 pairs of boots, should she buy them separately or together? Explain.

Answer : _____

⑬   Jacket A costs $98.27. Jacket B costs $102.95. If Eric wants to buy a cheaper jacket, which one should he buy?

Answer : _____

Donna and her friends went to a new candy store to buy their favourite candies. The prices included taxes.

⑭ Donna wanted to buy some lollipops. It was $0.97 each or $10.80 for a package of 12. How much would Donna save by buying a package of lollipops?

Answer : _____

⑮ Donna bought 2 packages of lollipops. What was her change from $25.00?

Answer : _____

⑯ Gary wanted some jellybeans. A box of 6 packages was sold at $3.24. How much did 1 package cost?

Answer : _____

⑰ Gary bought 18 packages of jelly-beans. What was his change from a $20 bill?

Answer : _____

⑱ Louis paid $23.76 to buy a package of lollipops and a few boxes of jelly-beans. How many boxes of jellybeans did Louis buy?

Answer : _____

⑲ There was a sign in the shop. 'Buy 2 chocolate bars at $1.26 each and get the third one free.' How much did each chocolate bar cost on average?

Answer : _____

⑳ Alexander took 9 chocolate bars. How much did he pay?

Answer : _____

㉑ Each jar of candies cost $12.96. Jeffrey had $40.00. Would he have enough money to buy 3 jars of candies?

Answer : _____

㉒ If Jeffrey bought 2 jars of candies, how much money would he have left?

Answer : _____

• For Question 18, follow the pattern to find the answer, e.g.

Read this first.

No. of boxes of jellybeans	1	2
Cost ($)	3.24	6.48

Help the candy store owner write out the profits in the past 4 weeks in numbers and in words. Then put the weeks in order.

Week 1	Week 2	Week 3	Week 4
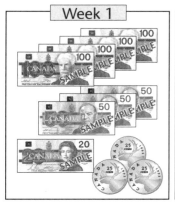		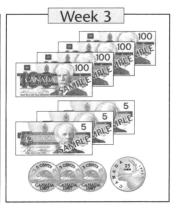	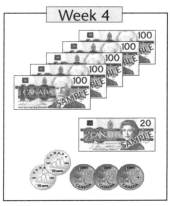

㉓ Money earned in week 1 : $ _____ ; the total amount earned in week 1 was

_____ .

㉔ Money earned in week 2 : $ _____ ; the total amount earned in week 2 was

_____ .

㉕ Money earned in week 3 : $ _____ ; the total amount earned in week 3 was

_____ .

㉖ Money earned in week 4 : $ _____ ; the total amount earned in week 4 was

_____ .

㉗ List the weeks in order from the greatest amount earned to the least.

Answer : _____

Mr Tiff buys 12 toy cars for $187.20 and re-sells them at $20.94 each.

① How much money will Mr Tiff get?   ② How much will he gain or lose?

Answer : _____   _Answer :_ _____

UNIT 2 Perimeter and Area

EXAMPLE

What is the perimeter and area of this figure?

Perimeter : 1.5 + 1.2 + 2 + 0.8 + 3.5 + 2 = 11

Area : (1.5 × 2) + (2 × 0.8) = 4.6

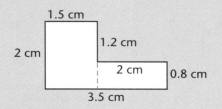

Answer : The perimeter of this figure is 11 cm and its area is 4.6 cm².

The diagrams below show the dimensions of 6 flower beds. Use the diagrams to solve the problems. Show your work.

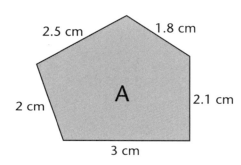

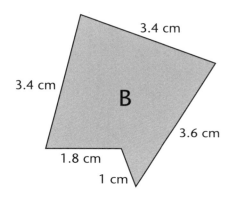

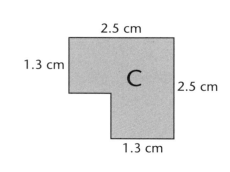

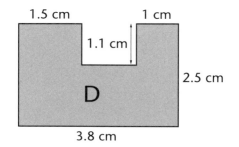

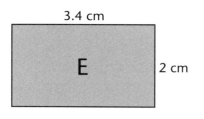

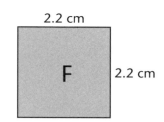

① What is the perimeter of A?

Answer : Its perimeter is _____ .

② What is the perimeter of B?

Answer : _____

③ What is the perimeter of C?

Answer : _____

④ What is the perimeter of D?

Answer : _____

⑤ What is the perimeter of E?

Answer : _____

⑥ What is the perimeter of F?

Answer : _____

⑦ The actual size of each garden is 100 times bigger than the diagram. Find the actual perimeter of each garden and write in metres.

Garden	A	B	C	D	E	F
Actual Perimeter						

Darren wants to divide his backyard into parts. The actual size is 100 times greater than the diagram below. Measure the diagram to solve the problems. Show your work.

Q T

P

R

S

⑧ What is the actual perimeter of P?

Answer : _____

⑨ What is the actual perimeter of Q?

⑩ What is the actual perimeter of R?

Answer : _____

⑪ What is the actual perimeter of S?

Answer : _____

⑫ What is the actual perimeter of T?

Answer : _____

⑬ Put the parts in order from the greatest perimeter to the smallest.

Answer : _____

Answer : _____

Look at the floor plan and dimensions of the first floor of Darren's house. All the ceilings are 2.8 m high. Solve the problems. Show your work.

	Dimension		Dimension
Library	5 m × 6.5 m	Side Garden	2.3 m × 5 m
Porch	5 m × 2.9 m	Wash-room	2.6 m × 5 m
Dining Room	5 m × 13 m	Living Room	7.9 m × 7.9 m
Hall	3 m × 7.3 m	Kitchen	5 m × 6.4 m

⑭ What is the area of the library?

Answer : _____

⑮ What is the area of the hall?

Answer : _____

⑯ What is the area of the living room?

Answer : _____

⑰ How many times of the area of the washroom is the area of the dining room?

Answer : _____

⑱ What is the area of the first floor of Darren's house?

Answer : _____

⑲ How many square metres of carpet would cover the living room and the library?

Answer : _____

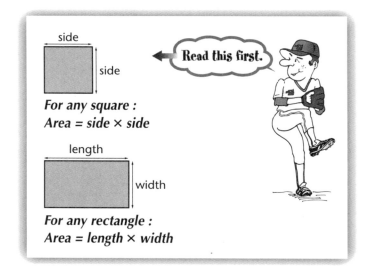

side
side
For any square :
Area = side × side

length
width
For any rectangle :
Area = length × width

Read this first.

⑳ If 1 m² of carpet costs $2.00, how much does Darren need to pay for the carpet for his living room and library?

Answer : _____

㉑ Darren wants to paint 2 adjacent walls in the kitchen. If 1 L of paint covers 4 m², how many litres of paint are needed for the 2 walls?

Answer : _____

㉒ If paint comes in 2 L cans, how many cans of paint does Darren need to buy?

Answer : _____

Solve the problems. Show your work.

㉓ A table is 2.5 m long and 1.2 m wide. What is its perimeter and area?

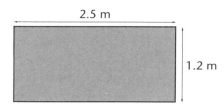

Answer : _____

㉔ The length of a square coffee table is 60 cm. What is its perimeter and area?

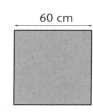

Answer : _____

㉕ A square has a perimeter of 120 cm. How long is each side?

Answer : _____

㉖ A rectangular backyard has an area of 450 m². If its length is 25 m, what is its width?

Answer : _____

㉗ A piece of rectangular cardboard has a perimeter of 45 cm. If its width is 5 cm, what is its area?

Answer : _____

CHALLENGE

The outside dimensions of a framed picture are 25 cm by 40 cm. If the border is 2 cm wide,

① what is the length and width of the picture?

Answer : _____

② what is the area and perimeter of the picture?

Answer : _____

EXAMPLE

School starts at 8:45 a.m. and finishes at 3:20 p.m. How long is the school day?

1st From 8:45 a.m. to noon : 3 h 15 min

2nd From noon to 3:20 p.m. : 3 h 20 min

Total time : 3 h 15 min + 3 h 20 min = 6 h 35 min

1st	
12 h 00 min	
− 8 h 45 min	
3 h 15 min	

2nd	
3 h 20 min	
− 0 h 00 min	
3 h 20 min	

Answer : The school day is 6 h 35 min.

Solve the problems. Show your work.

Jimmy and his grandparents like to walk for exercise. Last Saturday, they left home at 9:40 a.m. for the park, which took 57 minutes at their usual pace. After spending 40 minutes there, they walked to the convenience store for groceries, which took 32 minutes. After shopping, they arrived home at 12:42 p.m.

① At what time did Jimmy and his grandparents reach the park?

They reached the park
Answer : at _____ .

② At what time did they leave the park?

Answer : _____

③ At what time did they reach the convenience store?

Answer : _____

④ They shopped in the store for 35 minutes. At what time did they leave the store?

Answer : _____

⑤ How long did they take to walk home after shopping?

Answer : _____

⑥ It took Jimmy's grandmother 26 min to cook their lunch. If she finished cooking at 1:17 p.m., at what time did she start?

Answer : _____

⑦ Larry has an assignment due on Nov. 29. If he starts to work on it on Nov. 3, how many days does he have to complete the assignment?

Answer : _____

⑧ If Larry starts doing his assignment at 8:16 a.m. and stops at 4:05 p.m., how long has he worked on it?

Answer : _____

⑨ Larry spent 2 h 20 min looking for reference materials in the school library. He left there at 5:32 p.m. When did he start working in the library?

Answer : _____

⑩ Mrs Smith has an appointment with her doctor at 2:15 p.m. It takes her 23 minutes to walk to the doctor's office. If Mrs Smith leaves home at 1:48 p.m., will she be there on time?

Answer : _____

⑪ Ben's favourite TV show starts at 11:45 a.m. and lasts 1 h 35 min, when will the show be over?

Answer : _____

⑫ Movie A lasts 1 h 43 min; movie B lasts 1 h 16 min. If movie A starts at 11:45 a.m. and movie B starts at 12:10 p.m., which movie finishes first?

Answer : _____

⑬ Peter travelled from City A to City B in 170 h. How many days and hours did he spend on travelling?

Answer : _____

⑭ Gary wanted to go to the theatre. He left home at 11:26 a.m. First he took a bus for 37 min. Then he walked for 16 min. At what time did he reach the theatre?

Answer : _____

A flight from Jonesville to Littletown takes 2 h 16 min. A flight from Norhead to Littletown takes 1 h 45 min. If flight A leaves Jonesville for Littletown at 11:55 a.m., about what time must flight B leave Norhead to reach Littletown at the same time as flight A?

Answer : _____

EXAMPLE

Mr Ford drove his car at an average speed of 60 km/h. Mr Coleman drove his car at an average speed of 75 km/h. They both started at the same time from the same place but drove in opposite directions. How far apart would they be after 3 hours?

Distance travelled by Mr Ford : 60 × 3 = 180

Distance travelled by Mr Coleman : 75 × 3 = 225

Distance apart : 180 + 225 = 405

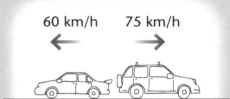

Answer : They would be 405 km apart after 3 hours.

Solve the problems. Show your work.

Sally and her family were going on a motoring trip. They planned to drive to Centretown, a distance of 600 km, and from there to Middleberg, a distance of 880 km and then drive the 780 km home.

① If they drove at an average speed of 60 km/h, how long would it take to drive from home to Centretown?

Answer : It would take _____ .

② If they drove at an average speed of 80 km/h, how long would it take to drive from Centretown to Middleberg?

Answer : _____

③ The trip from Middleberg to home took 10 hours. What was their average speed on this part of the trip?

Answer : _____

④ If they drove at an average speed of 60 km/h, how long would it take to drive from Middleberg to home?

Answer : _____

⑤ If they drove at an average speed of 80 km/h, how long would it take to drive the whole trip?

Answer : _____

⑥ If they took 20 hours to complete the trip, what would be the average speed?

Answer : _____

Doris can cycle at 20 km/h and run at 12 km/h. Use the diagram to solve the problems. Show your work.

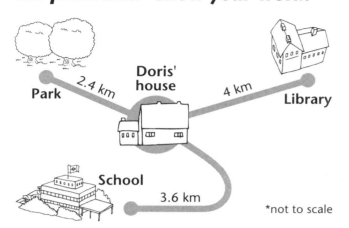

Park — 2.4 km — Doris' house — 4 km — Library

School — 3.6 km

*not to scale

Don't forget :

$1 h = 60 min$; $h \xrightleftharpoons[\div 60]{\times 60} min$

Read this first.

e.g. $0.3 h = 18 min$

$$\begin{array}{r} 0.3 \\ \times\ 6\,0 \\ \hline 1\,8.0 \end{array}$$

$42 min = 0.7 h$

$$\begin{array}{r} 0.7 \\ 6\,0\,\overline{)\,4\,2.0} \\ \underline{4\,2\,0} \end{array}$$

⑦ How long will Doris take to cycle to and from the library?

Answer : _____

⑧ How long will Doris take to run to the park from home?

Answer : _____

⑨ How many minutes can Doris save by riding the bicycle to the park instead of running?

Answer : _____

⑩ How many minutes will Doris take to cycle to school?

Answer : _____

⑪ Last Thursday, Doris took 15 min to cycle to school. What was her cycling speed in kilometres per minute?

Answer : _____

⑫ What was her cycling speed in kilometres per hour?

Answer : _____

Ricky, Raymond and Sam each have a 180-page story book. Ricky plans to read 20 pages each day. Raymond plans to read 36 pages every 2 days. Sam plans to read 15 pages every half day. How many days does each of them take to finish the whole book? Who is the first to finish the book?

Answer : _____

EXAMPLE

Gary has an aquarium 50 cm long, 30 cm wide and 45 cm high. What is its volume? How many litres of water does it hold?

Volume : 50 × 30 × 45 = 67500

Capacity : 67500 ÷ 1000 = 67.5

Answer : The volume of his aquarium is 67 500 cm^3. It holds 67.5 L of water.

Solve the problems. Show your work.

Sandy had a new aquarium 60 cm long, 25 cm wide and 40 cm high. She was told to fill it with 20 L of water on Monday, 15 L of water on Wednesday and 10 L of water on Friday. On Saturday, she could put her fish in the aquarium.

① Before filling the aquarium with water, what was the volume of air inside?

Answer : _____

② How many litres of water could the aquarium hold?

Answer : _____

③ What volume of air would be in the aquarium on Monday?

Answer : _____

④ What volume of air would be in the aquarium on Wednesday?

Answer : _____

cm^3 / mL $\underset{\times 1000}{\overset{\div 1000}{\rightleftharpoons}}$ L

← Read this first.

e.g.   415 mL = 0.415 L

5.12 L = 5120. mL

⑤ What volume of air would be in the aquarium on Friday?

Answer : _____

⑥ Sandy's old aquarium was 45 cm long, 15 cm wide and 20 cm high. How many more litres of water could the new aquarium hold than the old one?

Answer : _____

Alan has a tank full of 160 000 cm³ of water. He is trying to empty it with a pail in the shape of a rectangular prism. The pail is 25 cm long, 20 cm high and 10 cm wide.

⑦   What is the volume of the pail?

Answer : _____

⑧   How many litres of water does the pail hold?

Answer : _____

⑨   How many litres of water does the tank hold?

Answer : _____

⑩   After Alan has removed 8 pailfuls of water, what volume of air will be in the tank?

Answer : _____

⑪   How many litres of water will remain in the tank?

Answer : _____

⑫   How many pailfuls of water must be removed to half empty the tank?

Answer : _____

⑬   How many pailfuls of water must be removed to empty the entire tank?

Answer : _____

⑭   If Alan was emptying the water into an aquarium 1 m long and 0.25 m wide, how high would it be to just hold all the water from the tank?

Answer : _____

⑮   If Alan puts 6 metal balls into the tank and 75 000 cm³ of water overflows, what is the volume of each metal ball?

Answer : _____

Carol has 2 aquariums. The big one is 1 m long, 0.5 m wide and 0.6 m high. The small one is only 0.6 m long, but has the same height and width as the big one.

⑯ How much water can the big aquarium hold?

Answer : _____

⑰ How much water can the small aquarium hold?

Answer : _____

⑱ How much more water does the big aquarium hold than the small one?

Answer : _____

⑲ Each side of a cube is 10 cm long. If Carol tries to put the cubes into the small aquarium, how many cubes can the small aquarium hold?

Answer : _____

⑳ If Carol pumps 25 000 cm^3 of water each minute into the big aquarium, how long does it take to fill up the whole aquarium?

Answer : _____

㉑ If it takes Carol 30 minutes to fill up the small aquarium with pails of water, how much water will she pour into the aquarium in one minute?

Answer : _____

• **For Question 19:**

Small aquarium

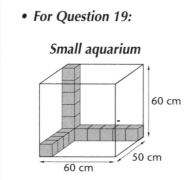

• **For Questions 20 and 21, first find the volume of the big aquarium and the small aquarium in cubic centimetres (cm^3). Then use division to find the answers.**

Read this first.

Look at the floor plan of Francis' new house. All the ceilings are 3 m high. Use the table to solve the problems. Show your work.

Washroom

Bedroom 1		Living Room
Bedroom 2	Hall	
	Dining Room	Kitchen

	Dimension
Bedroom 1	4 m × 7 m
Bedroom 2	8 m × 7 m
Washroom	2.3 m × 2.8 m
Dining room	4 m × 6.4 m
Kitchen	4 m × 5 m
Living room	5.6 m × 8.6 m

㉒ How much air is in the living room?

Answer : _____

㉓ How much air is in bedroom 2?

Answer : _____

㉔ How much more air is in bedroom 1 than in the washroom?

Answer : _____

㉕ Francis' father has built a store room in the kitchen. The area of the store room is one-eighth of the kitchen. What is its volume in cubic metres?

Answer : _____

㉖ What is the volume of the store room in cubic centimetres?

Answer : _____

CHALLENGE

Tina used 60 cubes each to build 2 models as shown. Each side of the cube was 1 cm long. Help her complete the table.

	Model	Volume (cm³)	Capacity (mL)
①	A		
②	B		

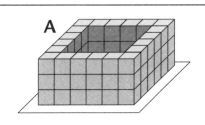
A

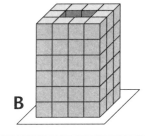
B

EXAMPLE

Kari was at position (2, 1). First she went 6 units right and 4 units up. Then she went 4 units left and 3 units down. Finally, she went 1 unit right and 2 units up. Show Kari's route on the grid and tell where she is now.

1st : 6 units right & 4 units up ⟶ (8, 5)

2nd : 4 units left & 3 units down ⟶ (4, 2)

Final: 1 unit right & 2 units up ⟶ (5, 4)

Answer : She is at position (5, 4) now.

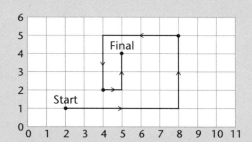

Solve the problems. Show your work.

Jerry calls out numbers and Lori has to guess the shape he is describing. Help Lori graph each set of ordered pairs and join them to form polygons. Then identify each polygon.

① (9, 5), (9, 1), (1, 1), (1, 5)

Answer : It is a _____ .

③ (3, 5), (10, 5), (9, 1), (2, 1)

Answer : _____

② (6, 1), (9, 4), (2, 5)

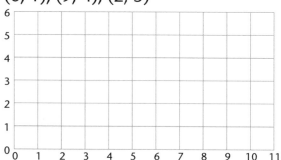

Answer : _____

④ (2, 5), (8, 5), (6, 1), (4, 1)

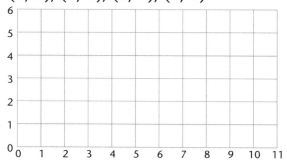

Answer : _____

Jerry draws some incomplete shapes on the grid. Help Lori find the missing vertex to complete each shape and solve the problems.

⑤ The missing vertex is 3 units right and 2 units up from (7, 3).

a.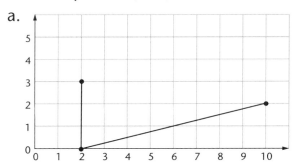

b. What is the ordered pair of the missing vertex?

Answer : _____

c. What shape is it?

Answer : _____

⑥ The missing vertex is 2 units right and 3 units up from (0, 2).

a.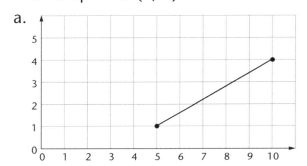

b. What is the ordered pair of the missing vertex?

Answer : _____

c. What shape is it?

Answer : _____

⑦ The missing vertex is 2 units up from (3, 0).

a.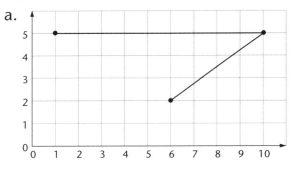

b. What is the ordered pair of the missing vertex?

Answer : _____

c. What shape is it?

Answer : _____

⑧ The missing vertex is between the ordered pairs (0, 4) and (4, 4).

a.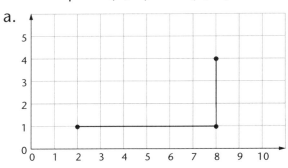

b. What is the ordered pair of the missing vertex?

Answer : _____

c. What shape is it?

Answer : _____

Dory's class is having a treasure hunt. They have a grid drawn over the map of an island. To find the treasure, they should follow Dory's instructions. Help the children find the coordinates of all the places and locate the traps on the grid. Then complete Dory's instructions and draw the route on the grid.

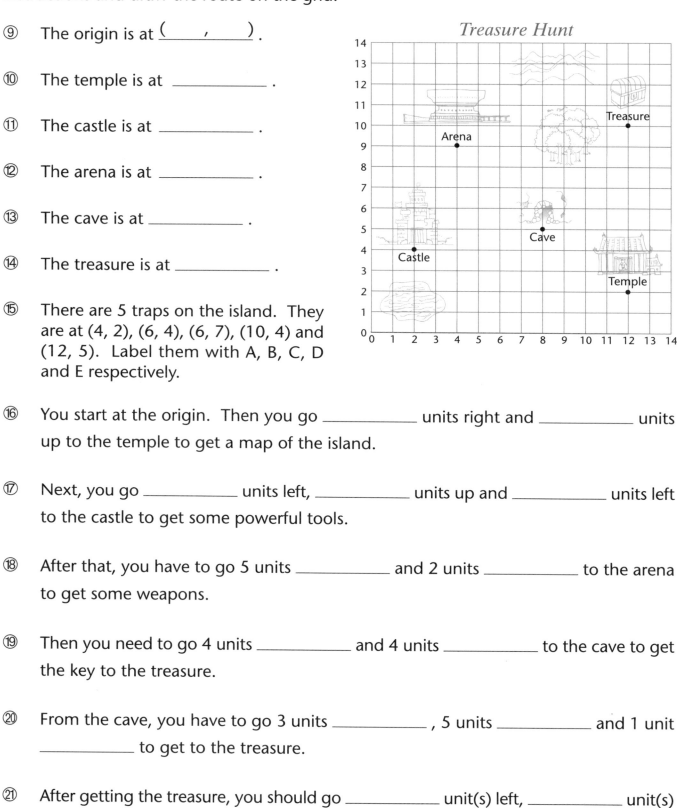

Treasure Hunt

⑨ The origin is at (___ , ___) .

⑩ The temple is at _____ .

⑪ The castle is at _____ .

⑫ The arena is at _____ .

⑬ The cave is at _____ .

⑭ The treasure is at _____ .

⑮ There are 5 traps on the island. They are at (4, 2), (6, 4), (6, 7), (10, 4) and (12, 5). Label them with A, B, C, D and E respectively.

⑯ You start at the origin. Then you go _____ units right and _____ units up to the temple to get a map of the island.

⑰ Next, you go _____ units left, _____ units up and _____ units left to the castle to get some powerful tools.

⑱ After that, you have to go 5 units _____ and 2 units _____ to the arena to get some weapons.

⑲ Then you need to go 4 units _____ and 4 units _____ to the cave to get the key to the treasure.

⑳ From the cave, you have to go 3 units _____ , 5 units _____ and 1 unit _____ to get to the treasure.

㉑ After getting the treasure, you should go _____ unit(s) left, _____ unit(s) down and _____ unit(s) left to the origin to leave the island.

Use the clues to find the seats for the children. Write their names in the boxes and find the ordered pairs.

- Mary is sitting 2 units left from Lori; Daisy is sitting 2 units right from Lori.
- Matthew is sitting between Daisy and Jerry.
- George is sitting 2 units up from the origin; Susan is sitting 1 unit down from George.
- Alvin is sitting between Mary and Gary; Ray is sitting 1 unit left from Alvin.
- Walk 2 units down and 1 unit left from Michael and you can find Amy's seat.
- Emily is sitting between Michael and Sarah; Jessica is sitting 1 unit right from Emily.
- John is sitting 1 unit up from Jessica, and Emily is sitting between John and Elaine.

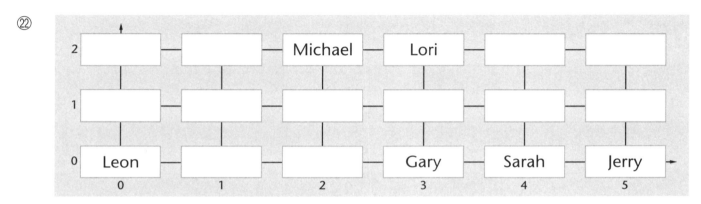

22

24 George _____   26 Alvin _____

24 Susan _____   27 Jessica _____

25 Elaine _____   28 Mary _____

CHALLENGE

A and B are two vertices of a square. Write out the possible coordinates for the other two vertices and plot them on the grid.

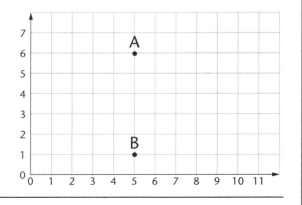

Answer : _____

Solve the problems. Show your work.

Wilma went to the mall to buy some containers and an aquarium. She left home at 10:47 a.m. and travelled at an average speed of 50 km/h to get to the mall.

① Wilma reached the mall at 11:11 a.m. How long did she take to go from her home to the mall?

Answer : _____

② How far away was the mall from her house?

Answer: _____

③ Wilma shopped in the mall for 2 hours and 18 minutes. She then had lunch there for 45 minutes. At what time did she leave the mall?

Answer : _____

④ Wilma travelled at 40 km/h back home. At what time did she reach home?

Answer : _____

⑤ Wilma bought 1 box and 1 aquarium. The box cost $18.27 and the aquarium cost $52.49. What was her change from a $100 bill?

Answer : _____

⑥ How much more did the aquarium cost than the box?

Answer : _____

⑦ The box was 45 cm wide, 60 cm long and 50 cm high. Wilma wanted to cover the bottom of the box with felt. How much felt would she need?

Answer : _____

⑧ Wilma wanted to decorate the edges of the top sides of the box by drawing a border. How long would her border be?

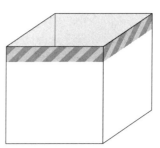

Answer : _____

⑨ What was the volume of the box?

Answer : _____

⑩ A box of tissue was 9 cm wide, 20 cm long and 10 cm high. How many boxes of tissue would the box hold?

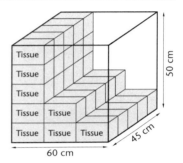

Answer : _____

⑪ The aquarium was 20 cm wide, 40 cm long and 30 cm high. How many litres of water could the aquarium hold?

Answer : _____

⑫ Wilma turned on the tap to fill the aquarium with water from 4:29 p.m. until 4.34 p.m. How long did it take to fill up the whole aquarium?

Answer : _____

⑬ Wilma poured some water from the aquarium until the water level in the aquarium dropped 5 cm. How much water was in the aquarium?

Answer : _____

⑭ Wilma put 8 pebbles into the aquarium and the water level rose 0.5 cm. On average, what was the volume of each pebble?

Answer : _____

Darlene has a grid drawn over the map of her neigbourhood. Follow Darlene's instructions to write the places in the boxes.

⑮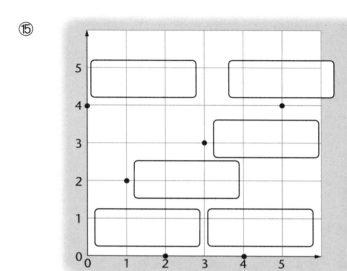

- The library is 1 unit up and 2 units right of Darlene's house.

- The park is 5 units left of the shopping mall.

- The school is 2 units down and 3 units right of Darlene's house.

- The shopping mall is 1 unit right and 4 units up of the school.

- The convenience store is 2 units left of the school.

⑯ Darlene's house is at (___ , ___) .

⑰ The park is at _____ .

⑱ The shopping mall is at _____ .

⑲ The convenience store is at _____ .

⑳ The school is at _____ .

㉑ The library is at _____ .

㉒ If the bus travels at an average speed of 50 km/h and it takes Darlene 15 minutes to get to the mall, how far away is the mall from the bus stop?

Answer : _____

㉓ If Darlene gets on the bus at11:56a.m., when will she arrive at the mall?

Answer : _____

㉔ A student ticket costs $1.28 each or 10 for $10.40. How much will Darlene save if she buys 10 tickets?

Answer : _____

㉕ Darlene buys 12 student tickets. How much does she pay?

Answer : _____

㉖ Darlene spends $12.84 for food and $31.39 for stationery. How much does she spend in all?

Answer : _____

㉗ Darlene has spent $32.97 altogether. Now she has $22.81 left. How much did she have at the begining?

Answer : _____

Circle the correct answer in each problem.

㉘ Gary is drawing a square on a grid. The vertices of the square are at (2, 0), (6, 0) and (2, 4). Where is the 4th vertex?

A. (4, 6)   B. (0, 6)   C. (6, 4)   D. (0, 4)

㉙ John is drawing a rectangle on a grid. The vertices of the rectangle are at (6, 2), (3, 5) and (1, 3). Where is the 4th vertex?

A. (0, 4)   B. (4, 0)   C. (5, 0)   D. (0, 5)

㉚ How much water would it take to half fill a rectangular box 1.6 m long, 0.6 m wide and 0.8 m high?

A. 384 L   B. 38.4 L   C. 3.84 L   D. 0.384 L

㉛ A bicycle and a car start at the same time from Bayville to Meadowview. The average speeds of the bicycle and the car are 20 km/h and 55 km/h. How far ahead is the car after 1 hour and 30 minutes?

A. 45.5 km   B. 54.5 km   C. 52.5 km   D. 30 km

㉜ A car takes 3 h 16 min to travel from Bayville to Meadowview. It leaves Bayville at 3:47 p.m. When will it arrive at Meadowview?

A. 6:33 p.m.   B. 8:03 p.m.   C. 6:03 p.m.   D. 7:03 p.m.

㉝ Georgia is planting her garden. Her plot is 4.2 m long and 3.5 m wide. She wants to put a fence around her plot. What length of fencing will she need?

A. 7.7 m   B. 14.7 m   C. 16.1 m   D. 15.4 m

㉞ If the fence costs $2.5 per metre, what will the cost of fencing be?

A. $19.25   B. $38.50   C. $36.75   D. $40.25

㉟ Georgia wants to plant one-seventh of her garden as lettuce. How much space will the lettuce take up?

A. 2.1 m^2 B. 7.7 m^2 C. 13 m^2 D. 14.7 m^2

EXAMPLE

What motion is shown in each set of diagrams? Write translation, reflection or rotation to describe each motion.

a. Before   After

b. Before   After

c. Before   After

Answer : a. Translation   b. Rotation   c. Reflection

Solve the problems. Show your work.

① Draw the reflection image of each polygon.

a.

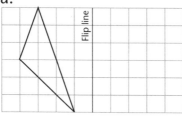

b.

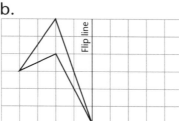

c.

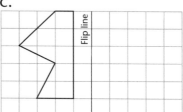

② Draw the rotation image of each polygon.

a. $\frac{1}{4}$ turn clockwise

b. $\frac{1}{2}$ turn clockwise

c. $\frac{1}{4}$ turn counterclockwise

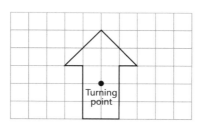

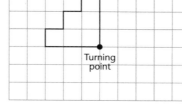

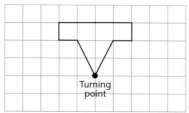

③ Draw the translation image of each polygon.

a. 2 units right
   1 unit down

b. 3 units right
   1 unit up

c. 3 units left
   2 units down

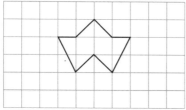

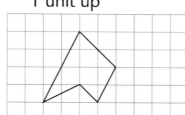

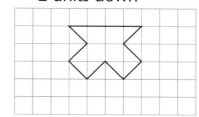

④ Draw the flip line for the reflection image of each shaded polygon.

a. 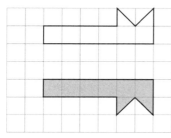 b. 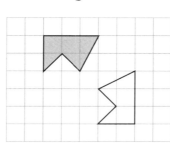 c.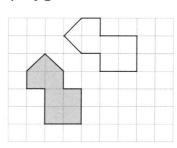

⑤ Draw the turning point for the rotation image of each shaded polygon and tell whether the turn is $\frac{1}{4}$ turn, $\frac{1}{2}$ turn or $\frac{3}{4}$ turn clockwise.

a. 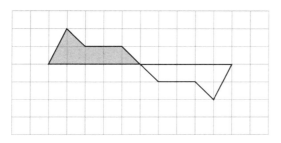 b.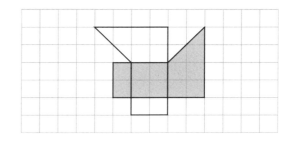

Answer : _____   Answer : _____

⑥ Describe the translation image of each shaded polygon.

a. 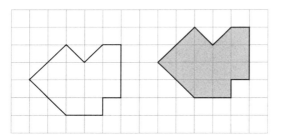 b.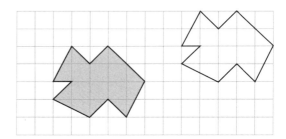

Answer : _____   Answer : _____

⑦ Draw the reflection image of each shaded polygon over the flip lines *l*, *m* and *n*.

a. 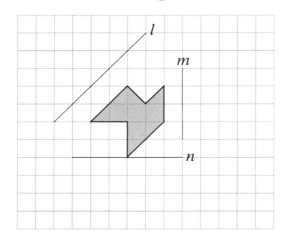 b.

Solve the problems.

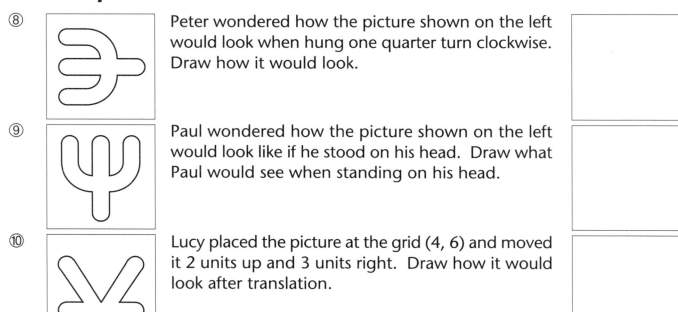

⑧ Peter wondered how the picture shown on the left would look when hung one quarter turn clockwise. Draw how it would look.

⑨ Paul wondered how the picture shown on the left would look like if he stood on his head. Draw what Paul would see when standing on his head.

⑩ Lucy placed the picture at the grid (4, 6) and moved it 2 units up and 3 units right. Draw how it would look after translation.

⑪ Katie placed a mirror beside the picture. Draw what Katie would see on the mirror.

← mirror

Look at the polygons on the grid. Solve the problems. Show your work.

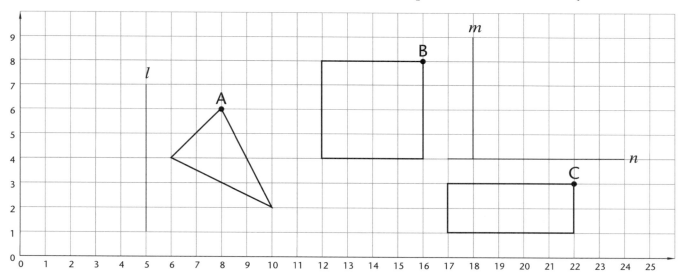

⑫ If Darren makes a $\frac{1}{4}$ turn clockwise about the point (6, 4) of the triangle, what will be the ordered pair of vertex A of the turned image?

Answer : _____

⑬ If Darren flips the triangle over line *l*, what will be the ordered pair of vertex A of the flipped image?

Answer : _____

⑭ If the ordered pair of the translation image of vertex B is (10, 6), describe how Terry translates the square to its image.

Answer : _____

⑮ If Terry flips the square over the line *m*, what will be the ordered pair of vertex B of the flipped image?

Answer : _____

⑯ If Grace makes a $\frac{1}{4}$ turn counterclockwise about the point (17, 3) of the rectangle, what will be the ordered pair of vertex C of the turned image?

Answer : _____

⑰ If the ordered pair of the translation image of vertex C is (23, 7), describe how Grace translates the rectangle to its image.

Answer : _____

⑱ If Grace flips the rectangle over line *n*, what will be the ordered pair of vertex C of the flipped image?

Answer : _____

 CHALLENGE

Sam is turning his sticker counterclockwise. Which set of the diagrams below shows the movement of the sticker? Circle the correct answer.

A.

B.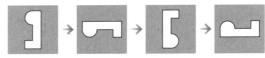

C.

D.

Line Graphs

EXAMPLE

Mary used a line graph to show the number of stamps she had. How many more stamps did Mary have in December than in August?

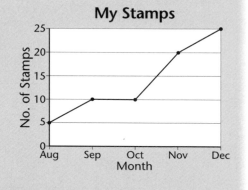

My Stamps

No. of stamps in Dec : 25

No. of stamps in Aug : 5

Difference : 25 – 5 = 20

Answer : Mary had 20 more stamps in December than in August.

Use the graphs to solve the problems. Show your work.

Larry recorded the number of toy cars produced by the factory last week.

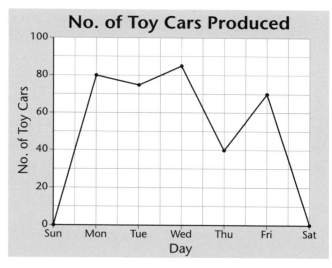

No. of Toy Cars Produced

① How many toy cars were produced last Monday?

Answer :   toy cars were produced last Monday.

② How many toy cars were produced last Friday?

Answer : _____

③ How many more toy cars were produced on Wednesday than on Thursday?

Answer : _____

④ One of the production lines in the factory broke down last week. Which day did it happen? Explain.

Answer : _____

⑤ On which days was the factory closed? Explain.

Answer : _____

⑥ On average, how many toy cars were produced each working day?

Answer : _____

Larry's factory produces 3 types of toy cars. He kept track of the production in the past year.

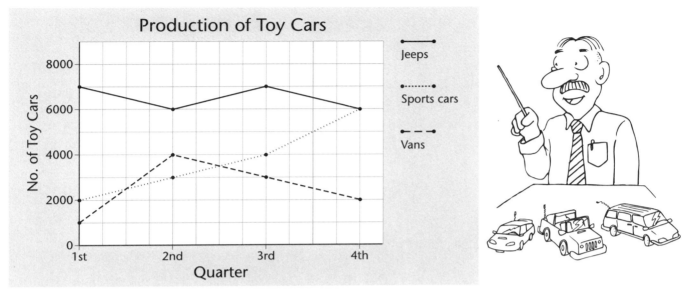

⑦ How many sports cars were produced in the 1st quarter?

Answer : _____

⑧ How many vans were produced in the 2nd quarter?

Answer : _____

⑨ How many jeeps were produced in the 3rd quarter?

Answer : _____

⑩ How many more vans were produced in the 4th quarter than in the 1st quarter?

Answer : _____

⑪ How many jeeps were produced from the 1st quarter to the 4th quarter?

Answer : _____

⑫ How many vehicles were produced in the 4th quarter?

Answer : _____

⑬ In which quarter was the number of jeeps 3 times the number of vans?

Answer : _____

⑭ In which quarter did Larry's factory produce more vans than sports cars?

Answer : _____

⑮ What did the line for sports cars indicate?

Answer : _____

⑯ If Larry wanted to cut one of his production lines, which one should be cut? Explain.

Answer : _____

Darcy and Horace wanted to buy a gift for their sister. They used a table to record their savings. Use their table to make a line graph and solve the problems.

⑰ **Darcy's and Horace's Savings**

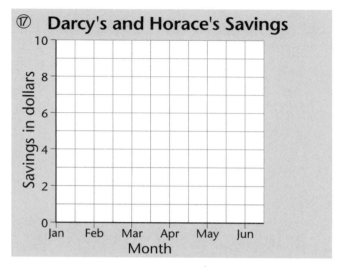

	Darcy's savings	Horace's savings
JAN	$4.50	$4.50
FEB	$2.00	$6.00
MAR	$8.50	$3.50
APR	$4.50	$7.00
MAY	$7.00	$6.00
JUN	$6.50	$5.50

⑱ How much more did Darcy save than Horace in March?

Answer : _____

⑲ How much more did Horace save than Darcy in February?

Answer : _____

⑳ In which months did Darcy save more than Horace?

Answer : _____

㉑ How many months were Darcy's savings more than Horace's?

Answer : _____

㉒ In which month were their savings the same?

Answer : _____

- Don't forget to label the lines on the line graph. e.g.

Read this first.

Amy
John

㉓ How much did Darcy save in the six months?

Answer : _____

㉔ How much did Horace save in the six months?

Answer : _____

㉕ If the birthday gift for their sister cost $65.39, would they have enough money to buy it?

Answer : _____

Mrs Harding sold her nuts in bags. She recorded the sales of cashews and almonds in the past year. Use her table to make a line graph and solve the problems.

	JAN	FEB	MAR	APR	MAY	JUN	JUL	AUG	SEP	OCT	NOV	DEC
No. of bags of cashews sold	250	350	300	450	350	300	250	250	250	300	200	200
No. of bags of almonds sold	150	150	100	150	200	250	300	300	350	400	400	450

㉖
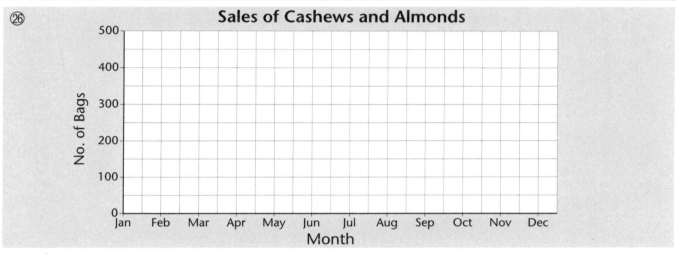

㉗ How many more bags of cashews were sold than almonds in April?

Answer : _____

㉘ How many more bags of almonds were sold than cashews in September ?

Answer : _____

㉙ How many bags of nuts did Mrs Harding sell in June?

Answer : _____

㉚ During which month did the sales of cashews increase the most?

Answer : _____

CHALLENGE

Look at the above line graph. Describe the trend of sales of cashews and the trend of sales of almonds.

Answer : _____

EXAMPLE

Dora's parents were looking at Dora's circle graph. It showed the time she was awake and the time she spent sleeping. They said that Dora should be getting more sleep. How did they know?

Answer : They found that only $\frac{1}{4}$ of the circle represented sleeping. Since $\frac{1}{4}$ of 24 hours is 6 hours, they thought that Dora did not have enough sleep.

Dora's Day

Awake

Sleeping

Solve the problems. Show your work.

Karin loves fruit. She kept track of the amount of money she spent on fruit each week and drew the circle graph.

① Which fruit did Karin spend the most money on?

Answer : Karin spent the most money on _____ .

② Which section represents the fruit that Karin spent the most money on? Colour it red.

③ Which fruit did Karin spend the least money on?

Answer : _____

④ Which section represents the fruit that Karin spent the least money on? Colour it green.

⑤ If Karin spent $100.00 on fruit, how much would she spend on pears?

Karin's Spending on Fruit

Bananas
Pears
Grapes
Apples

⑥ List the fruits from the one Karin spent the most money on to the one she spent the least money on.

Answer : _____

Answer : _____

Gary's teacher, Mr Milne, made a circle graph to represent the number of students in each group that scored an A on the test.

⑦ Which group had the most As?

Answer : _____

⑧ Which group had the fewest As?

Answer : _____

Students with As

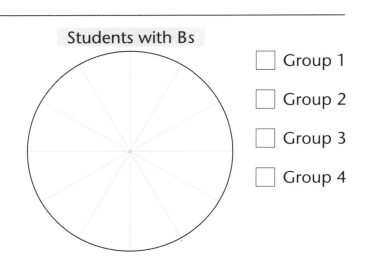

⑨ Altogether, there were 12 students who scored an A. How many students with an A were in group 4?

Answer : _____

⑩ How many students with an A were in group 1?

Answer : _____

⑪ Half of the students in group 4 got an A on the test. How many students were there in group 4?

Answer : _____

⑫ Each group had the same number of students. How many students took the test?

Answer : _____

⑬ There were 5 students with Bs in group 1, 1 in group 2, 4 in group 3 and 2 in group 4. Colour the circle graph and the boxes with matching colours to show the number of students in each group that scored a B on the test.

Students with Bs

☐ Group 1

☐ Group 2

☐ Group 3

☐ Group 4

Four groups of children sold apples to raise money for charity. Lori, John, Mario and Shirley were the group representatives. Their teacher, Mrs Carter, recorded the results in the circle graph.

⑭ Which group raised the second most money?

Answer : _____

⑮ Which group raised the least money?

Answer : _____

⑯ List the group representatives from the most money raised to the least.

Answer : _____

⑰ John's group raised $24.00. How much money did Mario's group raise?

Answer : _____

⑱ How much money did Shirley's group raise?

Answer : _____

⑲ How much money did Lori's group raise?

Answer : _____

⑳ How much money did the children raise altogether?

Answer : _____

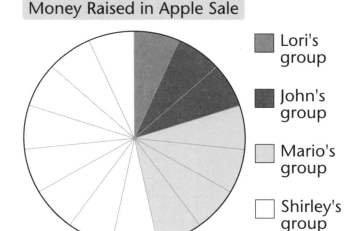

Money Raised in Apple Sale

- Lori's group
- John's group
- Mario's group
- Shirley's group

㉑ If the cost of each apple was the same, which group sold the most number of apples? Explain.

Answer : _____

㉒ Which group sold the second most number of apples? Explain.

Answer : _____

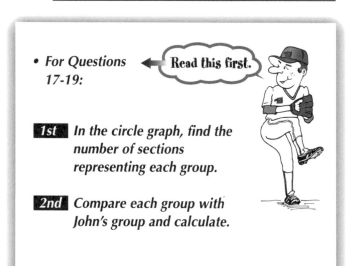

- **For Questions 17-19:**   ← Read this first.

  1st *In the circle graph, find the number of sections representing each group.*

  2nd *Compare each group with John's group and calculate.*

Willy drew a circle graph to show how much time he spent on video games each day last week.

㉓ Which day did Willy spend the most time on video games?

Answer : _____

㉔ Which day did he spend the second most time on video games?

Answer : _____

㉕ Which days did he not play video games?

Answer : _____

㉖ Willy spent 1 hour playing video games on Friday. How many hours did he play video games on Monday?

Answer : _____

Time Spent on Video Games

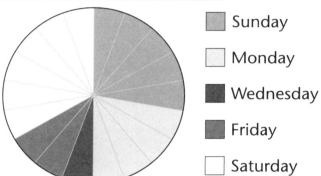

- ▨ Sunday
- ☐ Monday
- ■ Wednesday
- ▦ Friday
- ☐ Saturday

㉗ How many hours did he play video games on Saturday?

Answer : _____

㉘ How many more hours did he play video games on Sunday than on Wednesday?

Answer : _____

CHALLENGE

Katie had $20.00. She spent $8.00 on clothing, $5.00 on entertainment, $3.00 on food and $4.00 on transportation. Which of the circle graphs below is the best to show Katie's spending? Explain.

A. Katie's Spending

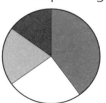

B. Katie's Spending

C. Katie's Spending

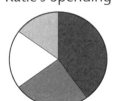

- ■ clothing
- ▦ entertainment
- ▨ transportation
- ☐ food

Answer : _____

EXAMPLE

Ken got his report card with the following marks : 87, 75, 78, 56, 78 and 88. What were his mean and mode marks?

Mean : (87 + 75 + 78 + 56 + 78 + 88) ÷ 6 = 462 ÷ 6 = 77

Mode : 87, 75, 78, 56, 78, 88 —————— 78 occurs the most often.

Answer : His mean mark was 77 and his mode mark was 78.

Solve the problems. Show your work.

Lori was trying to improve her running speed. She practised in the park every morning for the past 4 weeks. Her times were recorded in the table.

① What was Lori's mean running time in the 1st week?

Her mean running time was

Answer :   s.

Lori's Running Time				
Day \ Week	1st	2nd	3rd	4th
Sun	127s	110s	124s	100s
Mon	117s	126s	106s	125s
Tue	120s	112s	98s	105s
Wed	105s	104s	110s	104s
Thu	110s	108s	106s	100s
Fri	105s	110s	106s	104s
Sat	100s	121s	106s	104s

② What was her mean running time in the 2nd week?

Answer :

③ What was her mean running time in the 3rd week?

Answer :

④ What was her mean running time in the 4th week?

Answer :

⑤ What was her mode running time in the 3rd week?

Answer :

⑥ What was her mode running time in the 4th week?

Answer :

Mr Layton grouped the children and listed their allowances.

Group A		Group B		Group C		Group D	
Frank	$5.00	Ron	$6.80	George	$3.83	Lily	$4.75
Kelly	$6.75	Amy	$9.15	Ringo	$7.37	Donny	$8.13
Ray	$5.37	Rachel	$4.16	Elaine	$3.83	Terry	$4.75
Peter	$5.00	Beatrice	$4.16			Cindy	$4.75
		Tim	$4.18			Mark	$8.13
						Wayne	$0.69

⑦ Who had the highest allowance in the class?

Answer :

⑧ Who had the lowest allowance in the class?

Answer :

⑨ What was the mean allowance received by the students in group A?

Answer :

⑩ What was the mean allowance received by the students in group C?

Answer :

⑪ Was the mean allowance received by the students in group B higher than that by group D?

Answer :

⑫ What was the mode allowance in group B?

Answer :

⑬ What was the mode allowance in group D?

Answer :

⑭ If Tim was placed in group A, what would the mean allowance of group A be?

Answer :

⑮ If one of the students in group D joined group C and changed the mean allowance of group C to $5.79, who were the possible students?

Answer :

Henry, Larry, Michael and Elaine were comparing their trading cards. Henry had 258 cards, Larry 426, Michael 426 and Elaine 678.

⑯ What was the mean number of cards that the 4 children had?

Answer : _____

⑰ What was the mode number of cards that the 4 children had?

Answer : _____

⑱ If Elaine gave Henry 126 cards, what would be the mean number of cards that the 4 children had?

Answer : _____

⑲ What would be the mode number of cards that the 4 children had?

Answer : _____

⑳ If Larry gave Michael 252 cards, what would be the mean number of cards that the 4 children had?

Answer : _____

㉑ What would be the mode number of cards that the 4 children had?

Answer : _____

㉒ If Michael gave Larry 60 cards and Henry gave Elaine 40 cards, what would be the mean number of cards that the 4 children had?

Answer : _____

㉓ If Larry bought 28 cards and Henry bought 120 cards, what would be the mean number of cards that the 4 children had?

Answer : _____

㉔ If Elaine lost 88 cards, what would be the mean number of cards that the 4 children had?

Answer : _____

㉕ If the 4 children gave 160 cards to their friends, Ray, what would be their mean number of cards afterwards?

Answer : _____

㉖ If Michael lost 48 cards and Henry bought 12 cards, what would be the mean number of cards that the 4 children had?

Answer : _____

㉗ Tim has an average of 135 cards in 4 boxes. Which 4 of these boxes are his?

A 110 **B** 150 **C** 120 **D** 130 **E** 180

Answer : _____

㉘ If all the above boxes belonged to Tim, what would be the mean number of cards in each box?

Answer : _____

㉙ Elaine has an average of 12.35 kg of flour in 4 bags. Which 4 of these bags are hers?

A Flour 10.68 kg **B** Flour 12.37 kg **C** Flour 13.25 kg **D** Flour 11.89 kg **E** Flour 14.46 kg

Answer : _____

㉚ If all the above bags belonged to Elaine, what would be the mean amount in each bag?

Answer : _____

CHALLENGE

Don spilled some hot chocolate onto his report card, covering his mark in Math. He got 78 in English, 86 in Social Studies, 92 in Science and 68 in Physical Education. His average mark was 76.

① What was his mark in Math?

Answer : _____

② If he wanted an average mark of 77, how much would he have to get in Math?

Answer : _____

UNIT 11 Probability

EXAMPLE

Harry has a bag with 5 red balls and 7 blue balls. If he takes out one ball, what is the probability that the ball will be red?

Think : There are 12 balls altogether; 5 out of 12 balls are red.

Answer : The probability that the ball will be red is 5 out of 12, or $\frac{5}{12}$.

Solve the problems. Show your work.

Donny and Sari drew a circle on a piece of cardboard and divided it into 4 sections. Then they mounted a pointer in the centre and spun 100 times.

Section	Ice cream	Pop	Lollipop	Popsicle
No. of times occurred	40	10	30	20

① Complete the bar graph to show the number of times each outcome occurred.

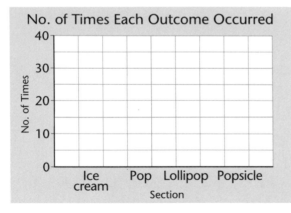

No. of Times Each Outcome Occurred

② What fraction of times did the pointer stop on 'ice cream'?

Answer : _____

③ What fraction of times did the pointer stop on 'pop'?

Answer : _____

④ What fraction of times did the pointer stop on 'lollipop'?

Answer : _____

⑤ On which section do you think the spinner is least likely to stop?

Answer : _____

⑥ On which section do you think the spinner is most likely to stop?

Answer : _____

See how many marbles each child has. Help them solve the problems. Show your work.

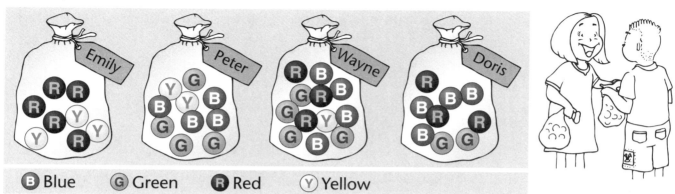

B Blue   G Green   R Red   Y Yellow

⑦   If Emily draws out a marble from her bag, what is the probability that the marble will be red?

Answer : _____

⑧   If Peter draws out a marble from his bag, what is the probability that the marble will be blue?

Answer : _____

⑨   If Wayne draws out a marble from his bag, what is the probability that the marble will be green?

Answer : _____

⑩   If Doris draws out a marble from her bag, what is the probability that the marble will be yellow?

Answer : _____

⑪   If Emily puts all her marbles into Peter's bag and draws out a marble from his bag, what is the probability that the marble will be blue?

Answer : _____

⑫   Doris says, 'If I draw out a marble from my bag, the most likely marble is red.' Is she correct? Explain.

Answer : _____

Solve the problems. Show your work.

The Fisher King Restaurant is holding a 'Spin and Win' event to attract customers. For every ten dollars spent, a customer can spin one of the spinners once to see what he or she can get.

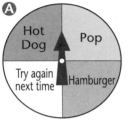  

⑬ For spinner A, what is the probability that the spinner will stop on 'hamburger'?

Answer : _____

⑭ For spinner B, what is the probability that the spinner will stop on 'sandwich'?

Answer : _____

⑮ For spinner C, what is the probability that the spinner will stop on 'pop'?

Answer : _____

⑯ For spinner C, what is the probability that the spinner will stop on 'hot dog'?

Answer : _____

⑰ Which spinner has the greatest probability that the spinner will stop on 'hot dog'?

Answer : _____

⑱ Which spinner has the least probability that the spinner will stop on 'try again next time'?

Answer : _____

⑲ Michael spends $20.08 in the restaurant. How many times can he spin?

Answer : _____

⑳ If Michael wants to have a free hot dog, which spinner should he spin? Explain.

Answer : _____

㉑ If Michael chooses spinner A, what is the probability that the spinner will stop on 'hot dog', 'pop', 'hamburger' or 'try again next time'?

Answer : _____

㉒ If Michael chooses spinner C, what is the probability that the spinner will stop on 'coffee'?

Answer : _____

• **The sum of the probability of all possible outcomes must be equal to 1.**

• **If an event never occurs, then the probability is zero.**

Read this first.

Joe has 1 yellow marble, 1 blue marble and 1 red marble in his bag. Tim has a penny. They try to take a marble from the bag and flip the coin once.

㉓ Complete the tree diagram to show all the possible outcomes.

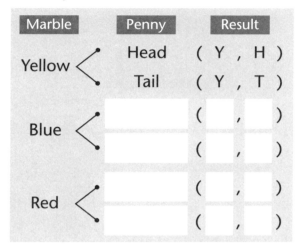

Marble	Penny	Result
Yellow	Head	(Y , H)
	Tail	(Y , T)
Blue		(,)
		(,)
Red		(,)
		(,)

㉔ How many possible outcomes are there?

Answer : _____

㉕ What is the probability that they will get a red marble and a head?

Answer : _____

㉖ What is the probability that they will get a blue marble and a tail?

Answer : _____

㉗ Joe says, 'The probability of getting a blue marble and a head is greater than the probability of getting a red marble and a tail.' Is he correct? Explain.

Answer : _____

㉘ If Joe and Tim played the games 60 times, about how many times would they get a yellow marble and a head?

Answer : _____

CHALLENGE

Which 2 of the 4 spinners below show the same probability of getting each letter? Explain.

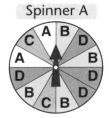

Spinner A

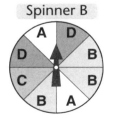

Spinner B

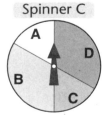

Spinner C

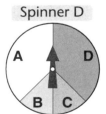

Spinner D

Answer : _____

Solve the problems. Show your work.

Mrs Quinn, the convenience store owner, was packing cereal boxes into a carton 20 cm wide, 60 cm long and 90 cm high.

① What was the volume of the carton?

Answer : _____

② Each cereal box was 5 cm wide, 15 cm long and 30 cm high. How many boxes of cereal would the carton hold?

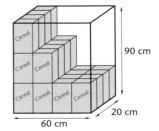

Answer : _____

③ If each box of cereal cost $2.99, how much would the carton cost when it was packed full?

Answer : _____

④ Mrs Quinn filled the carton with 18 boxes of bran flakes, 8 boxes of rice flakes, 10 boxes of corn flakes and some boxes of granola. How many boxes of granola were there?

Answer : _____

⑤ If Mrs Quinn took out 1 box of cereal from the carton, what would be the probability that it was a box of rice flakes?

Answer : _____

⑥ If Mrs Quinn took out 1 box of cereal from the carton, what would be the probability that it was not a box of corn flakes?

Answer : _____

⑦ Which type of cereal had the greatest probability that it would be taken out by Mrs Quinn? Explain.

Answer : _____

⑧ Mrs Quinn wanted to use a circle graph to show the different kinds of cereal in the carton. Each sector in the circle graph represents 2 boxes. Colour the circle graph and the boxes with matching colours to show the number of each kind of cereal in the carton.

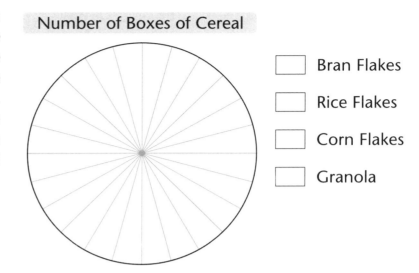

Number of Boxes of Cereal

☐ Bran Flakes

☐ Rice Flakes

☐ Corn Flakes

☐ Granola

Mrs Quinn recorded the number of cartons of cereal sold last year. Use the table to make a line graph.

	Jan	Feb	Mar	Apr	May	Jun	Jul	Aug	Sep	Oct	Nov	Dec
No. of cartons of cereal sold	125	100	150	50	25	75	150	125	100	100	75	125

⑨

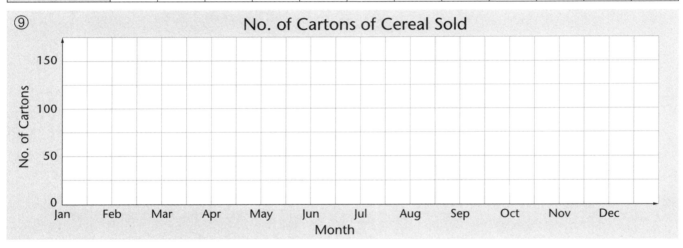

No. of Cartons of Cereal Sold

⑩ How many more cartons were sold in August than in May?

Answer :

⑪ On average, how many cartons were sold each month?

Answer :

⑫ If the delivery charge for 1 carton was $0.25, how much would be the cost of delivery in November?

Answer :

Look at the report cards of some of the students in Miss Bliss' class.

Sarah	
English :	80
Math :	86
French :	86
Art :	75
Science :	79
Drama :	86

Molly	
English :	78
Math :	91
French :	78
Art :	65
Science :	85
Drama :	89

Stanley	
English :	76
Math :	88
French :	97
Art :	72
Science :	76
Drama :	83

Elaine	
English :	82
Math :	97
French :	69
Art :	96
Science :	80
Drama :	80

⑬ What was Sarah's mean mark?

Answer : _____

⑭ What was Molly's mean mark?

Answer : _____

⑮ What was Stanley's mean mark?

Answer : _____

⑯ What was Elaine's mean mark?

Answer : _____

⑰ What was Sarah's mode mark?

Answer : _____

⑱ Which students had their mean mark higher than their mode mark?

Answer : _____

⑲ What was the mean mark in English for these 4 students?

Answer : _____

⑳ What was the mean mark in Drama for these 4 students?

Answer : _____

㉑ The children shuffled their report cards and placed them face down. If Elaine picked a card, what was the probability that she would pick her own card?

Answer : _____

㉒ If Molly picked a card, what was the probability that she would not pick her own card?

Answer : _____

㉓ If Stanley played the game 40 times, about how many times would he get his own card?

Answer : _____

Circle the correct answer in each problem.

㉔ Which of the diagrams below is the same as its reflection image?

A. ◎ ⟋Filp line   B. ¢ ⟋Filp line   C. ⏀ ⟋Filp line   D. $ ⟋Filp line

㉕ Which set of the diagrams below shows a translation?

A.   B.   C.   D.

㉖ Which set of the diagrams below shows a $\frac{1}{2}$ turn clockwise about the turning point?

A.   B.   C.   D.

㉗ Gary started doing his homework at 7:15 p.m. He finished at 9:04 p.m. How long did he take to do his homework?

A. 1 h 49 min   B. 1 h 39 min   C. 1 h 19 min   D. 49 min

㉘ Mr Louis took 2 h 30 min to complete his trip of 180 km. What was his average speed per hour?

A. 450 km/h   B. 60 km/h   C. 90 km/h   D. 72 km/h

㉙ Marcus puts 3 red balls, 2 yellow balls and 4 blue balls into a bag. If Marcus draws a ball from the bag, what is the probability that he will get a red ball?

A. $\frac{2}{3}$ B. $\frac{2}{9}$ C. $\frac{4}{9}$ D. $\frac{1}{3}$

㉚ What is the probability that Marcus will get either a red ball or a blue ball?

A. $\frac{2}{3}$ B. $\frac{5}{9}$ C. $\frac{7}{9}$ D. $\frac{1}{3}$

㉛ How many minutes are there from 11:49 a.m. to 1:07 p.m.?

    A. 68 minutes   B. 78 minutes   C. 18 minutes   D. 118 minutes

㉜ Paul is looking at his watch. The 6 is nearest to him. If he gave the watch a quarter turn counterclockwise, what number would be farthest away from him?

    A. 3   B. 6   C. 9   D. 12

㉝ Kelly has a swimming pool 16 m long, 12 m wide and 2 m deep. She wants to fill it right up to the top with water. How many cubic metres of water will she need?

    A. 384 m³   B. 192 m³   C. 30 m³   D. 768 m³

㉞ The hose carries 6 cubic metres of water a minute. How many minutes will it take to fill Kelly's swimming pool?

    A. 5 minutes   B. 32 minutes   C. 64 minutes   D. 128 minutes

㉟ Look at the shape on the right. What is the perimeter of the shape?

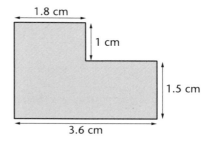

    A. 10.4 cm   B. 9.7cm

    C. 7.9 cm   D. 12.2 cm

㊱ What is the area of the shape?

    A. 4.5 cm²   B. 7.2 cm²   C. 6.48 cm²   D. 5.4 cm²

㊲ The heights of three boys are 1 m 2 cm, 1 m 9 cm and 1 m 16 cm. What is their average height?

    A. 1 m 4 cm   B. 1 m 5 cm   C. 1 m 6 cm   D. 1 m 9 cm

1. Large Numbers

→ Children learn how to write and read large numbers up to a hundred million.

→ Advise children to start writing a number from the ones digit, and leave a space between every three numerals counted from the right.

Example   Write 14 803 765 instead of 14803765.

→ When rounding a number to a certain place value, the digit immediately to the right of that place has to be considered.

Example   Round 14 803 765 and 2 497 382 to the nearest thousand.

14 803 765 ← The hundreds digit 7 is greater than 5, so round up to 14 804 000.

2 497 382 ← The hundreds digit 3 is less than 5, so round down to 2 497 000.

2. Distributive Property of Multiplication

→ Encourage children to apply the distributive property of multiplication to simplify their calculation.

Example   42 x 7 + 42 x 3   42 x 7 + 42 x 3

= 294 + 126 ← Multiply in the usual   = 42 x (7 + 3) ← Apply the distributive
= 420   way; then add.   = 42 x 10   property of multiplication.

                                        = 420

→ Remind children that the distributive property does not apply to division.

Example   24 ÷ 2 + 24 ÷ 4   24 ÷ 2 + 24 ÷ 4

= 12 + 6   = 24 ÷ (2 + 4)

= 18 ✔   = 24 ÷ 6

                                        = 4 ✗

3. Prime and Composite Numbers

→ Children learn the difference between prime and composite numbers. Parents may emphasize the following points:

a. 1 is neither a prime number nor a composite number.

b. All prime numbers except 2 are odd numbers.

c. All numbers with the ones digit equal to 5 are composite numbers except for 5.

d. A number with only 1 and itself as factors is a prime number.

e. A number with more than two factors is a composite number.

f. A number which can form a rectangle is a composite number.

4. Fractions

→ Remind children that the value of a fraction equals 1 if its numerator and denominator are equal, and that any whole number can be written as an improper fraction.

→ Make sure that children understand equivalent fractions have the same numerical value.

- To add or subtract fractions with like denominators, children should add or subtract the numerators only and keep the denominator the same. To add or subtract mixed numbers, they can either add or subtract the whole numbers and fractions separately, or change the mixed numbers to improper fractions before calculation.

- Reduce 1 to an improper fraction if necessary when subtracting fractions.

- To multiply two fractions, multiply their numerators and denominators respectively. To divide a fraction by another fraction, invert the fraction immediately after the ÷ sign and change ÷ to x.

- If the divisor is a whole number, remind children to change it to a fraction with denominator 1 before doing the division.

  Example $\frac{4}{5} \div 2 = \frac{4}{5} \div \frac{2}{1} = \frac{\cancel{4}^2}{5} \times \frac{1}{\cancel{2}_1} = \frac{2}{5}$

5. Decimals

- Remind children to align the decimal points when doing vertical addition or subtraction.

- The number of decimal places in the product is the same as that in the question. Add enough "0"s before the non-zero digits if necessary to locate the decimal point, and the "0"s at the end of the product can be deleted after locating the decimal point.

  Example   0.5 x 0.08 = ?

  $$\begin{array}{r} 0.0\,8 \\ \times\quad 0.5 \\ \hline 4\,0 \end{array} \longrightarrow \begin{array}{r} 0.0\,8 \\ \times\quad 0.5 \\ \hline 0.0\,4\,0 \end{array}$$

  This "0" can be deleted after locating the decimal point.

  Add 2 "0"s to locate the decimal point.

- When dividing, don't forget to add a "0" before the decimal point if necessary to locate the decimal point. If there is a remainder, add "0"s to the right of the dividend after the decimal point and continue to divide until the remainder is zero or there are enough decimal places.

  Example   4.8 ÷ 5 = ?

  $$\begin{array}{r} 9 \\ 5\,)\overline{4.8} \\ 4\,5 \\ \hline 3 \end{array} \longrightarrow \begin{array}{r} 9 \\ 5\,)\overline{4.8\,0} \\ 4\,5 \\ \hline 3\,0 \end{array} \longrightarrow \begin{array}{r} 9\,6 \\ 5\,)\overline{4.8\,0} \\ 4\,5 \\ \hline 3\,0 \\ 3\,0 \end{array} \longrightarrow \begin{array}{r} 0.9\,6 \\ 5\,)\overline{4.8\,0} \\ 4\,5 \\ \hline 3\,0 \\ 3\,0 \end{array}$$

  There is a remainder.   Add a "0" to the right of the dividend and bring down.   Continue to divide until the remainder is zero.   Add a "0" to locate the decimal point.

- Encourage children to check if their answers are reasonable by rounding the decimals to the nearest whole numbers and estimating the answers.

6. Decimals and Fractions

➻ Remind children that a decimal is another way to represent a fraction, with a denominator of 10, 100, 1000 etc., and that a fraction can be changed to a decimal by first writing its equivalent fraction with a denominator of 10, 100, 1000 etc.

➻ A fraction can also be converted to a decimal by dividing the numerator by the denominator.

Example

$$7.5 = 7\frac{5}{10}$$

$$(0.5 = \frac{5}{10})$$

$$7\frac{1}{4} = 7\frac{25}{100} = 7.25 \;\leftarrow\; (\frac{25}{100} = 0.25)$$

$$(\frac{1}{4} = \frac{1 \times 25}{4 \times 25} = \frac{25}{100})$$

7. Percent

➻ Children learn the conversion among percents, decimals and fractions. Parents should encourage them to make observations of the application of percent in everyday situations.

➻ Children should note that $1 = 100\%$ (one hundred percent) $= \frac{100}{100}$

8. Simple Equations

➻ Children may encounter difficulties in determining the value of an unknown in an equation using guess-and-test method. Parents can explain to them the balance principle in solving a simple equation, and encourage them to check the answer by substituting the answer for the unknown.

Example

1.
$$y + 30 = 70 \quad \leftarrow \text{an addition equation}$$
$$y + 30 - 30 = 70 - 30 \quad \leftarrow \text{subtract the same amount from both sides of the equation}$$
$$y = 40$$

2.
$$y \times 4 = 28 \quad \leftarrow \text{a multiplication equation}$$
$$y \times 4 \div 4 = 28 \div 4 \quad \leftarrow \text{divide both sides of the equation by the same number}$$
$$y = 7$$

9. Time and Speed

➻ Children recognize how to write the time and find a duration on a 12-hour clock and a 24-hour clock. Parents may remind children that when calculating a duration, they should trade 1 hour for 60 minutes if necessary.

10. Perimeter and Area

➻ Children practise using formulas to find the perimeter and area of some 2-D shapes. They may sometimes mistake the hypotenuse of a triangle or the slanted side of a parallelogram for the height. Remind them that the height of a 2-D shape must make a right angle with its base.

11. Factorization

➻ Children learn how to write a number as a product of prime factors, and determine the G.C.F. and L.C.M. of two numbers.

12. Inverse Proportion

➻ Make sure that children understand the difference between direct and inverse proportion. Encourage them to think and estimate whether one quantity is increasing or decreasing while the other quantity is increasing before writing the mathematical sentence for calculation. Remind them to check if their answers are reasonable.

13. Circles

➻ Children recognize the circumference, centre, radius, and diameter of a circle. At this stage, parents should not introduce to children the concept of π and the relationship between circumference and diameter/radius.

14. Volume and Capacity

➻ Children use a formula to calculate the volume of a cube. The method of determining the volume of an irregular object using the amount of water displaced is also practised.

➻ Point out to children that cm^3 is used to measure smaller volumes while m^3 is used to measure larger volumes.

15. Graphs

➻ Children learn to read bar graphs presenting data in large numbers.

➻ Besides learning to read and draw line graphs, children should be encouraged to make predictions following the trend of a line graph, and estimate data which have not been collected.

➻ At this stage, children learn to read and complete circle graphs divided into simple fractions only.

16. Transformations and Coordinate Systems

➻ When reading coordinates on a grid, children should read the number on the horizontal axis first, and then the number on the vertical axis.

17. Money

➻ Children practise how to write the amount of money using decimals and perform mathematical operations to find the change or money spent.

18. Probability

➻ At this stage, children are required to represent the probability of an event happening as a simple fraction.

Example   The probability of getting a 2 by rolling a die is $\frac{1}{6}$.

1 Operations with Whole Numbers

1. 700   2. 570   3. 800   4. 70000
5. 290   6. 90   7. 200   8. 620
9. 100   10. 300   11. 1000   12. 40
13. 6580   14. 111   15. 6753   16. 8229
17. 85   18. 2512   19. 73

20.
```
    6 5
5 ) 3 2 5
    3 0
    2 5
    2 5
```
21.
```
    2 9 1
3 ) 8 7 3
    6
    2 7
    2 7
      3
      3
```
22.
```
    9 2
8 ) 7 3 6
    7 2
    1 6
    1 6
```

23. 4833   24. 5124   25. 1065
26. 7002 + 499 = 7501   27. 984 - 578 = 406

28.

A 2	1	0		
B 5	2		C 3	0
	D 2	0	7	0
E 4		F 7	5	0
6		6		

29. 2   30. 0   31. 1   32. 0
33. 4   34. 2   35. 9 ; 9
36. 11 - 7 = 4 ; 4
37. 12 + 12 + 2 + 2 = 28 ; Its perimeter is 28 m.
38. 66 x 60 = 3960 ; It beats 3960 times in an hour.
39. 240 ÷ 12 = 20 ; 20 x 2 = 40 ; He earns $40 per day.

Just for Fun
1a. 110 , 121 , 132   b. 108 , 120 , 132
2. 5790 ; 4563

2 Introducing Decimals

1. $\frac{52}{100}$ 2. 0.05   3. 0.3   4. $\frac{9}{100}$
5. 7.2   6. $4\frac{1}{10}$
7.

```
O  D   C     A B              E    1
```
8. 0.01 , 0.02 , 0.1 , 0.15 , 0.2   9. 1.05 , 1.4 , 1.45 , 1.50 , 1.54
10. 5.88 , 5.80 , 5.08 , 0.58 , 0.55 , 0.50
11. 3.2 , 2.93 , 2.9 , 2.39 , 2.3 , 2.09
12. 0.05   13. 0.10   14. 0.75   15. 0.40
16. 3.16   17. 3.7   18. T   19. F
20. T   21. T   22. F   23. F
24. 7.02   25. 3.57   26. 0.16   27. 2.35
28. 0.05   29. 0.25   30. 0.7   31. 1.15
32. 1.75   33. 2   34. tenths ; 0.5
35. hundredths ; 0.07   36. tens ; 20
37. ones ; 3   38. hundredths ; 0.06
39. hundreds ; 100   40. 5.7
41. 0.9   42. 2.0   43. 12.3   44. 5.94
45. 2.70   46. 3.10   47. 6.01   48. <
49. <   50. >   51. >
52a. 3 hours 58.5 minutes   b. Yes
53. She spent $64.
54. (Suggested answers)
a. 8 (10¢)
b. 1 (25¢) ; 4 (10¢) ; 3 (5¢)
55. One hundred ninety-five dollars and fifty-five cents.

Just for Fun
▨ = 3 or 1   ♠ = 1 or 3
◆ = 7   ♥ = 8

3 Adding Decimals

1. 1.5   2. 10.6   3. 46.8   4. 65.0
5. 22.9   6. 13.7   7. 58.21   8. 34.23
9. 30.91   10. 107.14   11. 8.83   12. 108.10
13. 6.40   14. 326.00   15. 158.01   16. 26.23
17. 12.8   18. 6.68   19. 7.63   20. 8.23
21. 14.63   22. 7.93   23. 52.57   24. 29.15
25. 162.13   26. 811.82   27. 167.45   28. 370.42
29. 16.18   30. 115.9   31. 30.65   32. 9.09
33. 21.83   34. 21.14   35. 980
36. 20 + 5 + 0.8 + 0.07   37. 10 + 2 + 0.9 + 0.03
38. 570.8   39. 108.64   40. $10.27   41. $11.17
42. $11.32   43. $11.14   44. $60.07   45. $71.44
46. $69.83   47. $11.17 , $11.32 , $60.07 , $71.44
48. $154.00   49. $154.00   50. 18.7   51. 24.6
52. 23.3   53. 17.4   54. + ; +
55. 5.50 + 5.50 + 3.75 + 1.2 + 1.2 = 17.15 ; $17.15
56. 6.75 + 5.9 + 6.5 + 5 = 24.15 ;
She gets $24.15 over the 4 week period.
57. 25.2 + 22.1 + 24.8 + 28.2 = 100.3 ;
He cycled 100.3 km during the week.

Just for Fun
5 ; 7 ; 5

4 Subtracting Decimals

1. 0.5   2. 56.5   3. 6.3   4. 1.2
5. 28.4   6. 33.8   7. 5.04   8. 0.69
9. 3.06   10. 579.16   11. 23.71   12. 1.98
13. 5.03   14. 3.77   15. 8.27   16. 3.02
17. 11.38   18. 7.87   19. 1.82   20. 0.88
21. 0.22   22. 0.26   23. 0.81   24. 0
25. 0.06   26. 32.47   27. 26.4   28. 150.77
29. 50   30. 19.78   31. 199.4   32. 3
33. 1   34. 40   35. 9   36. 14
37. 14   38. 2.7   39. 1.8   40. 11.1
41. 18.4   42. 34.3   43. 12.6   44. 1.4
45. 8.0   46. 3.36   47. 2.4   48. 1.9
49. 2.61   50. 4.2   51. 1.23   52. 7
53. 0.6   54. 7.7   55. 7.38   56. 14.13
57. 9.46

58.

11.4	7.7	7.38	7.0	6.94
17.0	5.8	1.4	10.6	9.17
7.5	0.2	14.13	5.2	3.61
15.1	9.3	4.2	14.0	15.2
14.8	3.63	9.46	41.11	12.3
12.3	22.3	2.61	2.60	11.36
2.63	0.6	8.0	1.23	3.27

59. I
60. 35 - 32.85 ; 2.15 ; $2.15
61. 45.2 - 41.5 = 3.7 ; Sue is 3.7 kg heavier than her sister.
62. 0.55 - 0.19 = 0.36 ; The CN Tower is 0.36 km taller.
63. 12.13 - 11.87 = 0.26 ; Carl took 0.26 seconds longer.

Just for Fun

4	9	2
3	5	7
8	1	6

5 More Addition and Subtraction of Decimals

1. 19.5   2. 2   3. 6.99   4. 14
5. 10.5   6. 1.5   7. 0   8. 15
9. 10   10. 28   11. 0.5   12. 17.5
13. 10   14. 100   15. 15.45   16. 3.28
17. 8.8   18. 5.01   19. 4.69   20. 4.8
21. 109.25   22. 20.33   23. 243.6   24. 1003.8

25. 0.93　　26. 100.27　　27. 14.56　　28. 10.66
29. $15.44　　30. $73.10　　31. $24.80　　32. $98
33. $10.24　　34. $11.52　　35. 59¢　　36. 33¢
37. 22¢　　38. 7¢　　39. 8.1　　40. 1.67
41. 1.5　　42. 20　　43. 0.65　　44. 3.44
45. 25.00 - 4.55 - 6.99 = 13.46 ; $13.46
46. 35.00 - 5.95 - 17.45 = 11.60 ; She has $11.60 left.
47. 6.50 + 19.95 + 7.50 - 2.00 = 31.95 ; Each of them spent $31.95.
48. 17.5 + 17.5 + 17.5 = 52.50 ; 20.95 + 20.95 + 6.30 = 48.20 ;
    They have enough money.

Just for Fun

1¢ + 2¢ + 4¢ + 8¢ + 16¢ + 32¢ + 64¢ = 127¢ ($1.27)

6 Multiplying Decimals by Whole Numbers

1. 1　　2. 32　　3. 0.7　　4. 0.08
5. 12　　6. 9.9　　7. 24.06　　8. 540
9. 91.5　　10. 0.1　　11. 10　　12. 93
13. 200.8　　14. 8　　15. 6.2　　16. 1
17. 248　　18. 1　　19. 14.1　　20. 10.76
21. 54.5　　22. 45.29　　23. 44.40　　24. 65.7
25. 34.3　　26. 97.6　　27. 28.60　　28. 59.34
29. 10.8　　30. 3.92　　31. 33.81　　32. 1.62
33. 29.25　　34. 9.66　　35. 23.2　　36. 506.1
37. 29.97　　38. 4.56　　39. 35 ; 36.4
40. 8 ; 7.4　　41. 50 ; 49.05　　42. 48 ; 49.38
43. 12 ; 11.25　　44. 3.2 ; 2.88　　45. 1.8 ; 1.53
46. 32 ; 33.76　　47. 13.86　　48. ✓　　49. 3.09
50. 100　　51. 3　　52. 10　　53. 100
54. 159　　55. 30.9　　56. 23.99 x 3 ; 71.97 ; $71.97
57. 89.50 x 4 = 358 ; The total cost is $358.
58. 2.3 x 5 = 11.5 ; He walks 11.5 km in a 5-day week.
59. 3.2 x 8 = 25.6 ; They occupy 25.6 cm.
60. 12.95 x 3 = 38.85 ; 39.99 x 2 = 79.98 ; 38.85 + 79.98 = 118.83 ;
    She pays $119 altogether.

Just for Fun

444 + 44 + 4 + 4 + 4 = 500

7 Dividing Decimals by Whole Numbers

1. 0.98　　2. 0.032　　3. 0.75　　4. 0.0092
5. 0.328　　6. 0.0005　　7. 0.008　　8. 1.5493
9. 3.1645　　10. 17.6　　11. 0.12　　12. 2.04
13. 0.52

14.
```
       1 . 1 5
   7 ) 8 . 0 5
       7
       1 0
         7
         3 5
         3 5
```
15.
```
       7 . 4
   9 ) 6 6 . 6
       6 3
         3 6
         3 6
```
16.
```
      1 0 . 5
   7 ) 7 3 . 5
       7
         3 5
         3 5
```
17.
```
       1 . 4 2
   6 ) 8 . 5 2
       6
       2 5
       2 4
         1 2
         1 2
```
18.
```
       0 . 0 6
   4 ) 0 . 2 4
         2 4
```
19.
```
      2 0 . 1
   8 ) 1 6 0 . 8
       1 6
           8
           8
```
20.
```
       4 . 0 3
   3 ) 1 2 . 0 9
       1 2
           9
           9
```
21.
```
      1 0 . 5 3
   5 ) 5 2 . 6 5
       5
         2 6
         2 5
           1 5
           1 5
```
22.
```
       4 . 5 5
   8 ) 3 6 . 4
       3 2
         4 4
         4 0
           4 0
           4 0
```

23.
```
      1 7 . 6
   4 ) 7 0 . 4
       4
       3 0
       2 8
         2 4
         2 4
```
24.
```
       2 . 0 8
   5 ) 1 0 . 4
       1 0
         4 0
         4 0
```
25.
```
       2 . 1 5
   9 ) 1 9 . 3 5
       1 8
         1 3
           9
         4 5
         4 5
```
26.
```
       2 . 3
   4 ) 9 . 2
       8
       1 2
       1 2
```
27.
```
       0 . 1 9
   3 ) 0 . 5 7
         3
         2 7
         2 7
```
28.
```
       2 . 5 5
   2 ) 5 . 1
       4
       1 1
       1 0
         1 0
         1 0
```
29.
```
       5 . 1 2
   7 ) 3 5 . 8 4
       3 5
           8
           7
         1 4
         1 4
```
30.
```
      1 5 2 . 1
   5 ) 7 6 0 . 5
       5
       2 6
       2 5
         1 0
         1 0
           5
           5
```
31.
```
       7 . 0 1
   5 ) 3 5 . 0 5
       3 5
           5
           5
```
32.
```
       1 . 3
   8 ) 1 0 . 4
       8
       2 4
       2 4
```
33.
```
      5 4 . 3
   7 ) 3 8 0 . 1
       3 5
         3 0
         2 8
           2 1
           2 1
```
34.
```
     1 2 5 . 8 5
   4 ) 5 0 3 . 4
       4
       1 0
         8
         2 3
         2 0
           3 . 4
           3 . 2
             2 0
             2 0
```
35.
```
       0 . 0 9
   5 ) 0 . 4 5
         4 5
```
36.
```
       6 . 5 3
   9 ) 5 8 . 7 7
       5 4
         4 7
         4 5
           2 7
           2 7
```
37.
```
      8 3 . 7 3
   6 ) 5 0 2 . 3 8
       4 8
         2 2
         1 8
           4 3
           4 2
             1 8
             1 8
```

38. LITTLE STARS　　39. 32.5 ÷ 10 ; 3.25 ; 3.25 kg
40. 7350 ÷ 100 = 73.5 ; He travelled 73.5 km each hour.
41. 36.4 ÷ 8 = 4.55 ; Each part is 4.55 m.
42. 394 ÷ 8 ; $49.25 ; Each student pays $49.25.
43. 13.5 ÷ 3 = 4.5 ; The length of each side is 4.5 cm.

Just for Fun

21 ; 34 ; 55

8 More Multiplying and Dividing of Decimals

1. 73.4　　2. 0.923　　3. 1.234　　4. 1.21
5. 12.3　　6. 120　　7. 0.03　　8. 10.1
9. 3.429　　10. 34 290　　11. 125　　12. 0.002
13. 4　　14. 11.8　　15. 4　　16. 0.0125
17. 0.2　　18. 635

19.
```
      2 3 . 6
   4 ) 9 4 . 4
       8
       1 4
       1 2
         2 4
         2 4
```
20.
```
       1 . 0 4
   7 ) 7 . 2 8
       7
         2 8
         2 8
```
21.
```
      1 5 . 0 3
   3 ) 4 5 . 0 9
       3
       1 5
       1 5
           9
           9
```
22.
```
       3 . 9 2
   x       4
     1 5 . 6 8
```
23.
```
      1 0 . 3
   x       7
     7 2 . 1
```
24.
```
       5 . 9 1
   x       6
     3 5 . 4 6
```

25.
$$1.32$$
$6\,)\,\overline{7.92}$
6
19
18
12
12

26.
$$1.9$$
$9\,)\,\overline{17.1}$
9
81
81

27.
$$1.24$$
$5\,)\,\overline{6.2}$
5
12
10
20
20

28.
$$0.47 \times 8 = 3.76$$

29.
$$18.2 \times 9 = 163.8$$

30.
$$36.7 \times 2 = 73.4$$

31. 10 32. 7 33. 0.17 34. 2.6
35. 27.72 36. 25.6 37. 89 38. 190
(39, 44 : products < 15)
40. 15.8 41. 15.2 42. 17.1 43. 15.5
(46, 47 : quotients > 2)

45.

$$1.4$$
$9\,)\,\overline{12.6}$
9
36
36

48.
$$1.9$$
$3\,)\,\overline{5.7}$
3
27
27

49.
$$1.8$$
$6\,)\,\overline{10.8}$
6
48
48

50.
$$1.9$$
$7\,)\,\overline{13.3}$
7
63
63

51. 100 52. 10 53. 3.42 54. 2
55. 6.2 56. 9.1 57. 100 58. 10
59. 58.2 ÷ 3 = 19.4 ; $19.40
60. 19.95 x 3 = 59.85 ; 12.45 x 2 = 24.90 ;1.25 x 10 = 12.50 ;
59.85 + 24.90 + 12.50 = 97.25 ; She pays $97.25 altogether.
61. 12.99 x 2 = 25.98 ; 1.29 x 2 = 2.58 ; 1.49 x 2 = 2.98 ;
25.98 + 2.58 + 2.98 = 31.54 ; 31.54 ÷ 5 = 6.308 ;
They must pay $6.31 each.
62. 29.40 ÷ 3 = 9.80 ; 39.50 ÷ 5 = 7.90 ;
A 5-kg bag for $39.50 is the better buy.

Just for Fun
0.5

Midway Review
1. 18.95 2. 11.76 3. 67.2 4. 1.05
5. 16.26 6. 0.62 7. 209.04 8. 3.2
9. 954.1 10. 14.59 11. 968.69 12. 149.5
13. 54.19 14. 95.31 15. 520 ; 5.2 16. 7 ; 0.07
17. 1.2 ; 0.012 18. 7.5 ; 0.75 19. 0.3 ; 0.03 20. 8 ; 80
21. 150 ; 1500 22. D 23. C 24. C
25. C 26. B 27. D 28. B
29. C 30. A 31. B 32. B
33. C 34. C 35. 9.0 + 3.2 + 3.2 = 15.4 ; 15.4
36. 20 x 15.4 = 308 ; The total cost is $308.
37. 9 + 3.2 + 9 + 3.2 = 24.4 ; The perimeter is 24.4 m.
38. 9 x 3.2 = 28.8 ; The area is 28.8 m².
39a. New length = 9.0 x 2 = 18.0 ; New width = 3.2 x 2 = 6.4 ;
18.0 + 18.0 + 6.4 + 6.4 = 48.8 = 24.4 x 2 ;
The perimeter is doubled as well.
b. 9 x 2 x 3.2 x 2 = 9 x 3.2 x 2 x 2 = 28.8 x 4 ;
The area is 4 times larger than before.

9 Introducing Fractions
1. $\frac{1}{6}$ 2. $\frac{1}{3}$ 3. $\frac{2}{3}$ 4. $\frac{5}{6}$
5. $\frac{1}{6}$ 6. $\frac{4}{6} = \frac{2}{3}$ 7. $\frac{5}{8}$ 8. $\frac{6}{16} = \frac{3}{8}$
9. $\frac{3}{8}$ 10. $\frac{1}{4}$
11. [image] 12. [image] 13. [image]

14. [image] 15. [image] 16. [image]
17. number line with $\frac{1}{20}$, $\frac{1}{10}$, $\frac{2}{5}$, $\frac{1}{2}$, $\frac{4}{5}$, $\frac{9}{10}$ (0 to 1)
18. $\frac{5}{9}$ 19. $\frac{5}{8}$ 20. $\frac{8}{11}$
21. [image] 22. [image] 23. [image]
24. 5 25. 12 26. 6 27. 2
28. 2 29. 4 30. $\frac{3}{4}$ 31. $\frac{1}{3}$
32. $\frac{1}{2}$ 33. $\frac{2}{3}$ 34. $\frac{3}{8}$ 35. $\frac{4}{5}$
36. (Suggested answers) $\frac{1}{8}$; $\frac{1}{4}$; $\frac{1}{3}$
37a. $\frac{35}{100} = \frac{7}{20}$ b. $\frac{60}{100} = \frac{3}{5}$ 38. $\frac{3}{24} = \frac{1}{8}$ 39. $\frac{2}{8} = \frac{1}{4}$
40. $\frac{50}{250} = \frac{1}{5}$ 41. $\frac{15}{45} = \frac{1}{3}$ 42. $\frac{21}{26}$ 43. $\frac{18}{30} = \frac{3}{5}$
44. $\frac{50}{120} = \frac{5}{12}$ 45. $\frac{12}{16} = \frac{3}{4}$ 46a. $\frac{87}{100}$ b. $\frac{13}{100}$

Just for Fun
1. $\frac{1}{16}$; $\frac{1}{32}$; $\frac{1}{64}$ 2. No

10 Equivalent Fractions and Ordering of Fractions
1. 25 2. 25 3. 15 4. 75
5. 2 6. 77 7. $\frac{5}{6}$ 8. $\frac{1}{2}$
9. $\frac{2}{11}$ 10. $\frac{3}{7}$ 11. $\frac{1}{4}$ 12. $\frac{2}{3}$
13. $\frac{3}{4}$ 14. $\frac{1}{3}$ 15. $\frac{1}{6}$ 16. $\frac{2}{3}$
17. $\frac{8}{21}$ 18. $\frac{11}{15}$ 19. $\frac{1}{10} < \frac{1}{5} < \frac{1}{2} < \frac{3}{5} < \frac{7}{10} < \frac{4}{5}$
20. $\frac{1}{4} < \frac{1}{3} < \frac{2}{4} < \frac{2}{3} < \frac{3}{4}$ 21. T 22. F
23. T 24. F 25. 3 ; 12
26. 5 ; 2 27. 2 ; 4 28. 55 ; 4
29. - 32. (Suggested answers) 29. $\frac{2}{16}$; $\frac{3}{24}$; $\frac{4}{32}$
30. $\frac{4}{6}$; $\frac{6}{9}$; $\frac{8}{12}$ 31. $\frac{2}{8}$; $\frac{3}{12}$; $\frac{4}{16}$ 32. $\frac{10}{14}$; $\frac{15}{21}$; $\frac{20}{28}$
33. $\frac{7}{8} > \frac{3}{4} > \frac{5}{8} > \frac{1}{2} > \frac{3}{8} > \frac{1}{4} > \frac{3}{16}$
34. $\frac{5}{6} > \frac{13}{18} > \frac{2}{3} > \frac{1}{2} > \frac{7}{18} > \frac{1}{3} > \frac{1}{6}$
35. < 36. = 37. > 38. <
39. < 40. > 41. $\frac{3}{4}$ 42. $\frac{3}{5}$
43. $\frac{5}{6}$ 44. $\frac{4}{9}$ 45. $\frac{7}{9}$ 46. $\frac{6}{7}$
47. $\frac{200}{450}$; $\frac{75}{125}$; $\frac{15}{20}$; $\frac{14}{18}$; $\frac{45}{54}$; $\frac{150}{175}$
48. 14 ; 14 49. 8 ; 8 50. 88 ; 88
51. Nadine : $\frac{9}{12} = \frac{27}{36}$; Danielle : $\frac{14}{18} = \frac{28}{36}$; Danielle
52a. $\frac{682}{5421}$; $\frac{1583}{8474}$ b. Increasing
c. $\frac{512}{5421}$; $\frac{542}{8474}$ d. Decreasing

Just for Fun
$\frac{1}{16}$; $\frac{1}{25}$; $\frac{1}{36}$

11 Adding Fractions with the Same Denominator

1. 1
2. 1
3. $\frac{2}{3}$
4. $\frac{2}{5}$
5. $\frac{5}{9}$
6. $\frac{4}{7}$
7. $\frac{4}{5}$
8. 1
9. 1
10. $\frac{8}{9}$
11. $\frac{11}{13}$
12. $\frac{8}{11}$
13. $\frac{7}{8}$
14. $\frac{13}{20}$
15. $\frac{9}{17}$
16. $\frac{9}{19}$
17. $\frac{21}{25}$
18. $\frac{10}{12} = \frac{5}{6}$
19. $\frac{17}{21}$
20. $\frac{8}{15}$
21. $\frac{6}{16} = \frac{3}{8}$
22. $\frac{2}{4} = \frac{1}{2}$
23. $\frac{12}{18} = \frac{2}{3}$
24. $\frac{22}{23}$
25. $\frac{4}{6} = \frac{2}{3}$
26. $\frac{25}{27}$
27. $\frac{13}{20}$
28. $\frac{12}{15} = \frac{4}{5}$
29. $\frac{3}{9} = \frac{1}{3}$
30. $\frac{12}{14} = \frac{6}{7}$
31. $\frac{6}{8} = \frac{3}{4}$
32. $\frac{6}{10} = \frac{3}{5}$
33. $\frac{8}{16} = \frac{1}{2}$
34. $\frac{6}{12} = \frac{1}{2}$
35. $\frac{4}{20} = \frac{1}{5}$
36. $\frac{2}{6} = \frac{1}{3}$
37. $\frac{4}{7}$
38. $\frac{3}{18} = \frac{1}{6}$
39. $\frac{6}{24} = \frac{1}{4}$
40. $\frac{8}{32} = \frac{1}{4}$
41. $\frac{7}{7} = 1$
42. $\frac{11}{11} = 1$

43. $\frac{4}{8} = \frac{1}{2}$
44. $\frac{1}{3} + \frac{2}{3} = \frac{3}{3} = 1$
45. $\frac{3}{6} + \frac{1}{6} = \frac{4}{6} = \frac{2}{3}$
46. $\frac{1}{4} + \frac{1}{4} = \frac{2}{4} = \frac{1}{2}$
47. $\frac{1}{3} + \frac{2}{3} = \frac{3}{3} = 1$
48. $\frac{1}{5} + \frac{2}{5} = \frac{3}{5}$

49. $\frac{2}{7}$
50. $\frac{1}{11}$
51. $\frac{5}{6}$
52. $\frac{7}{8}$
53. $\frac{1}{4}$
54. $\frac{1}{8}$
55. $\frac{1}{15}$
56. $\frac{1}{10}$
57. $\frac{11}{20}$
58. $\frac{5}{12}$
59. $\frac{11}{25}$
60. $\frac{2}{9}$

61. $\frac{1}{4} + \frac{1}{4} + \frac{1}{4} = \frac{3}{4}$; $\frac{3}{4}$

62a. $\frac{2}{6} + \frac{2}{6} + \frac{1}{6} = \frac{5}{6}$; They eat $\frac{5}{6}$ pizza.

 b. $\frac{5}{6} < 1$; There is some pizza left.

63a. $\frac{5}{8} + \frac{1}{8} = \frac{6}{8} = \frac{3}{4}$; She needs $\frac{3}{4}$ m altogether.

 b. $\frac{3}{4} < 1$; She will have enough ribbon.

64a. $\frac{3}{10} + \frac{1}{10} = \frac{4}{10} = \frac{2}{5}$; She has spent $\frac{2}{5}$ of her allowance.

 b. $\frac{2}{5} + \frac{3}{5} = 1$; She has $\frac{3}{5}$ of her allowance left.

Just for Fun

$\frac{8}{15}$	$\frac{1}{15}$	$\frac{6}{15}$
$\frac{3}{15}$	$\frac{5}{15}$	$\frac{7}{15}$
$\frac{4}{15}$	$\frac{9}{15}$	$\frac{2}{15}$

12 Improper Fractions and Mixed Numbers

1. $2\frac{1}{7}$
2. $\frac{27}{8}$
3. $3\frac{2}{3}$
4. $\frac{45}{4}$
5. $1\frac{2}{5}$
6. $\frac{4}{7}$; $\frac{5}{20}$; $\frac{7}{9}$; $\frac{11}{12}$
7. $\frac{9}{9}$; $\frac{25}{20}$; $\frac{15}{8}$; $\frac{16}{7}$
8. $3\frac{3}{10}$; $3\frac{1}{2}$; $1\frac{5}{20}$; $1\frac{2}{5}$

9. $2\frac{2}{3}$; $\frac{8}{3}$
10. $1\frac{1}{6}$; $\frac{7}{6}$

11.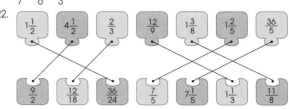

12. $\frac{8}{6} = \frac{4}{3}$
13. $\frac{13}{6}$
14. $\frac{15}{6} = \frac{5}{2}$
15. $\frac{16}{6} = \frac{8}{3}$
16. $\frac{20}{6}$; $\frac{10}{3}$
17. $\frac{23}{6}$
18. $\frac{15}{4} > \frac{7}{2} > \frac{7}{3} > \frac{9}{4} > \frac{5}{3}$
19. $\frac{17}{2} > \frac{17}{3} > \frac{17}{4} > \frac{17}{5} > \frac{17}{6}$
20. $\frac{23}{6}$; $\frac{19}{6}$; $\frac{7}{2}$
21. $\frac{60}{7}$; $\frac{49}{6}$; $\frac{25}{3}$

22.
    $1\frac{1}{2}$ $4\frac{1}{2}$ $\frac{2}{3}$ $\frac{12}{9}$ $1\frac{3}{8}$ $1\frac{2}{5}$ $\frac{36}{5}$
    $\frac{9}{2}$ $\frac{12}{18}$ $\frac{36}{24}$ $\frac{7}{5}$ $7\frac{1}{5}$ $1\frac{1}{3}$ $\frac{11}{8}$

23a. $2\frac{1}{2}$
 b. $\frac{5}{2}$
24. 9

25. $1\frac{3}{5}$
26. 9

27. False. Since $\frac{15}{4} = 3\frac{3}{4}$, $\frac{13}{3} = 4\frac{1}{3}$; So $\frac{13}{3} > \frac{15}{4}$

Just for Fun

56

13 Adding Improper Fractions and Mixed Numbers

1. 2
2. 3
3. 5
4. 3
5. 7
6. 3
7. 6
8. 7
9. 3
10. 2
11. 2
12. 3
13. 4
14. 2
15. $2\frac{1}{4}$
16. $6\frac{3}{5}$
17. $3\frac{2}{5}$
18. $5\frac{1}{2}$
19. $3\frac{2}{5}$
20. $3\frac{1}{2}$
21. $1\frac{1}{2}$
22. $4\frac{1}{3}$
23. $1\frac{3}{5}$
24. $2\frac{7}{8}$
25. $3\frac{1}{4}$
26. 2
27. $4\frac{3}{4}$
28. $2\frac{1}{3}$
29. $9\frac{2}{5}$
30. 6
31. $\frac{3}{4}$
32. $\frac{5}{8}$
33. $1\frac{4}{5}$
34. $1\frac{1}{2}$
35. $\frac{1}{2}$
36. $\frac{3}{5}$
37. $\frac{2}{3}$
38. $\frac{7}{6}$
39. $3\frac{1}{5}$
40. $\frac{3}{4}$
41. T
42. T
43. F
44. T
45. T
46. F
47. T
48. F
50, 51, 55 : sum < 3
49. $3\frac{1}{3}$
52. $3\frac{1}{2}$
53. $3\frac{1}{2}$
54. $3\frac{1}{5}$
56. $3\frac{5}{9}$

57. $1\frac{1}{4} + 2\frac{1}{4} + 1\frac{3}{4} = 5\frac{1}{4}$; They eat $5\frac{1}{4}$ cans of food per week.

58. $45\frac{3}{8} + 2\frac{1}{8} = 47\frac{1}{2}$; The new selling price is $47\frac{1}{2}$ ¢.

59a. $3\frac{1}{8} + 4\frac{3}{4} = 7\frac{7}{8}$; She must buy $7\frac{7}{8}$ m. b. Yes.

60. $1\frac{1}{4} + 1\frac{1}{4} + \frac{3}{4} + 1\frac{1}{4} + 2 + 1\frac{3}{4} + 2\frac{3}{4} = 11$;
She watched TV for 11 hours during the week.

Just for Fun
16

14 Subtracting Fractions with the Same Denominator

1. $\frac{2}{7}$ 2. $\frac{1}{12}$ 3. $\frac{7}{9}$ 4. $\frac{2}{11}$
5. $\frac{2}{7}$ 6. $\frac{1}{10}$ 7. $\frac{3}{17}$ 8. 0
9. $\frac{1}{15}$ 10. $\frac{1}{4}$ 11. $\frac{2}{13}$ 12. $\frac{2}{7}$
13.   14.   15.   16.
17. $\frac{1}{2}$ 18. $\frac{1}{2}$ 19. $\frac{1}{3}$ 20. $\frac{1}{4}$
21. $\frac{2}{3}$ 22. $\frac{3}{4}$ 23. $\frac{1}{2}$ 24. $\frac{4}{7}$
25. $\frac{2}{3}$ 26. $\frac{1}{4}$ 27. $\frac{3}{4}$ 28. $\frac{3}{5}$
29. $\frac{1}{3}$ 30. $\frac{2}{5}$ 31. $\frac{1}{2}$ 32. $\frac{1}{4}$
33. $\frac{3}{4}$ 34. $\frac{1}{7}$ 35. $\frac{4}{7}$ 36. $\frac{2}{4}$
37. $\frac{1}{4}$ 38. $\frac{8}{9}$ 39. $\frac{1}{5}$ 40. $\frac{4}{9}$
41. $\frac{1}{6}$ 42. $\frac{3}{4}$ 43. $\frac{6}{9}$ 44. $\frac{2}{9}$
45. $\frac{2}{3}$ 46. $\frac{2}{5}$ 47. $\frac{3}{10}$ 48. $\frac{5}{11}$
49. $\frac{2}{5}$ 50. $\frac{1}{8}$ 51. $\frac{2}{7}$
52. $\frac{4+7-5}{12}$; $\frac{6}{12} = \frac{1}{2}$ 53. $\frac{11-7+1}{18}$; $\frac{5}{18}$
54. $\frac{5}{8} - \frac{3}{8} = \frac{2}{8} = \frac{1}{4}$; $\frac{1}{4}$
55. $\frac{3}{4} - \frac{1}{4} = \frac{1}{2}$; Ben takes $\frac{1}{2}$ hour longer.
56. $\frac{5}{6} - \frac{1}{6} = \frac{4}{6} = \frac{2}{3}$; Dave takes $\frac{2}{3}$ hour less.
57.a. $\frac{10}{40} = \frac{1}{4}$; She has done $\frac{1}{4}$ of the job.
b. $\frac{1}{4} + \frac{3}{4} = \frac{4}{4} = 1$; $\frac{3}{4}$ of the job still remains.
58a. $\frac{2}{10} = \frac{1}{5}$; $\frac{4}{10} = \frac{2}{5}$; $\frac{1}{5}$ are violet, $\frac{2}{5}$ are red.
b. $\frac{2}{5} + \frac{1}{5} + \frac{2}{5} = 1$; $\frac{2}{5}$ are neither red nor violet.

Just for Fun
8 ; 7 , 8 ; 8 , 3 , 8

15 Subtracting Improper Fractions and Mixed Numbers

1. $2\frac{1}{7}$ 2. $2\frac{2}{5}$ 3. $\frac{7}{9}$ 4. $\frac{1}{8}$
5. $\frac{3}{4}$ 6. $\frac{3}{4}$ 7. 0 8. $\frac{2}{9}$
9. 3 10. $\frac{1}{9}$ 11. $\frac{3}{13}$ 12. 1
13. $\frac{7}{8}$ 14. $\frac{2}{3}$ 15. $\frac{4}{6} = \frac{2}{3}$ 16. 5
17. 0 18. $2\frac{1}{2}$ 19. 1 20. $1\frac{1}{2}$

21. $\frac{1}{2}$ 22. $\frac{1}{4}$ 23. 2 24. $\frac{2}{5}$
25. $\frac{1}{3}$ 26. 1 27. $1\frac{1}{4}$ 28. 0
29. 1 30. $1\frac{2}{3}$ 31. 3 32. $1\frac{1}{5}$
33. $\frac{1}{2}$ 34. $\frac{4}{5}$ 35. $\frac{1}{3}$ 36. 5
37. $1\frac{1}{2}$ 38. $\frac{3}{4}$ 39. 4 40. $\frac{5}{3} = 1\frac{2}{3}$
41. $\frac{3}{4}$ 42. $2\frac{3}{7}$ 43. $\frac{2}{5}$ 44. $3\frac{1}{2}$
45. $\frac{2}{3}$ 46. 1 47. $\frac{1}{2}$ 48. $\frac{4}{5}$
49. $3 + 4 - 2 + \frac{4+1-2}{6}$; $5\frac{1}{2}$ 50. $9 - 3 + 1 + \frac{2-1}{8}$; $7\frac{1}{8}$
51. $4 - 3 + 1 + \frac{1-3+4}{6}$; $2\frac{1}{3}$ 52. $3 + 2 - 1 + \frac{2+4-5}{7}$; $4\frac{1}{7}$
53. $3\frac{1}{4} - 2\frac{3}{4} = \frac{1}{2}$; Pat spent $\frac{1}{2}$ hour longer.
54. $8\frac{3}{8} - 6\frac{5}{8} = 1\frac{3}{4}$; He ran $1\frac{3}{4}$ km farther.
55. $3\frac{1}{5} - 2\frac{4}{5} = \frac{2}{5}$; The difference is $\frac{2}{5}$ dollar.
56. $1 - \frac{3}{8} - \frac{1}{8} = \frac{1}{2}$; The length of the third side is $\frac{1}{2}$ m.
57. $15\frac{1}{4} - 1\frac{1}{2} - 1\frac{1}{2} = 12\frac{1}{4}$; $10\frac{1}{2} - 1\frac{1}{2} - 1\frac{1}{2} = 7\frac{1}{2}$;
The dimensions of the unframed part of the picture are $12\frac{1}{4}$ cm by $7\frac{1}{2}$ cm.

Just for Fun
$\frac{1}{4}$

16 Relating Decimals and Fractions

1. 0.1 2. 0.7 3. 0.03 4. 0.49
5. 0.09 6. 0.73 7. $\frac{3}{10}$ 8. $\frac{7}{10}$
9. $\frac{9}{10}$ 10. $\frac{1}{100}$ 11. $\frac{9}{100}$ 12. $\frac{7}{100}$
13. $\frac{31}{100}$ 14. $\frac{19}{100}$ 15. $\frac{47}{100}$ 16. $\frac{3}{100}$
17. 0.5 18. 0.2 19. 0.75 20. 0.6
21. 0.125 22. 0.625 23. 0.375 24. 0.8
25. 1.63 26. 3.57 27. 12.8 28. 2.38
29. 3.83 30. 5.44 31. 1.67 32. 2.6
33. 4.25 34. 10.4 35. 8.86 36. 6.7
37. $\frac{13}{20}$ 38. $\frac{75}{100}$; $\frac{3}{4}$ 39. $\frac{5}{100}$; $\frac{1}{20}$ 40. $\frac{12}{100}$; $\frac{3}{25}$
41. $\frac{45}{100}$; $\frac{9}{20}$ 42. $\frac{36}{100}$; $\frac{9}{25}$ 43. $1\frac{45}{100}$; $1\frac{9}{20}$ 44. $6\frac{55}{100}$; $6\frac{11}{20}$
45. $2\frac{8}{10}$; $2\frac{4}{5}$ 46. $2\frac{25}{100}$; $2\frac{1}{4}$ 47. 25 48. 75
49. 40 50. 60 51. 70 52. 90
53. 0.65 54. 0.9 55. $1\frac{2}{5}$ 56. $\frac{2}{3}$
57. 4.26 58. 0.57 59. 3.69 60. 8.38
61. $6\frac{3}{8}$ 62. 1.54 ; $1\frac{7}{8}$; $1\frac{8}{9}$
63. $2\frac{4}{7}$; $2\frac{3}{5}$; 2.68 64. $5\frac{4}{5}$; 5.83 ; $5\frac{9}{10}$
65. 0.125 ; 0.25 ; 0.75 ; 0.375 ; 0.875 ; 0.2 ; 0.7
66. $\frac{1}{8}$; $\frac{1}{5}$; $\frac{1}{4}$; $\frac{3}{8}$; $\frac{7}{10}$; $\frac{3}{4}$; $\frac{7}{8}$ 67. $\frac{6}{25}$
68a. $\frac{5}{8}$ b. 0.625 69a. 0.4 b. 30¢

Just for Fun
$\frac{3}{9}$; $\frac{3}{8}$; 0.56 ; $\frac{5}{6}$; $\frac{8}{9}$

Final Review

1. B   2. C   3. D   4. A

5. B   6. D   7. A   8. C

9. B   10. $\frac{3}{4}$; 0.75   11. $1\frac{2}{5}$; 1.4   12. $\frac{1}{5}$; 0.2

13. $\frac{3}{20}$; $\frac{1}{4}$; $\frac{1}{2}$; $\frac{3}{5}$; $\frac{4}{5}$ 14. 0.15 ; 0.25 ; 0.5 ; 0.6 ; 0.8

15. $3\frac{3}{4}$ 16. $1\frac{1}{2}$ 17. $3\frac{2}{5}$ 18. $2\frac{1}{9}$

19. $1\frac{1}{3}$ 20. $3\frac{1}{2}$ 21. $4\frac{2}{3}$ 22. $4\frac{1}{6}$

23. $4\frac{3}{8}$ 24. $1\frac{3}{4}$ 25. $2\frac{3}{5}$ 26. $4\frac{4}{5}$

27.

28. 0   29. 2   30. 4   31. $1\frac{1}{4}$

32. $4\frac{2}{5}$ 33. 9   34. $\frac{1}{2}$ 35. $\frac{3}{5}$

36. $7.60 - $5.40 = $2.20

37a. $6.85 x 5 ; $34.25   b. $7.60 x 5 ; $38

38. $38 - $34.25 ; $3.75

39a. $6\frac{9}{10}$ b. $\frac{69}{10}$ 40. $5.90 + $0.75 ; $6.65

41a. 1969 , $21\frac{3}{10}$; 1994 , $29\frac{1}{5}$

b. 29.2 - 21.3 = 7.9 or $7\frac{9}{10}$; The increase was 7.9 or $7\frac{9}{10}$ million.

c. 29.2 + 7.9 = 37.1 ;

The population of Canada in 2019 will be 37.1 million.

42a. $\frac{35}{100} = \frac{7}{20} = 0.35$; He has run $\frac{7}{20}$ or 0.35 of his monthly goal.

b. 100 - 35 = 65 ; He still has to run 65 km.

c. $1 - \frac{7}{20} = \frac{13}{20} = 0.65$;

He still has to run $\frac{13}{20}$ or 0.65 of the total distance.

d. $\frac{65 - 35}{100} = \frac{30}{100} = \frac{3}{10}$;

The difference between the fractions of the total distance run in the first week and during the rest of the month is $\frac{3}{10}$.

43a. $2\frac{1}{4} + 3\frac{3}{4} = 6$; They drink 6 cups of tea.

b. $3\frac{3}{4} - 2\frac{1}{4} = 1\frac{1}{2}$; The difference is $1\frac{1}{2}$ cups.

c. $2\frac{1}{4} = 2.25$; 2.25 x 7 = 15.75 ;

Mr King will drink 15.75 cups per week.

d. $3\frac{3}{4} = 3.75$; 3.75 x 7 = 26.25 ;

Mrs King will drink 26.25 cups per week.

44a. $8\frac{1}{5} + 9\frac{3}{5} + 7\frac{1}{5} = 25$; They watch TV for 25 hours in a week.

b. $9\frac{3}{5} - 8\frac{1}{5} = 1\frac{2}{5}$; David watches TV for $1\frac{2}{5}$ hours longer than Peter.

c. $9\frac{3}{5} - 7\frac{1}{5} = 2\frac{2}{5}$; David watches TV for $2\frac{2}{5}$ hours longer than Ruth.

d. $7\frac{1}{5} - 1\frac{3}{5} = 5\frac{3}{5}$; She can watch TV for $5\frac{3}{5}$ hours now.

1 Large Numbers

1. 282 000
2. 164 300
3. 1 343 200
4. 275 300
5. 5 000 000
6. 600 000
7. 20 000 000
8. 70 000

	hundred	thousand	ten thousand
9.	123 200	123 000	120 000
10.	174 200	174 000	170 000
11.	246 500	247 000	250 000
12.	477 100	477 000	480 000
13.	1 205 100	1 205 000	1 210 000
14.	985 800	986 000	990 000

Activity

A, D

2 Prime and Composite Numbers

1. 8; composite
2. 7; prime
3. 5; prime
4. 4; composite
5. composite
6. prime
7. composite
8. composite
9. prime
10. prime

11 – 13.

orange   red   yellow

14. 25; prime
15. composite
16. True
17. True
18. False

Activity

1. 7 + 13 (or 17 + 3)
2. 5 + 19 (or 17 + 7;13 + 11)
3. 13 + 19 (or 29 + 3)
4. 31 + 67 (or 19 + 79; 37 + 61)

3 Fractions

1. $\dfrac{4 \times 2}{1 \times 3}$

   $\dfrac{8}{3} = 2\dfrac{2}{3}$

   $2\dfrac{2}{3}$

2. $\dfrac{3}{2}$

   $\dfrac{1 \times 3}{2 \times 2} = \dfrac{3}{4}$

   $\dfrac{3}{4}$

3. $1\dfrac{1}{5}$
4. $1\dfrac{2}{7}$
5. $\dfrac{1}{6}$
6. $\dfrac{4}{27}$
7. $8\dfrac{1}{2}$
8. $\dfrac{1}{2}$
9. $\dfrac{1}{6}$
10. $1\dfrac{3}{7}$
11. 16
12. $\dfrac{1}{2}$
13. $\dfrac{1}{15}$
14. $\dfrac{2}{7}$
15. $\dfrac{1}{18}$
16. $\dfrac{1}{12}$
17. $\dfrac{2}{3}$
18. $\dfrac{2}{5}$
19. 4
20. 6
21. 12
22. 20
23. $7\dfrac{1}{2}$
24. $4\dfrac{1}{2}$
25. 10
26. $\dfrac{6}{7}$
27. 6
28. $3\dfrac{1}{2}$
29. $\dfrac{5}{6}$

Activity

1. +
2. x
3. ÷
4. –

4 Distributive Property of Multiplication

1. 10 + 6
   16
2. 2 x 8
   16
3. Yes

4. 7 x 3 + 7 x 5
   21 + 35
   56
5. 4 x 18 – 4 x 7
   72 – 28
   44

6. 5 x (12 – 7)
   5 x 5
   25

7. 5 x (70 + 3)
   5 x 70 + 5 x 3
   350 + 15
   365
8. 6 x (100 – 2)
   6 x 100 – 6 x 2
   600 – 12
   588

9. 714   10. 441   11. 558
12. 332   13. 558   14. 395

Activity

1. $10 \times (5 + \frac{1}{5})$

   $10 \times 5 + 10 \times \frac{1}{5}$

   $50 + 2$

   52

2. $6 \times (50 + 4 + \frac{1}{5})$

   $6 \times 50 + 6 \times 4 + 6 \times \frac{1}{5}$

   $300 + 24 + \frac{6}{5}$

   $325\frac{1}{5}$

5   Simple Equations

1. $5 + y = 12$ 2. $n - 6 = 8$
3. $3 \times m = 12$ 4. $k \div 5 = 2$

5. $50 + 10$
   $60 - 20$
   40 Check: $40 + 20 = 60$
   40

6. $50 + 20$
   $70 \div 2$
   35 Check: $35 \times 2 = 70$
   35

7. $x + 3 - 3 = 12 - 3$
   9
   $9 + 3 = 12$

8. $7 \times n \div 7 = 28 \div 7$
   4
   $7 \times 4 = 28$

9. $m \div 2 \times 2 = 9 \times 2$
   18
   $18 \div 2 = 9$

10. $p - 9 + 9 = 26 + 9$
    35
    $35 - 9 = 26$

11. $q \times 5 \div 5 = 35 \div 5$
    7
    $7 \times 5 = 35$

12. $n \times 2 = 10; 5$
13. $n \times 2 = 14; 7$
14. $n \times 2 = 18; 9$
15. $n \times 2 = 36; 18$
16. $m \div 6 = 4; 24$
17. $m \div 6 = 6; 36$
18. $m \div 6 = 8; 48$
19. $m \div 6 = 9; 54$
20. $m \div 3 = 5$
    $m \div 3 \times 3 = 5 \times 3$
    15
    15 Check: $15 \div 3 = 5$

21. $p - 0.5 = 0.125$
    $p - 0.5 + 0.5 = 0.125 + 0.5$
    0.625
    0.625 Check: $0.625 - 0.5 = 0.125$

Activity
A, D

6   Time

1. 30   2. $\frac{1}{3}$
3. 90   4. 1 h 35 min
5. 100   6. 1 h 45 min
7. 110   8. 2 h 15 min
9. 65   10. 1 h 25 min
11. 4 h 10 min   12. 2 h 23 min   13. 0 h 40 min
14. 09:10   15. 02:47   16. 07:00
17. $05:00 - 01:05 = 03:55$ 3:55
18. $09:15 - 07:30 = 01:45$ 1 h 45 min

Activity
1. 35 min   2. 12:50 p.m.   3. 3:45 p.m.

7   Area

	Height	Base	Area
1.	3	5	$7\frac{1}{2}$
2.	3	6	9
3.	3	3	$4\frac{1}{2}$
4.	3	3	9
5.	3	4	12
6.	2	3	6

7. 9, 7, 63   8. 10, 12, 120
9. 12.6, 5, 63   10. 8, 11.2, 89.6
11. 17, 5, 85   12. 12, 7, 42
13. 8, 6, 24   14. 3, 9, 13.5
15. 6, 2.4, 7.2   16. 6.4, 2, 6.4
17. 100, 35, 135
18. 48   19. 23
20. 48   21. 42

Activity
1. 21   2. 19

8   Directions

1. south
2. west
3. north
4. east
5. east
6. west, south
7. north-east
8. south-east
9. south-west
10. north-west
11. south-west
12. north-west

Activity

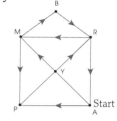

9   Graphs

1. 2000, 1000, 3000, 3000, 4000, 5000

2.

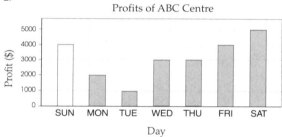

Profits of ABC Centre

3. Saturday
4. Tuesday
5. 2
6. August
7. 3
8. 40 000
9. 2

Activity

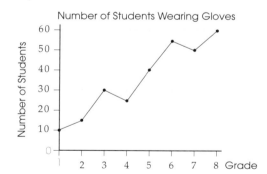

Number of Students Wearing Gloves

10   Factorization

1.

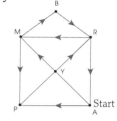

2. 199
3. prime
4. composite
5. prime
6. composite
7. composite
8. prime
9. 3 x 7, 3 x 7
10. 5 x 7, 5 x 7
11. 4
   2 x 2 x 7
   2 x 2 x 7
12. 5
   3 x 3 x 5
   3 x 3 x 5
13. 2 x 2 x 3 x 3
14. 2 x 3 x 3 x 3
15. 2 x 2 x 2 x 2 x 2 x 2
16. 2 x 2 x 2 x 3 x 3
17. 2 x 13
   3 x 13
   13
   13
18. 2 x 3 x 5
   3 x 3 x 5
   3, 5
   3 x 5 = 15
19. 2 x 2 x 7
   2 x 3 x 7
   2, 7
   2 x 7 = 14
20. 2 x 5 x 5
   3 x 5 x 5
   5, 5
   5 x 5 = 25
21. 4
22. 6
23. 20
24. 8
25. 2 x 2 x 3
   2 x 3 x 3
   2 x 2 x 3 x 3
   36
26. 3 x 5
   3 x 7
   3 x 5 x 7
   105
27. 30
28. 72
29. 48
30. 40

Activity

1. 199
2. 109

Midway Test

1. Twenty thousand six hundred eighty-one
2. Four hundred thirty-three thousand
3. 387 425, 387 245, 378 425, 378 245
4. 941 756, 941 576, 914 756, 914 576
5. 500 000   6. 1 000 000
7. n + 6 = 15   8. 3 x m = 18   9. k – 5 = 9
10. y + 2 – 2 = 21 - 2   11. m – 6 + 6 = 5 + 6
    19   11
12. 4 x n ÷ 4 = 24 ÷ 4   13. p ÷ 9 x 9 = 3 x 9
    6   27
14. 700 000, 900 000, 300 000, 200 000
15.

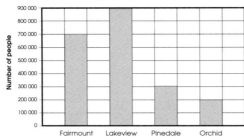

Population of Cities

16. 1500   17. August   18. 7000
19. 4500   20. 1500
21. 60   22. 77   23. 26
24. 12   25. 30   26. 38
27. $5\frac{1}{3}$ 28. $\frac{2}{7}$ 29. 14
30. 4   31. $1\frac{1}{2}$ 32. 1
33. $\frac{2}{3}$ 34. $\frac{1}{16}$ 35. $\frac{1}{2}$
36. $\frac{1}{2}$
37. 2 x 3 x 7   38. 2 x 2 x 2 x 2
    2 x 2 x 2 x 3 x 3   2 x 2 x 2 x 3
    6   8
39. 3 x 5   40. 2 x 2 x 5
    3 x 3 x 5   2 x 2 x 2 x 2 x 2
    15   4
41. 2 x 2 x 7   42. 2 x 3 x 3
    5 x 7   2 x 2 x 5
    140   180
43. 2 x 2 x 2 x 3   44. 2 x 3 x 5
    2 x 2 x 3 x 3   2 x 2 x 2 x 5
    72   120
45. north-east   46. south   47. south-west
48. Library   49. 100   50. 1 h 35 min
51. 11:10

11 Inverse Proportion

1. 12   2. 24 ÷ 3 = 8
3. 24 ÷ 4 = 6   4. 24 ÷ 6 = 4
5. 24 ÷ 8 = 3   6. 24 ÷ 12 = 2
7. 60 x 3 ÷ 6 = 30   8. 60 x 3 ÷ 9 = 20
    30   20
9. No. of groups: 6, 8, 12
   No. of people: 24, 16, 12

Activity

1. 10   2. 12   3. 15
4. 20   5. 30   6. 60

12 Decimals and Fractions

1. 16.25   2. 14.062   3. 15.2
4. 13.424   5. 17.07
6. 0.03   7. 0.005
8. 0.006   9. 10
10. $16\frac{3}{10}$ 11. $18\frac{1}{5}$ 12. $19\frac{2}{5}$
13. $13\frac{4}{25}$ 14. $13\frac{3}{4}$ 15. $18\frac{1}{50}$
16. $18\frac{1}{40}$ 17. $14\frac{433}{500}$ 18. $9\frac{21}{200}$
19. 25; 0.25   20. 12; 0.12
21. 0.625   22. 0.35   23. 0.36
24. 1.2   25. 2.15   26. 12.192
27. A. 0.5   B. 1.25   C. 2.13
    D. 3.57   E. 4.17   F. 6.07
    G. 9.85
28. 2.08   29. 6.30
30. 1.116   31. 1.2150

32.
```
    1.3
x   1.9
  ─────
    117
    130
  ─────
   2.47
```
33.
```
    3.06
x    1.4
  ──────
    1224
    3060
  ──────
   4.284
```
34.
```
    0.06
x   0.12
  ──────
      12
      60
  ──────
  0.0072
```

35. 0.868   36. 1.488
37. 0.75   38. 2.106
39. 1.236   40. 0.609

41.
```
      1.47
  6 ) 8.82
      6
      2 8
      2 4
        4 2
        4 2
```
42.
```
        0.111
  18 ) 1.998
        18
        1 9
        1 8
          1 8
          1 8
```
43.
```
      2.13
  7 ) 14.91
      14
        9
        7
        2 1
        2 1
```

44.
```
       0.46
  12 ) 5.52
       4 8
         7 2
         7 2
```
45.
```
      3.47
  8 ) 27.76
      24
      3 7
      3 2
        5 6
        5 6
```
46.
```
      3.65
  9 ) 32.85
      27
      5 8
      5 4
        4 5
        4 5
```

47. 5.51   48. 1.22
49. 0.45   50. 1.36
51. 0.85   52. 3.29
53. 2.73   54. 12.44
55. 3.14
56. 2.59; 2.59
57. $3.78 \div 6 = 0.63$ 58. $8.62 \div 2 = 4.31$
    0.63   4.31

Activity

13 More about Simple Equations

1. $50 + 2 \times k - 50 = 90 - 50$ 2. $3 \times p + 12 - 12 = 48 - 12$
   $2 \times k = 40$ $3 \times p = 36$
   $2 \times k \div 2 = 40 \div 2$ $3 \times p \div 3 = 36 \div 3$
   20   12
   20

3. $9 \times q - 16 + 16 = 29 + 16$ 4. $m \div 4 + 13 - 13 = 19 - 13$
   $9 \times q = 45$ $m \div 4 = 6$
   $9 \times q \div 9 = 45 \div 9$ $m \div 4 \times 4 = 6 \times 4$
   5   24

5. $n \div 5 - 12 + 12 = 8 + 12$
   $n \div 5 = 20$
   $n \div 5 \times 5 = 20 \times 5$
   100

6. $2y - 9 = 3, y = 6$ 7. $4m \div 2 = 6, m = 3$
8. $2p + 5 = 7, p = 1$

Activity

1. a. 40   b. 30
2. a. 10   b. 70

14 Percent

1. $\frac{46}{100}$; 0.46; 46   2. $\frac{18}{100}$; 0.18; 18

3. 13%   4. 9%   5. 80%

6. 35%   7. 75%   8. 32%

9. 50%   10. $\frac{19}{50}$ 11. $\frac{3}{5}$

12. $\frac{2}{25}$ 13. $\frac{1}{25}$ 14. $1\frac{7}{20}$

15. $2\frac{17}{20}$ 16. $\frac{80}{100}$; 80   17. $\frac{76}{100}$; 76

18. $\frac{70}{100}$; 70   19. a, d, e, f, h, i, j; $\frac{7}{10}$; 70

20. 55   21. 25
22. 20   23. 25
24. 55   25. 20

26.

0.16	0.45	0.25	1.2	1.34
16%	45%	25%	120%	134%
$\frac{4}{25}$	$\frac{9}{20}$	$\frac{1}{4}$	$1\frac{1}{5}$	$1\frac{17}{50}$

27. $1 - 60\%$ 28. $1 - 30\% - 25\%$
    $100\% - 60\%$ $100\% - 30\% - 25\%$
    40% 45%
    40   45

Activity

1. Baseball
2. a. 30   b. 50   c. 20

15 More about Time

1. 04:30   2. 23:45
3. 18:15   4. 21:20
5. 3:35 p.m.   6. 9:28 a.m.

7. 9:19 p.m.　　　8. 1:06 p.m.

9. 6:55 a.m.　　　10. 12:05 p.m.

11. 8:25 p.m.　　　12. 8:57 a.m.

13. 1:40 p.m.　　　14. 8:00 a.m.

15. 1:25　　　16. 3:00

17. 80　　　18. 45

19. 50

Activity

1. C　　　2. E　　　3. A

4. D　　　5. B

16 Circles

1. a. diameter　b. radius　　c. circumference
   d. centre

2. 6　　　3. 3　　　4. 3

5. 5　　　6. 2　　　7. AOB

8. 3 cm　　　9. 9cm　　　10. 3

Activity

2. a. many　　b. bigger

17 Volume and Capacity

1. 8　　　2. 4　　　3. 10

4. 12　　　5. 14

6. a. 12　　b. 6　　　c. 4
   d. 12 x 6 x 4 = 288

7. a. 7　　b. 5　　　c. 9
   d. 7 x 5 x 9 = 315

8. 12.5 x 2.2 x 2 = 55　　　9. 0.75 x 0.6 x 1.7 = 0.765

10. 0.6; 600　　11. 1; 1000　　12. 0.4; 400

13. 60 x 40 x 20　　　14. 30 x 20 x 15
    48 000　　　　　　　　9 000

15. 50 x 20 x 15cm³
    15 000

16. 3　　　17. 2

Activity

1. 2.3　　　2. 1 000 000

18 Line Graphs

1. 3　　　2. 6

3. 20　　　4. 28

5. 40　　　6. 40, 35, 25, 20, 15

7.

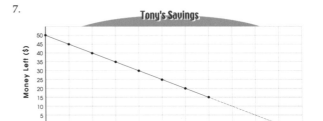

8. 2　　　9. 5

10. 35　　　11. 10

Activity

1. 2002　　　2. Tony

19 Transformations and Coordinates

1. Reflection　　2. Translation　　3. Rotation

4. Rotation　　5. Reflection　　6. Translation

7.　　　　　　　　　8.

A (2, 5)　　　　　B (3, 6)

9.

Turning point

C (6, 1)

Activity

1. (3,2)　　　2. (4, 1)　　　3. (2, 3)

20 Money

1. 40.04; 4.96　　2. 44.88; 5.12　　3. 76.11; 90.00

4. 56.01; 70.00　　5. 61.95　　6. 142.54

7. 3 350　　　8. 2 500　　　9. 4 650

10.　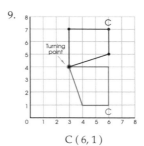

11. 10, 20, 50, 100, 400　　12. 5, 10, 25, 50, 200

Activity
8

21 Probability

1. Blue
2. Yellow
3. No
4. maybe
5. Blue
6. Yellow
7. $\frac{4}{8}$
8. $\frac{1}{8}$
9.
10.
11. $\frac{7}{8}$
12. $\frac{5}{8}$

Activity
(Suggested answer)

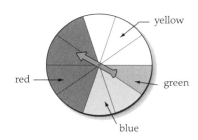

Final Test

1. 8, 6, 4, 3
2. No. of hours: 8, 12
    No. of days: 24, 16
3. 14.267
4. 5.42
5. 10.025
6. 0.002
7. 0.86
8. 1.4
9. 3.83
10. 2.56
11. 3.68
12. 1.4355
13. 0.0186
14. 0.426
15. 0.1436
16. 206
17. 14.1
18. 47
19. 90

20. $2 \times q + 6 - 6 = 10 - 6$
    $2 \times q = 4$
    $2 \times q \div 2 = 4 \div 2$
    2

21. $5 \times k - 2 + 2 = 18 + 2$
    $5 \times k = 20$
    $5 \times k \div 5 = 20 \div 5$
    4

22. $3 \times p + 1 - 1 = 10 - 1$
    $3 \times p = 9$
    $3 \times p \div 3 = 9 \div 3$
    3

23. $m \div 4 + 3 - 3 = 5 - 3$
    $m \div 4 = 2$
    $m \div 4 \times 4 = 2 \times 4$
    8

24. diameter
25. centre
26. radius
27. circumference
28. 1, 2
29. 2.5, 5
30. $\frac{43}{100}$; 0.43; 43%
31. $\frac{67}{100}$; 0.67; 67%
32. $\frac{4}{12}$
33. $\frac{6}{12}$
34. $\frac{2}{12}$
35. 32
36. 34
37. 34
38. 32
39. 68
40. 10:30 a.m.
41. 4:40 p.m.
42. The Journey
43. Rumble
44. 4:07 p.m.
45. 88
46. 34.85
47. 31.24
48. 25
49. 100
50. 2.50
51. 50
52. 11
53. 14
54. 120
55. 36
56. 500
57. 1200
58. 750

59.
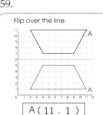
Flip over the line.

A (11 , 1)

60.
$\frac{1}{2}$ turn about the turning point.

B (2 , 1)

61.
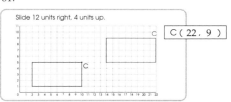
Slide 12 units right, 4 units up.

C (22 , 9)

Unit 1

1. No. of pencils : 28 x 3 = 84   84
2. No. of books : 28 x 5 = 140   Difference : 140 – 84 = 56
   There are 56 more books than pencils given out at the beginning of the year.
3. No. of chairs : 28 + 2 = 30   No. of stacks : 30 ÷ 5 = 6
   There would be 6 stacks of chairs.
4. No. of pencils belonging to girls : 21 x (3 – 2) = 21
   There would be 21 pencils belonging to the girls.
5. No. of rows : 28 ÷ 7 = 4   There would be 4 rows of chairs.
6. No. of panes of glass : 9 x 8 = 72
   There are 72 panes of glass in the doors.
7. No. of panes of glass : 19 x 2 = 38
   Total no. of panes of glass : 72 + 38 = 110
   There are 110 panes of windows.
8. Cost : 72 ÷ 2 x 3 = 108
   It would cost $108.00 to clean the panes of glass in the doors.
9. Cost : 38 x 5 + 108 = 298
   It would cost $298.00 to clean all the glass in the house.
10. Value : 11 x 34 = 374
    The value of Sally's pennies was 374¢ ($3.74).
11. Value : 135 ÷ 9 = 15   Each nickel was worth 15¢.
12. Value : 14 x 31 = 434
    The value of her collection of dimes was 434¢ ($4.34).
13. Value : 116 x 5 + 76 x (19 – 5) = 1644
    The value of her quarters was 1644¢ ($16.44).
14. Value : 374 + 135 + 434 + 1644 = 2587
    The value of her collection was 2587¢ ($25.87).
15. Value : 25 x (34 + 9 + 31 + 19) = 2325 (2325 < 2587)
    No, it would not be a good idea.
16. No. of hours : 30 x 2 = 60
    She spent 60 hours on doing homework in September.
17. No. of hours : 30 x 2 x 17 = 1020
    The girls spent 1020 hours on doing homework in September.
18. No. of hours : 60 ÷ 20 = 3
    3 hours of homework would be assigned each school day.
19. No. of hours : 25 x 30 ÷ 15 = 50
    Wanda would do 50 hours of homework in September.
20. No. of hours : 50 x 17 = 850
    All the girls would do 850 hours of homework in September.
21. Money spent : 4 x 7 x 3 ÷ 2 = 42
    Lisa spends $42.00 each week on phone calls.
22. No. of phone calls : 4 x 31 = 124
    She would make 124 phone calls in January.
23. Cost : 4 x 31 x 3 ÷ 2 = 186
    Her phone calls would cost $186.00 in October.
24. Money saved : 4 ÷ 2 x 300 – 4 x 46 = 416
    She could save 416¢ ($4.16).
25. Money saved : 4200 – 500 x 7 = 700
    She would save 700¢ ($7.00) each week.
26. Time taken : 936 x 36 = 33696
    It takes 33 696 seconds to dust all the paperback books.
27. Time taken : 882 x 36 = 31752
    It takes 31 752 seconds to dust all the hardcover books.
28. No. of shelves : 936 ÷ 26 = 36
    There will be 36 shelves of paperback books.
29. No. of shelves : 882 ÷ 21 = 42
    There will be 42 shelves of hardcover books.
30. No. of books : 936 + 882 = 1818
    No. of books in each box : 1818 ÷ 6 = 303
    303 books are in each box.
31. Weight : 1242 ÷ 6 = 207
    There are 207 g of raisins in each bag.
32. Weight : 1896 ÷ 8 = 237
    There are 237 g of peanuts in each serving.
33. Weight : 63 x 4 x 15 = 3780   Allan's figs weigh 3780 g.
34. No. of days : (5 x 32) ÷ (4 x 2) = 20   They will last 20 days.
35. No. of cookies : 486 ÷ 6 = 81   Each person gets 81 cookies.
36. In bags of 5 : 486 ÷ 5 = 97...1   In bags of 7 : 486 ÷ 7 = 69...3
    To put in bags of 7.
37. No. of figs : 63 x 4 ÷ 3 = 84   Difference : 84 – 63 = 21
    Each bag holds 21 more figs than before.
38. No. of bags : 1896 ÷ 25 = 75...21   He needs 76 bags.
39. No. of portions of 18 grams : 1242 ÷ 18 = 69
    Cost : 69 x 12 = 828   Allan's raisins cost 828¢ ($8.28).
40. No. of pebbles : 308 ÷ 4 = 77
    She would have to carry 77 pebbles each day.
41. Time spent : 17 x 4 x 1 x 12 = 816
    He would spend 816 hours in a year listening to the CDs.
42. No. of shelves : 1648 ÷ 24 = 68...16
    He would need 69 shelves.
43. No. of plants : 35 x 23 = 805   Peter needed 805 plants.
44. Amount of water : 45 x 31 = 1395   Peter will use 1395 L of water.

Challenge

Day	Mon	Tue	Wed	Thu
No. of ants	100	200	400	800

x2 x2 x2

There might be 800 ants on Thursday.

Unit 2

1. Difference : 19 – 18 = 1   1 m
2. Total distance : 12 + 18 + 14 + 19 + 16 = 79
   They threw 79 m altogether.
3. Mario & Jimmy : 12 + 19 = 31   Sandy & Dolores : 18 + 16 = 34
   Sandy & Dolores threw the ball farther.
4. Danny : 14 + 14 = 28   Difference : 34 – 28 = 6
   The winning team threw 6 m farther than Danny did.
5. Jimmy : 19 x 5 = 95   Sandy : 18 x 3 = 54
   Dolores : 16 x 1 = 16
   Jimmy got the highest number. The number is 95.
6. No. of days : 31 + 29 + 31 + 30 + 31 + 30 + 31 + 31 + 30 + 31 +
   30 + 31 = 366   There are 366 days in a leap year.
7. No. of marbles : 56 x 6 = 336   Frank would have 336 marbles.
8. No. of people : 47 x 12 = 564   564 people would fill 12 rows.
9. No. of packages : 1371 ÷ 250 = 5...121
   He must buy 6 packages of paper.
10. Total time : 60 + 20 = 80   No. of times : 80 ÷ 4 = 20
    He can ride around the park 20 times.
11. No. of stamps : 482 + 561 + 398 = 1441
    She has 1441 stamps in all.
12. Cost : 75 x 2 + 34 x 3 = 252   He should pay $252.00.
13. No. of pieces of lumber : 2352 + 598 + 28 = 2978
    They had 2978 pieces of lumber in all.
14. Difference : 2352 – 28 = 2324
    They had 2324 more pieces of pine than maple.
15. Difference : 2352 – 598 = 1754
    They had 1754 more pieces of pine than oak.
16. Length : 2978 x 2 = 5956
    They had 5956 metres of lumber at the lumber yard.
17. Length : (598 – 269) x 2 = 658
    They had 658 metres of oak left to sell.
18.

No. of days	1	2	3
Length of pine sold (m)	1568	3136	4704

It would take 3 days to sell all their pine pieces.

19. No. of pieces of oak left : $414 \div 2 = 207$
No. of pieces of oak sold : $598 - 207 = 391$
391 pieces of oak were sold.
20. Money earned : $2 \times 9 \times 5 = 90$ She earned $90.00.
21. Time taken : $25 + 17 + 28 = 70$; (70 min = 1 h 10 min)
He finished at 5:10 p.m.
22. Cost : $15 + 18 = 33$
Money Mario had : $20 + 10 + 5 = 35$ ($35 > 33$)   Yes, he could.
23. Time saved : $(20 - 14) \times 2 \times 5 = 60$
She could save 60 minutes each week.
24. There are 3 7 years in 21 years.   No. of times : $2 \times 2 \times 2 = 8$
It should be worth 8 times its present value in 21 years.

Challenge
1. There are 3 leap years and 8 years.
No. of days : $366 \times 3 + 365 \times 8 = 1098 + 2920 = 4018$
He is 4018 days old.
2. There are 3 quarters in 9 months.   Charge : $158920 \times 3 = 476760$
The client would pay them $476 760.00.

Unit 3
1. $6\frac{1}{2} = 6\frac{1 \times 4}{2 \times 4} = 6\frac{4}{8}$; $6\frac{4}{8} > 6\frac{3}{8}$ Peter
2. $\frac{1}{2}$ of an hour = 30 minutes (30 minutes < 42 minutes)
Mary read the chapter faster.
3. Douglas : $25 + 10 + 3 = 38$ Jill : $10 + 5 \times 6 + 1 = 41$
Douglas had $\frac{38}{100}$ of a dollar; Jill had $\frac{41}{100}$ of a dollar. Jill had the larger fraction of a dollar.
4. Cake served : $\frac{2}{7} = \frac{2 \times 4}{7 \times 4} = \frac{8}{28}$
Cake kept : $\frac{1}{4} = \frac{1 \times 7}{4 \times 7} = \frac{7}{28}$

No, she didn't save more cake than she served.
5. Henry ate : $\frac{1}{3} = \frac{1 \times 5}{3 \times 5} = \frac{5}{15}$
Ann ate : $\frac{2}{5} = \frac{2 \times 3}{5 \times 3} = \frac{6}{15}$ ($\frac{6}{15} > \frac{5}{15}$)   Henry ate less.
6. ($1 = 100¢); She had $\frac{63}{100}$ of a dollar.
7. Money Dolores had : $100 + 25 \times 7 = 275$
(275¢ = $2\frac{75}{100}$) She had $2\frac{75}{100}$ of a dollar.
8. Money Milly had : $25 + 10 \times 4 + 5 \times 12 = 125$
(125¢ = $1\frac{25}{100}$) She had $1\frac{25}{100}$ of a dollar.
9. Money Gerry had : $25 \times 7 + 10 \times 2 + 5 \times 6 = 225$
(225¢ = $2\frac{25}{100}$) He had $2\frac{25}{100}$ of a dollar.
10. Dolores raised the most money for charity.
11. Total amount : $\frac{63}{100} + 2\frac{75}{100} + 1\frac{25}{100} + 2\frac{25}{100} = 6\frac{88}{100}$
They raised 6\frac{88}{100}$ for charity in all.

Challenge
1. Sam : $\frac{21}{147} = \frac{1}{7}$ Hindy : $\frac{54}{216} = \frac{1}{4}$
Kelly : $\frac{28}{98} = \frac{2}{7}$ Oliver : $\frac{2}{166} = \frac{1}{83}$
Kelly had the largest fraction of valuable cards.
2. Sam had the second smallest fraction of valuable cards.
3. Kelly, Hindy, Sam, Oliver.

Unit 4
1. Total time : $1\frac{5}{6} + 1\frac{4}{6} + \frac{1}{6} = 3\frac{4}{6}$; $3\frac{4}{6}$
2. Difference : $1\frac{4}{6} - \frac{1}{6} = 1\frac{3}{6}$
Dolores spent $1\frac{3}{6}$ h more on the project than Mario.

3. Difference : $1\frac{4}{6} + 1\frac{5}{6} - \frac{1}{6} = 2\frac{9}{6} - \frac{1}{6} = 2\frac{8}{6} = 3\frac{2}{6}$
Ann and Dolores spent $3\frac{2}{6}$ h more on the project than Mario.
4. No. of hours : $1\frac{5}{6} + \frac{1}{6} = 1\frac{6}{6} = 2$
Ann and Mario spent 2 hours on the project in all.
5. Time Dolores spent : $1\frac{4}{6}$ Time Ann and Mario spent : 2
Ann and Mario together spent more time on the project than Dolores.
6. Difference : $1\frac{5}{6} - \frac{1}{6} = 1\frac{4}{6}$
Mario would spend $1\frac{4}{6}$ hours more.
7. No. of bags : $\frac{3}{7} + \frac{5}{7} + \frac{1}{7} = \frac{9}{7} = 1\frac{2}{7}$
Harry collected $1\frac{2}{7}$ bags of bottles in all.
8. No. of bags : $\frac{5}{7} + \frac{3}{7} + \frac{2}{7} = \frac{10}{7} = 1\frac{3}{7}$
Barry collected $1\frac{3}{7}$ bags of bottles in all.
9. No. of bags : $\frac{6}{7} + \frac{6}{7} + 1 = \frac{12}{7} + 1 = 2\frac{5}{7}$
Mary collected $2\frac{5}{7}$ bags of bottles in all.
10. Mary collected the most bottles.
11. No. of bags : $1\frac{2}{7} + 1\frac{3}{7} + 2\frac{5}{7} = 5\frac{3}{7}$
The children collected $5\frac{3}{7}$ bags of bottles in all.
12. Difference : $2\frac{5}{7} - 1\frac{2}{7} = 1\frac{3}{7}$
Mary collected $1\frac{3}{7}$ more bags of bottles than Harry.
13. Difference : $2\frac{5}{7} - 1\frac{3}{7} = 1\frac{2}{7}$
Mary collected $1\frac{2}{7}$ more bags of bottles than Barry.
14. No. of bags : $2 - 1\frac{2}{7} = \frac{5}{7}$
He needs to collect $\frac{5}{7}$ of a bag of bottles more.
15. No. of bags : $3 - 1\frac{3}{7} = 1\frac{4}{7}$
He needs to collect $1\frac{4}{7}$ more bags of bottles.
16. No. of bags : $5 - 2\frac{5}{7} = 4\frac{7}{7} - 2\frac{5}{7} = 2\frac{2}{7}$
She needs to collect $2\frac{2}{7}$ more bags of bottles.
17. Total amount : $\frac{2}{5} + \frac{4}{5} + \frac{3}{5} = \frac{9}{5} = 1\frac{4}{5}$
He had $1\frac{4}{5}$ boxes of cereal in all.
18. Difference : $\frac{4}{5} - \frac{2}{5} = \frac{2}{5}$
He had $\frac{2}{5}$ of a box more bran flakes than corn flakes.
19. Difference : $\frac{3}{5} + \frac{2}{5} - \frac{4}{5} = \frac{5}{5} - \frac{4}{5} = \frac{1}{5}$
He had $\frac{1}{5}$ of a box more rice and corn flakes than bran flakes.
20. Amount of cereal left :
$(\frac{2}{5} - \frac{1}{5}) + (\frac{4}{5} - \frac{1}{5}) + (\frac{3}{5} - \frac{1}{5}) = 1\frac{1}{5}$
$1\frac{1}{5}$ boxes of cereal would be left.
21. Total amount : $1\frac{4}{5} + 1 - \frac{1}{5} = 2\frac{3}{5}$
He would have $2\frac{3}{5}$ boxes of cereal altogether.
22. Total distance : $2\frac{7}{20} + 3\frac{19}{20} + 2\frac{11}{20} + 5 = 13\frac{17}{20}$
They ran $13\frac{17}{20}$ km in all.
23. Difference : $5 - 2\frac{7}{20} = 2\frac{13}{20}$ The person who ran the farthest ran $2\frac{13}{20}$ km farther than the one who ran the shortest distance.
24. Total distance : $2\frac{7}{20} + 2\frac{11}{20} = 4\frac{18}{20}$ Their team ran $4\frac{18}{20}$ km.

25. Distance : $3\frac{19}{20} + 2\frac{11}{20} = 6\frac{10}{20}$
    They ran $6\frac{10}{20}$ km in all.

26. Difference : $5 - 3\frac{19}{20} = 1\frac{1}{20}$ Toni ran $1\frac{1}{20}$ km farther than Lori.

27. Difference : $2\frac{11}{20} - 2\frac{7}{20} = \frac{4}{20}$ Freda ran $\frac{4}{20}$ km farther than Kim.

28. New magazines : $1 - (\frac{1}{19} + \frac{9}{19} + \frac{7}{19}) = \frac{19}{19} - \frac{17}{19} = \frac{2}{19}$
    $\frac{2}{19}$ of his magazines are new.

29. Fraction of magazines : $\frac{7}{19} + \frac{2}{19} = \frac{9}{19}$
    $\frac{9}{19}$ of his magazines were printed between 1980 and the present.

30. Fraction of magazines : $\frac{9}{19} + \frac{7}{19} = \frac{16}{19}$
    $\frac{16}{19}$ of his magazines were printed between 1970 and 1990.

31. Fraction of magazines : $\frac{9}{19} + \frac{1}{19} = \frac{10}{19}$
    $\frac{10}{19}$ of his magazines need protective envelopes.

32. Fraction of magazines : $1 - \frac{10}{19} = \frac{9}{19}$
    $\frac{9}{19}$ of his magazines do not need protective envelopes.

33. Fraction of magazines left : $1 - \frac{3}{8} = \frac{5}{8}$
    $\frac{5}{8}$ of his magazines are left.

34. $\frac{113}{190}$ of his magazines are in English.

35. No. of French magazines : $190 - 113 = 77$
    $\frac{77}{190}$ of his magazines are in French.

Challenge

$\frac{3}{13} + ? = \frac{9}{13} \longrightarrow ? = \frac{6}{13}$
The fraction under the chocolate stain is $\frac{6}{13}$.

Unit 5

1. Weight : $0.75 + 0.007 + 1.28 + 0.95 + 0.01 = 2.997$; 2.997 kg
2. Weight : $4 - 2.997 = 1.003$
   He could add 1.003 kg more to his dry ingredients.
3. Weight : $0.75 + 1.28 + 0.95 + 0.01 = 2.99$
   This recipe requires 2.99 kg of vegetables.
4. Weight : $0.01 + 1.28 = 1.29$
   This recipe requires 1.29 kg of herbs and spices.
5. Weight : $2.997 + 0.599 = 3.596$
   The entire dish would weigh 3.596 kg before cooking.
6. Money saved : $7.5 - 3.49 - 1.78 - 2 = 0.23$
   She saved $0.23 each week.
7. Money spent : $3.49 + 1.78 = 5.27$
   She spent $5.27 for entertainment and snacks each week.
8. Difference : $3.49 - 2 = 1.49$ She spent $1.49 more for entertainment than transportation each week.
9. Money saved : $0.23 + 0.68 = 0.91$ She would save $0.91 each week.
10. Money left : $3.49 - (2.23 - 1.78) = 3.04$
    She would have $3.04 left for entertainment.

Challenge

1. Distance : $1.97 - 1.78 = 0.19$ He would have to go 0.19 km farther.
2. Final balance : $15.02 + (5.78 - 0.15) + (1.99 - 0.15) - 3.14 - 0.15 - 2.67 - 0.15 = 16.38$ Her final balance was $16.38.

Unit 6

1. Money saved : $5.75 \times 12 = 69$ $(69 < 75.6)$;   wouldn't
2. Difference : $75.6 - 69 = 6.6$ He would be short of $6.60.
3. Money saved : $6.45 \times 12 = 77.4$ $(77.4 > 75.6)$
   Yes, that would allow him to buy the game on time.
4. He is short of $6.60. Extra money needed : $6.6 \div 12 = 0.55$
   He would have to save an extra $0.55 each month.

5. Difference : $69 - 59.88 = 9.12$
   Less money saved : $9.12 \div 12 = 0.76$
   He would save $0.76 less each month.
6. Money spent : $2.16 \times 2 = 4.32$ She would spend $4.32 for pine.
7. Money spent : $0.3 \times 4.7 = 1.41$ She would spend $1.41 for oak.
8. Money spent : $2.4 \times 5.65 = 13.56$
   She would spend $13.56 for walnut.
9. Money spent : $4.32 + 1.41 + 13.56 = 19.29$
   She would spend $19.29 for wood altogether.
10. Total cost : $(2.16 + 0.3 + 2.4) \times 0.5 = 2.43$
    The total cost would be $2.43.
11. Total cost : $19.29 + 2.43 = 21.72$
    The total cost for the wood plus finishing was $21.72.
12. Amount each paid : $21.72 \div 3 = 7.24$ Each person would pay $7.24.
13. Length : $2.16 \div 3 = 0.72$ Each part was 0.72 m long.
14. Length : $(2.4 - 0.04) \div 4 = 0.59$ Each part was 0.59 m long.
15. No. of metres of pine : $16.5 \div 2 = 8.25$
    I can buy 8.25 metres of pine.
16. Travel cost : $305 \times 0.06 = 18.3$
    The travel cost on Day 2 was $18.30.
17. Difference : $271 \times 0.04 - 186 \times 0.05 = 1.54$
    The difference in travel cost was $1.54.
18. Day 1 : $271 \times 0.04 = 10.84$ Day 2 : $305 \times 0.06 = 18.30$
    Day 3 : $652 \times 0.05 = 32.60$ Day 4 : $186 \times 0.05 = 9.30$
    Day 5 : $395 \times 0.04 = 15.80$
    The lowest travel cost was on Day 4. It was $9.30.
19. Day 3 was the highest.   The cost was $32.60.
20. Day 5 : $15.80 > 12.00$
    Yes, it would have exceeded his budget.
21. Day 2 : $18.30 > 12.00$ Day 3 : $32.60 > 12.00$
    Day 5 : $15.80 > 12.00$
    Days 2, 3 and 5 exceeded his travel budget.
22. Cost per km : $4 \div 100 = 0.04$ The cost per km would be $0.04.
23. Cost per km : $(4 + 2) \div 100 = 0.06$ The cost per km would be $0.06.
24. Cost : $8.76 \div 4 = 2.19$ Each box of juice costs $2.19.
25. Capacity : $1.25 \div 5 = 0.25$ The capacity of each glass is 0.25 L.
26. Capacity : $1.25 \times 7 = 8.75$ There is 8.75 L of juice in 7 boxes.
27. Regular size : $1.38 \div 2 = 0.69$ Jumbo size : $5.90 \div 10 = 0.59$
    Jumbo size is the better buy.
28. Cost : $1.38 \times 8 = 11.04$ He should pay $11.04.
29. Amount of water : $1.75 \times 7 = 12.25$
    He will drink 12.25 L of water in a week.

Challenge

Area : $16.8 \times 2.4 = 40.32$ Amount of paint : $40.32 \div 32 \times 2 = 2.52$
She will need 2.52 L of paint for the wall.

Midway Review

1. No. of helpers : $9 \times 4 + 12 \times 4 = 36 + 48 = 84$
   There were 84 helpers.
2. No. of pieces of cake : $64 \times 8 = 512$ She made 512 pieces of cake.
3. Cost : $0.75 \times 8 = 6.00$ A cake cost $6.00.
4. Cost : $2.16 \times 64 = 138.24$
   The total cost for baking all the cakes would be $138.24.
5. No. of doughnuts : $1064 + 898 = 1962$
   There were 1962 doughnuts in all.
6. No. of packages : $1064 \div 4 = 266$
   There were 266 packages of chocolate doughnuts.
7. No. of honey doughnuts sold : $898 - 159 = 739$
   739 honey doughnuts had been sold.
8. Cost : $5.04 \div 8 = 0.63$ 1 honey doughnut cost $0.63.
9. No. of cookies : $4 \times 6 \times 15 = 360$ There were 360 cookies.
10. No. of cookies left : $360 - 218 = 142$ 142 cookies were left.
11. Weight : $486.5 \div 5 = 97.3$ 1 cookie weighed 97.3 grams.

12. Amount of cake : $\frac{1}{8} + \frac{5}{8} = \frac{6}{8}$

They bought $\frac{6}{8}$ of the cake in all.

13. Difference : $\frac{5}{8} - \frac{1}{8} = \frac{4}{8}$

Sally bought $\frac{4}{8}$ more of the cake than Gary.

14. Change : 10 – 4.16 = 5.84   Her change was $5.84.

15. A bag of 5 bagels : 1.30 ÷ 5 = 0.26
A bag of 8 bagels : 1.76 ÷ 8 = 0.22
A bag of 8 bagels is a better buy.

16. Money collected : 459 x 8 = 3672
The stalls collected $3672.00 in all.

17. Money donated : 3672 ÷ 2 = 1836
Mr Stanley donated $1836.00 to the Children's Hospital.

18. Money Mr Stanley had : $1836 ($1836 > $1285)
Yes, he made a profit after the donation.

19. Profit : 1836 – 1285 = 551   He gained $551.00.

20. Amount of paint : 3.48 x 4 = 13.92
13.92 L of paint are needed for all the bedrooms.

21. No. of cans : 13.92 ÷ 4 = 3.48   She needs 4 cans.

22. No. of boxes of tiles needed : $1\frac{3}{5} + 1\frac{3}{5} + 1\frac{3}{5} = 4\frac{4}{5}$

$4\frac{4}{5}$ boxes of tiles are needed.

23. She needs to buy 5 boxes.

24. No. of boxes left : $5 - 4\frac{4}{5} = \frac{1}{5}$

$\frac{1}{5}$ of a box of tiles will be left over.

25. Money spent : 798.65 + 268.47 = 1067.12
They spend $1067.12 in all.

26. Store A : 102 x 6 = 612   Store B : 621 (621> 612)
Stores A offers a better buy.

27. Cost : 1295 + 612 = 1907   She will pay $1907.00.

28. B   29. C   30. D   31. A   32. C

33. A   34. D   35. C   36. A

Unit 7

1. Cost : 12.37 x 3 + 14.62 = 51.73; $51.73

2. Amount saved : (19.99 – 14.62) x 5 = 26.85
She would save $26.85.

3. Cost : 12.37 + 227.36 = 239.73 (239.73 > 230)   No, he cannot.

4. Change : 150 – 67.99 x 2 = 14.02   Her change was $14.02.

5. Average price : (12.37 + 14.62 + 67.99) ÷ 3 = 31.66
The average price is $31.66.

6. Money spent : 5.88 + 3.35 + 4.32 + 8.37 = 21.92
They spent $21.92 in all.

7. Change : 50 – 21.92 = 28.08   They should receive $28.08 change.

8. Amount each paid : 21.92 ÷ 2 = 10.96
Each person should pay $10.96.

9. They spent $21.92; there were 2 ten dollars.
Cost : 21.92 – 1.05 x 2 = 19.82   They would have paid $19.82.

10. Cost : 5.88 ÷ 6 = 0.98   The cost of 1 kg of apples was $0.98.

11. Cost : 8.37 ÷ 3 = 2.79   The cost of 1 kg of candies was $2.79.

12. Cost : 3.35 ÷ 5 = 0.67   The cost of 1 head of lettuce was $0.67.

13. 5-pound bag : 6.45 ÷ 5 = 1.29   8-pound bag : 9.28 ÷ 8 = 1.16
An 8-pound bag is a better buy.

14. Distance : 0.3 x 1000 = 300
Rachel lives the closest to the school. The distance is 300 m.

15. Distance : 1620 ÷ 1000 = 1.62
The distance between Sandra's house and Paul's house is 1.62 km.

16. Distance : 1.57 + 0.89 = 2.46
The distance from Debbie's house to the school is 2.46 km.

17. Shortest distance : 0.93 + 1.35 = 2.28 (via Sandra's house)
The shortest distance from Debbie's house to the school is 2280 m.

18. Rachel → School → Virginia → Debbie : 0.3 + 0.89 + 1.57 = 2.76
Rachel → School → Sandra → Debbie : 0.3 + 1.35 + 0.93 = 2.58
The shortest distance is 2.58 km.

19. Distance walked per minute : 1.35 ÷ 5 = 0.27
The average distance she walked per minute was 0.27 km.

20. Distance travelled per minute : (1.57 + 0.89) ÷ 6 = 2.46 ÷ 6 = 0.41
The average distance she travelled per minute was 0.41 km.

21. Distance travelled per minute : (2.82 + 1.32) ÷ 9 = 0.46
The average distance she travelled per minute was 0.46 km.

22. Distance travelled : 1.35 x 4 x 5 = 27
She will travel 27 km in 5 days.

23. Distance travelled : 0.89 + 1.35 + 0.3 x 2 = 2.84
They walk 2.84 km in total.

24. Actual distance : 2.5 x 0.3 = 0.75   The actual distance is 0.75 km.

Challenge

1. Cost : 3.75 x 25 + 6.90 = 93.75 + 6.90 = 100.65
They would have to pay $100.65 in total.

2. Cost : 3.75 x 35 – 12.60 = 118.65
They would have to pay $118.65 in total.

Unit 8

1. No. of seats : 26 x 48 = 1248
No. of empty seats : 1248 – 952 = 296   296

2. Total amount from children's tickets : 2475 – 462 x 4.5 = 396
No. of children's tickets : 396 ÷ 3 = 132
132 children's tickets were sold.

3. Amount each child paid : 3 + 2 = 5
Money collected : 1248 x 5 = 6240
$6240.00 would be collected for that show.

4. Amount each adult paid : 4.5 + 2 = 6.5
Money collected : 1248 x 6.5 = 8112
$8112.00 would be collected for that show.

5. She would have to buy 1 adult ticket, 4 children's tickets and 3 pop corns. Cost : 4.5 + 3 x 4 + 2 x 3 = 22.5   She would pay $22.50 in all.

6. Cost : 9 + 14 = 23   He would pay $23.00 for his purchases.

7. Cost : (18 ÷ 3 x 6 + 19) – 4 = 51   Change : 100 – 51 = 49
She would get $49.00 change.

8. Cost : (9 ÷ 2 x 4 + 18) – 4 = 32
Money needed : 32 – 20 – 10 = 2   She would need $2.00.

9. Cost : (14 x 2 + 9 ÷ 2 x 4) – 4 = 42
He would pay $42.00 for his purchases.

10. Cost : (18 ÷ 3 x 9 + 14 x 3) – 4 x 2 = 88
She would pay $88.00 for her purchases.

11. Cost : 19 x 4 = 76   Money needed : 76 – 50 = 26
She would need to borrow $26.00.

12. Price of 6 blouses : 18 ÷ 3 x 6 – 4 = 32   Price of 4 dresses : 19 x 4 = 76
Difference : 76 – 32 = 44   The price difference was $44.00.

13. Amount spent on dresses : 71 – 14 = 57
No. of dresses : 57 ÷ 19 = 3   She bought 3 dresses.

14. No. of shirts : 128 + 224 = 352   No. of packages : 352 ÷ 4 = 88
He made 88 packages of 4 in all.

15. No. of packages : 352 ÷ 3 = 117...1
He made 117 packages of 3 in all.

16. Time for ads and music in an hour : 8 x 2 + 16 x 2 = 48
Time for talk : 60 – 48 = 12 There will be 12 min of talk every hour.

17. There are 16 min of ads in an hour; 16 min have 32 30 seconds.
Cost : 120 x 32 = 3840   The station will earn $3840.00 per hour.

18. No. of songs in an hour : 16 x 2 ÷ 4 = 8
No. of songs between 4:00 p.m. and 9:00 p.m. : 8 x 5 = 40
40 songs can be played between 4:00 p.m. and 9:00 p.m.

19. Non-ad time in an hour : 60 – 8 x 2 = 44
Non-ad time in a day : 44 x 16 = 704
There will be 704 min of non-ad time in a day.

20. There are 12 min of talk in an hour; there are 72 10 seconds in 12 min.
    No. of words in an hour : 12 x 72 = 864
    He will say 864 words in each hour's talk time.
21. Cost : 0.46 x 4 = 1.84   Change : 5 – 1.84 = 3.16
    She would get $3.16 change.
22. Cost for Anna's friends : (0.46 x 4) x 4 = 7.36
    Total cost : 0.46 x 4 + 7.36 = 9.2
    They would have spent $9.20 in postage.
23.

    | 1st chain | 2nd chain |

    $1 \xrightarrow{x4} 4 \xrightarrow{x4} 16$

    No. of people involved: 1 + 4 + 16 = 21
    21 people were involved in the chain.
24. Cost : 85 x 0.46 = 39.1   They would pay $39.10 for postage.
25. Time each person spent on sending a letter : 6 + 2 = 8
    Total time spent : (4 + 16) x 8 = 160
    They would spend 160 minutes.

Challenge

1.

Day	Mon	Tue	Wed	Thu
No. of pages read	38	67	67	29

    No. of pages left : 249 – 38 – 67 – 67 – 29 = 48
    She would have 48 pages left to read on Thursday at noon.
2. Total amount for the payments : 92.6 x 24 = 2222.4
   Difference : 2222.4 – 2120.5 = 101.9
   Wayne pays $101.90 more by purchasing it on the instalment plan.

Unit 9

1. 1st : 4 + 2 = 6   2nd : 6 x 3 = 18   18
2. 1st : 6 + 2 = 8   2nd : 8 x 3 = 24   Dorothy would answer 24.
3. 1st : 5.5 + 2 = 7.5   2nd : 7.5 x 3 = 22.5
   Dorothy would answer 22.5.
4. A : 4 ÷ 2 = 2; 2 + 10 = 12 ✗   B : 4 x 6 = 24; 24 – 10 = 14 ✓
   C : 4 – 3 = 1; 1 x 10 = 10 ✗   D : 4 + 8 = 12; 12 ÷ 2 = 6 ✗
   B is correct.
5. 1st : 2.4 x 6 = 14.4   2nd : 14.4 – 10 = 4.4
   Gladys would answer 4.4.
6. Yes. He scored 2 more baskets each day.
7. $1 \xrightarrow{+2} 3 \xrightarrow{+2} 5 \xrightarrow{+2} 7 \xrightarrow{+2} 9$
   The numbers increase by 2 each time.
8. Billy would score 11 baskets on the 6th day.
9.

    | 6th | 7th | 8th | 9th | 10th |

    $11 \longrightarrow 13 \longrightarrow 15 \longrightarrow 17 \longrightarrow 19$

    Billy would score 19 baskets on the 10th day.
10. Total no. of baskets : 1 + 3 = 4
    Billy scored 4 baskets in the first 2 days.
11. Total no. of baskets : 1 + 3 + 5 = 9
    Billy scored 9 baskets in the first 3 days.
12. Total no. of baskets : 1 + 3 + 5 + 7 = 16
    Billy scored 16 baskets in the first 4 days.
13. Total no. of baskets : 1 + 3 + 5 + 7 + 9 = 25
    Billy scored 25 baskets in the first 5 days.
14.

Day	1	2	3	4	5	6	7	8	9
No. of baskets in all	1	4	9	16	25	36	49	64	81

    Billy would score 81 baskets in the first 9 days.
15.

Day	9	10	11
No. of baskets in all	81	100	121

    Billy would take 11 days.
16. $1 \xrightarrow{x3} 3 \xrightarrow{x3} 9 \xrightarrow{x3} 27 \xrightarrow{x3} 81 \xrightarrow{x3} 243$
    Each number is 3 times the previous number. The next 2 numbers are 81 and 243.

17. $1 \xrightarrow{+0.9} 1.9 \xrightarrow{+0.9} 2.8 \xrightarrow{+0.9} 3.7 \xrightarrow{+0.9} 4.6 \xrightarrow{+0.9} 5.5$
    The numbers increase by 0.9. The next 2 numbers are 4.6 and 5.5.
18. a $\underset{}{}$ b   c   d e   f   g h i   j   k l m n   o   p q r s t   u
    The letters skip 1 more letter than before. The next 2 letters are o and u.
19. $3 \xrightarrow{+3} 6 \xrightarrow{+4} 10 \xrightarrow{+5} 15 \xrightarrow{+6} 21 \xrightarrow{+7} 28$
    The numbers increase by 1 more each time. The next 2 numbers are 21 and 28.
20.

    1, 1, 2, 2, 2, 4, 3, 3, 6, 4, 4, 8, 5, 5, 10

    3 numbers are in a group.   The first 2 numbers in the group increase by 1, the last numbers increase by 2.
    The next 6 numbers are 4, 4, 8, 5, 5, and 10.
21.

    1+2 2+3 3+5 5+8 8+13 13+21 21+34
    1 , 2 , 3 , 5 , 8 , 13 , 21 , 34 , 55

    Each number is the sum of the previous 2 numbers.
    The next 2 numbers are 34 and 55.
22.

Day	1	2	3	4	5	6	7
Allowance	0.1	0.2	0.4	0.8	1.6	3.2	6.4

    Total allowance in a week :
    0.1 + 0.2 + 0.4 + 0.8 + 1.6 + 3.2 + 6.4 = 12.7 (12.7>12)
    To give $12.00 per week is a better deal for Hortense's parents.
23. Improvement : 58 – 52 = 6;   Final mark : 58 + 6 x 2 = 70
    Mr Finley would give Karen 70 for her next test.
24.

Age	12	22	32	42	52	62	72
Value of bond	25	50	100	200	400	800	1600

    It will be worth $1600.00 when Jerry is 72 years old.

Challenge

1. 40   2. Subtraction   3. Addition

Unit 10

1. 62.50, 125.00, 500.00, 2000.00, 4000.00
2.

Year	2000	2010	2020
Price ($)	4000.00	8000.00	16000.00

    The price of the savings bond in 2020 would be $16 000.00.
3.

Year	2000	2010	2020	2030	2040
Price ($)	4000.00	8000.00	16000.00	32000.00	64000.00

    It would be worth $64 000.00 in 2040.
4. No. of times : 250 ÷ 62.5 = 4   It was 4 times more.
5. Money earned : 16000 – 1000 = 15000
   I would have earned $15 000.00.
6. 6, 8, 5;   2.25, 3.60;   19, 24, 30, 38, 43
7.

Week	1	2	3	4	5	6	7	8	9
No. of cards	5	6	8	5	6	8	5	6	8

    He will buy 8 cards.
8.

Week	7	8	9	10
Money spent	2.25	2.70	3.60	2.25

    He will spend $2.25.
9. He will collect 19 cards.   10. He will collect 38 cards.
11.

Week	7	8	9
No. of cards bought	5	6	8
No. of cards in collection	43	49	57

    He will collect 57 cards.

12. No. of cards collected in 3 weeks : 5 + 6 + 8 = 19
No. of cards collected in 30 weeks : 19 x 10 = 190
He will collect 190 cards.
13. Following the pattern, Matthew should buy 6 cards next week.
He will buy 6 cards in week 23.
14. Total amount : 2.25 + 2.7 + 3.6 = 8.55   He will spend $8.55.
15. Money spent : (2.25 + 2.7 + 3.6) x 2 = 17.1
He will spend $ 17.10.
16. 14, 16, 18, 20, 22;   8, 11, 14, 17, 20
17. No. of yellow marbles : 22 + 2 = 24; 24
18. No. of blue marbles : 20 + 3 = 23
Tony has 23 blue marbles on the 7th day.
19.

Day	6th	7th	8th	9th	10th	11th
No. of yellow marbles	22	24	26	28	30	32

Tony takes 11 days to have 32 yellow marbles.
20.

Day	6th	7th	8th	9th	10th
No. of blue marbles	20	23	26	29	32

Tony takes 10 days to have 32 blue marbles.
21.

Day	6th	7th	8th
No. of yellow marbles	22	24	26
No. of blue marbles	20	23	26

The yellow and blue marbles will be the same in number on the 8th day.
22. No. of marbles : 22 + 20 = 42
Tony has 42 marbles in all in the first 6 days.
23. The number of yellow marbles increases by 2 every day. The number of blue marbles increases by 3 every day. The total number of marbles increases by 5 every day.
24. 0, 0;   6, 10;   4, 8, 12, 16, 24;   6, 12, 24, 30;
16, 24, 48;   40, 50
25. The numbers increase by 6 each time.
The next 3 numbers would be 36, 42 and 48.
26. The numbers increase by 4 each time.
The next 3 numbers would be 28, 32 and 36.
27. Column 5 has the same pattern as that in row 6.
The numbers increase by 10 each time.
28. Row 6 can show the counting pattern of Joe's cards.
He will have 50 cards after 5 days.
29. Row 5 can show the amount of money Raymond has spent.
He will have spent $32.00 after 4 days.
30. 4, 9, 14, 19, 24, 29   31. 2.50, 3.00, 3.50, 4.00, 4.50, 5.00
32.

Hour	6	7	8	9	10
Charge ($)	29.00	34.00	39.00	44.00	49.00

The charge was $49.00.
33. Charge : 19 + 3.5 = 22.5   The twins earned $22.50 for the service.
34. Cost : 4 + 2 x 4 = 12   Lily's bill was $12.00.
35. Charge for 8 hours of simple care : 29 + 5 + 5 = 39
Total bill : 39 + 39 x 2 = 117   Their total bill was $117.00.
36. $3.50, $4.50, $5.00
37. Cost : 12.50 + 12.00 + 0.75 x 6 = 29
His total bill was $29.00.
38. Charge for 7 hours' care : 17 + 4.5 + 4.5 + 4.5 = 30.5
Total bill : 30.5 + 10 = 40.5   Their total bill was $40.50.

Challenge

Hour	1	2	3	4	5
Charge ($) for children over 3	1	2.5	4	5.5	7
Charge ($) for children under 3	3	4.5	6	7.5	9

Cost : 7 + 9 = 16   Their bill would be $16.00.

Final Review

1. Area : 1.96 x 4 = 7.84   The area is 7.84 km².
2. Distance travelled : 1.4 x 3 = 4.2   She walked 4.2 km.
3. Distance travelled : 1.4 x 4 = 5.6   He walked 5.6 km.
4. Distance travelled : 1.4 x 3 x 2 = 8.4   They travelled 8.4 km in all.
5. Difference : 1.4 x 2 – 1.86 = 0.94   She would have to walk 0.94 km.
6. Distance travelled in 1 min : 1.4 ÷ 5 = 0.28
He would travel 0.28 km in 1 min.
7. Difference : 1.4 ÷ 4 – 1.4 ÷ 5 = 0.35 – 0.28 = 0.07
Doris would walk 0.07 km more than Bobby in 1 min.
8. 4.2, 5.6, 7, 8.4;   9, 12, 15, 18
9. The time taken increases by 3 minutes.
10. The distance travelled increases by 1.4 km.
11.

No. of blocks	6	7	8
Time (min)	18	21	24

He would take 24 min to travel 8 blocks.
12.

No. of blocks	6	7	8	9	10	11	12
Time (min)	18	21	24	27	30	33	36

He would pass 12 blocks.
13.

No. of blocks	6	7	8	9
Distance travelled (km)	8.4	9.8	11.2	12.6

He would travel 12.6 km.
14.

Time (min)	15	30	45	60	75
Water drunk (L)	$\frac{1}{4}$	$\frac{2}{4}$	$\frac{3}{4}$	1	$1\frac{1}{4}$

He would drink $1\frac{1}{4}$ L of water.
15.

Time (min)	75	90	105
Water drunk (L)	$1\frac{1}{4}$	$1\frac{2}{4}$	$1\frac{3}{4}$

He would have travelled 105 minutes (1 h 45 min) on his bike.
16. Cost : 29.45 – 7.15 = 22.3   I have to pay $22.30.
17. Price : 53.25 + 15.5 = 68.75   Its price is $68.75.
18. Cost : 10.8 x 3 = 32.4   He can save $7.15.
19. Cost before discount : 15.99 x 2 = 31.98
Cost after discount : 31.98 – 7.15 = 24.83   He will pay $24.83.
20. Cost before discount : 22.99 x 2 = 45.98
Change : 50 – (45.98 – 15.5) = 19.52   He will get $19.52 change.
21. Cost before discount : 59.99 + 3.99 = 63.98
Change : 60 – (63.98 – 15.5) = 11.52   She will get $11.52 change.
22. Cost after discount : 19.87 – 3.25 = 16.62
Money Gary has : 10 + 2 x 3 + 0.25 x 3 = 16.75 (16.75 > 16.62)
Yes. He will have enough money to buy a box of chocolates.
23. No. of male customers : 329 – 251 = 78
There will be 78 male customers.
24. Money collected : 215 x 5 = 1075
$1075.00 can be collected from 215 customers.
25. Sweater A : 34.87 – 7.15 = 27.72
Sweater B : 40.05 – 15.5 = 24.55
Difference : 27.72 – 24.55 = 3.17
The price difference between sweater A and sweater B after the discount is $3.17.
26. Ray should buy sweater B because it is cheaper.
27. B   28. C   29. A   30. B   31. D   32. C
33. B   34. A   35. B   36. D   37. C   38. B
39. B   40. D   41. D

Unit 1

1. Cost : 4.98 + 12.49 = 17.47 $17.47
2. Cost : 20.18 + 5.39 = 25.57   His bill would be $25.57.
3. Cost : 4.98 + 2.84 + 12.49 + 20.18 − 4.5 =35.99
   His bill would be $35.99.
4. Change : 100 − 35.99 = 64.01   He would get $64.01 change.
5. Raking leaves : 23.02 − 4.98 = 18.04 ✗
   Sweeping sidewalks : 23.02 − 2.84 = 20.18 (cleaning garage) ✓
   He swept Mrs Winter's sidewalk and cleaned her garage.
6. Change : 50 − 23.02 = 26.98   She would get $26.98 change.
7. Amount earned per hour : 20.18 ÷ 2 = 10.09
   Ben would earn $10.09 per hour.
8. Amount after donation : (37.65 + 35.94 + 31.53) − (37.65 + 35.94 + 31.53) ÷ 4 = 78.84   Ben would have $78.84 after his donation.
9. Change : 100 − (82.97 − 8 x 1.5) = 29.03   Ann's change is $29.03.
10. Change : 100 − (120.45 − 12 x (1.5 + 0.3)) = 1.15
    Tim's change is $1.15.
11. Cost : 16.99 x 3 = 50.97 ; Rebate : 5 x 1.5 = 7.5
    Change : 50 − (50.97 −7.5) = 6.53   Ray's change is $6.53.
12. Rebate for buying separately : 1.5 x 9 x 2 = 27
    Rebate for buying together : (1.5 + 0.3) x 9 x 2 = 32.4
    Sally can get more rebate by buying them together.
13. Jacket A : 98.27 − (9 x 1.5) = 84.77
    Jacket B : 102.95 − 10 x (1.5 + 0.3) = 84.95
    Eric should buy Jacket A.
14. Cost of 12 lollipops : 0.97 x 12 = 11.64 ;
    Money saved : 11.64 − 10.8 = 0.84   Donna would save $0.84.
15. Change : 25 − (10.8 x 2) = 3.4   Donna's change was $3.40.
16. Cost of 1 package : 3.24 ÷ 6 = 0.54   1 package cost $0.54.
17. Change : 20 − (0.54 x 18) = 10.28   Gary's change was $10.28.
18. Money spent on jellybeans : 23.76 − 10.8 = 12.96

No. of boxes of jellybeans	1	2	3	4
Cost ($)	3.24	6.48	9.72	12.96

   Louis bought 4 boxes of jellybeans.
19. Average cost : (1.26 x 2) ÷ 3 = 0.84
    Each chocolate bar cost $0.84 on average.
20. Cost : 1.26 x 6 = 7.56   Alexander paid $7.56.
21. Cost of 3 jars of candies : 12.96 x 3 = 38.88   (40 > 38.88)
    Yes, Jeffrey would have enough money to buy 3 jars of candies.
22. Money left : 40 − (12.96 x 2) = 14.08
    Jeffrey would have $14.08 left.
23. $570.75 ; five hundred seventy dollars and seventy-five cents.
24. $462.20 ; four hundred sixty-two dollars and twenty cents.
25. $415.40 ; four hundred fifteen dollars and forty cents.
26. $520.23 ; five hundred twenty dollars and twenty-three cents.
27. week 1, week 4, week 2, week 3

Challenge

1. Amount : 20.94 x 12 = 251.28   Mr Tiff will get $251.28.
2. Gain : 251.28 − 187.2 = 64.08   He will gain $64.08.

Unit 2

1. Perimeter : 1.8 + 2.1 + 3 + 2 + 2.5 = 11.4   11.4 cm
2. Perimeter : 3.4 + 3.6 + 1 + 1.8 + 3.4 = 13.2
   Its perimeter is 13.2 cm.
3. Perimeter : 2.5 + 2.5 + 1.3 + 1.2 + 1.2 +1.3 = 10
   Its perimeter is 10 cm.
4. Perimeter : 2.5 + 3.8 + 2.5 + 1.5 + 1.1 + 1.3 + 1.1 + 1 = 14.8
   Its perimeter is 14.8 cm.
5. Perimeter : (3.4 + 2) x 2 = 10.8   Its perimeter is 10.8 cm.
6. Perimeter : 2.2 x 4 = 8.8   Its perimeter is 8.8 cm.
7. 11.4 m , 13.2 m , 10 m , 14.8 m , 10.8 m , 8.8 m
8. Actual perimeter : (4 + 3 + 6) x 100 = 1300
   The actual perimeter is 1300 cm (13 m).

9. Actual perimeter : (4 + 2 +3.5 + 4) x 100 = 1350
   The actual perimeter is 1350 cm (13.5 m).
10. Actual perimeter : (2 + 3 + 2 + 3) x 100 = 1000
    The actual perimeter is 1000 cm (10 m).
11. Actual perimeter : (3 + 4 + 5) x 100 = 1200
    The actual perimeter is 1200 cm (12 m).
12. Actual perimeter : (6 + 4 + 3.5 + 3) x 100 = 1650
    The actual perimeter is 1650 cm (16.5 m).
13. T, Q, P, S, R
14. Area : 5 x 6.5 = 32.5   Its area is 32.5 m².
15. Area : 3 x 7.3 = 21.9   Its area is 21.9 m².
16. Area : 7.9 x 7.9 = 62.41   Its area is 62.41 m².
17. No. of times : (5 x 13) ÷ (2.6 x 5) = 5
    The area of the dining room is 5 times that of the washroom.
18. Area : (13 + 6.4) x (7.9 + 5) = 250.26   The area is 250.26 m².
19. Area : (7.9 x 7.9) + (5 x 6.5) = 94.91
    94.91 m² of carpet would cover the living room and the library.
20. Cost : 94.91 x 2 = 189.82   He needs to pay $189.82 for the carpet.
21. Amount of paint : (5 x 2.8 + 6.4 x 2.8) ÷ 4 = 7.98
    7.98 L of paint are needed for the 2 walls.
22. No. of cans : 7.98 ÷ 2 = 3.99   He needs to buy 4 cans.
23. Perimeter : (2.5 + 1.2) x 2 = 7.4   Area : 2.5 x 1.2 = 3
    Its perimeter is 7.4 m and its area is 3 m².
24. Perimeter : 60 x 4 = 240 ;   Area : 60 x 60 = 3600
    Its perimeter is 240 cm and its area is 3600 cm².
25. Length : 120 ÷ 4 = 30   Each side is 30 cm long.
26. Width : 450 ÷ 25 = 18   Its width is 18 m.
27. Length : (45 ÷ 2) − 5 = 17.5   Area : 17.5 x 5 = 87.5
    Its area is 87.5 cm².

Challenge

1. Length : 40 − (2 x 2) = 36   Width : 25 − (2 x 2) = 21
   The length is 36 cm and the width is 21 cm.
2. Area : 36 x 21 = 756 ;   Perimeter : (36 + 21) x 2 = 114
   Its area is 756 cm² and its perimeter is 114 cm.

✳ Unit 3

1. Time : 9 h 40 min + 57 min = 10 h 37 min   10:37 a.m.
2. Time : 10 h 37 min + 40 min = 11 h 17 min
   They left the park at 11:17 a.m.
3. Time : 11 h 17 min + 32 min = 11 h 49 min
   They reached the convenience store at 11:49 a.m.
4. Time : 11 h 49 min + 35 min = 12 h 24 min
   They left the store at 12:24 p.m.
5. Time taken : 12 h 42 min − 12 h 24 min = 18 min
   They took 18 min.
6. Time : 1 h 17 min − 26 min = 0 h 51 min
   She started at 12: 51 p.m.
7. No. of days : 29 − 3 = 26   Larry has 26 days.
8. Time taken : (12 h 0 min − 8 h 16 min) + 4 h 5 min = 7 h 49 min
   He has worked for 7 h 49 min.
9. Time : 5 h 32 min − 2 h 20 min = 3 h 12 min
   He started at 3: 12 p.m.
10. Time : 1 h 48 min + 23 min = 2 h 11 min (2:11 p.m.)
    Yes, she will be there on time.
11. Time : 11 h 45 min + 1 h 35 min = 13 h 20 min
    It will be over at 1:20 p.m.
12. Time movie A finishes :   Time movie B finishes :
    11 h 45 min + 1 h 43 min   12 h 10 min + 1 h 16 min
    = 13 h 28 min (1:28 p.m.)   = 13 h 26 min (1:26 p.m.)
    Movie B finishes first.
13. No. of days = 170 ÷ 24 = 7...2   He spent 7 days and 2 hours.
14. Time : 11 h 26 min + 37 min + 16 min = 12 h 19 min
    He reached the theatre at 12:19 p.m.